# THE SALESMAN AGAINST THE WORLD

By

Carson V. Heady

© 2010, 2014, 2016, 2017 Carson V. Heady

Copyright notice: All work contained within is the sole copyright of its author, 2010, and may not be reproduced without consent.

## Acknowledgements

To the readers and supporters of *Birth of a Salesman* for making that experience so rewarding, my parents, family and friends and, most of all, to my best friend, Madison.

Thank you to Jonathan Foreman and Switchfoot for writing and recording the song, "The Blues." It got me through some very challenging personal times.

"Success is often the result of taking a misstep in the right direction." - Al Bernstein

*Birth of a Salesman* and *The Salesman Against the World* are works of fiction, and any resemblance to any people living or deceased, or any corporations past or present, are purely coincidental.

# "The Surviving Game" by Vincent Scott
## INTRODUCTION –
### Sales: The Real Oldest Profession

In the annals of history, one common philosophy, thread and attribute binds together multiple facets of all professions, walks of life and means of communication. That commonality, pulsating through every vein of humankind is the psychology of sales.

While the pushy and the unethical in the trade give the love a bad name, "sales" itself is a necessary trait in communication - business and personal - and its characteristics are woven deeply into the very fabric of our existences.

Sales is the oldest profession in the world because it is in who we are, what we do, how we act and how we go about our daily lives. We're all in sales – some of us are fortunate enough to be paid handsomely for perfecting the ability.

Basic communication in business and personal relationships boils down to listening, asking specific questions, and learning how we can cure what ails those who come into our lives. Whether we are teaching or being taught, providing a customer service or receiving one, or we are enjoying some of the finest things in life, sales is involved - be it out in the open or behind the scenes.

To teach others, in whatever setting, the audience must be considered - what do they need? How can I meet those needs? From there, follow-up is required - is the curriculum taking care of the clientele in the best means possible?

To provide a service - hotel, restaurant, automobile - the potential customer is the central figure of the universe. What are they looking for in accommodations, amenities or appetizers?

Then, the "selling body" - be it a university, a hotel chain, restaurant chain, major corporation or a Mom and Pop store - must show that potential customer that they are the winning choice. They have to prove themselves to be the best fit for that need.

Supply and demand has been around since the dawn of time. The gathering and hunting, bartering and trading, negotiations amongst peoples - these are common themes in all eras of mankind. Sales tactics and techniques, listening, communicating and putting the "customer" at ease that we have their best interests at heart, understand their situation and are the answer when it comes to satisfaction of said needs go hand in hand.

Whatever profession you are in, whatever relationships you are a part of and whatever your daily routine, these same principles will be utilized regularly. You may think you want to distance yourself from the sales game, but that is where you are wrong; the day will never arrive where we are no longer called upon to sell something to someone. It could be selling your significant other on the restaurant for the evening, your child on using the potty as opposed to his/her diaper to do their business, or dazzling a potential employer to hire you - face it: that is sales.

The best at it can create a lot of opportunities in his/her life, so, no matter what your calling, station in life or aspirations, you should never stop striving to learn and conquer the selling game.

At its core, like the world we live in, sales is an honorable domain - a psychology and human understanding so intertwined with our daily lives that its essence is evident in many of the things we do and say.

While the world is full of evil elements and decay, you can put the windows down and drive south on the interstate with the sunlight beating down and the wind in your hair and all of those things go away – if even for a moment. There is enough beauty in the world to keep ourselves waking up every day. There is enough beauty in sales to keep us waking up to it every day as well; sometimes we just have to look a little harder to find it in the people we work with, the lessons we've learned and successes we've achieved.

Capitalism in its purest, utopian form makes our world function monetarily; supply and demand, meeting customer needs and servicing the customer effectively and with care keep the machine finely tuned. However, just like the world, when the seven deadly sins - namely greed - enter the picture, anything can take a turn for the worst.

It is our duty, as noble knights of the selling profession, to keep honor in the game. True salespeople are not cheaters, not liars, and not human manipulators; they are listeners, they are givers and they are more concerned with putting the needs of the many in front of their own. Unfortunately, there are a lot of unscrupulous salespeople, managers and above in the selling game. Our prime directive, however, is to maintain discipline and integrity and ethics in what is a sometimes dirty game.

Just as the world is not inherently bad or evil, neither is sales. A few bad apples give the orchard a lousy name. Always remember: we have a holy trinity of sales to satisfy on every transaction - be it a solitary call or visit, a negotiation or a long-lasting relationship. The customer, the company and the salesperson must be satisfied on every deal; short-change any of those three and the result is an unhealthy sales balance. Someone unnecessarily suffers.

Many companies talk out of both sides of their mouths; they dismiss shady selling out of one side, but on the other they promote it by doing nothing about it or commending great performances that were brought about unethically. Stay strong. Find ways to creatively weave everything into your arsenal without crossing the line. Once you cross, there is no going back. And superior, ethical sales *can* be accomplished.

Remember: we are compensated to make money for our company. This does involve knowing all of the nooks and crannies and idiosyncrasies of the playing field. It can involve manipulation of the playing field – but never manipulation of the customer or company.

Much of sales can be the words we choose to use, handling sales objections, overcoming fear and usage of statistics to further our cause of satisfying that holy trinity. However, when you start skipping steps, when you bend the rules, fudge the numbers, tell half-truths and slick your way to the sale, no one wins.

Think about it: sure, you may get to mark that stick tally on the board today and ring the bell. You may get that pat on the back from your boss. But when the product or service fails to deliver for the customer, who wins? When you or your company or your goods get a bad name because of that failure, who wins? What will be the potential fallout in the black eye of a faulty reputation?

The best salespeople see the big picture of all of their words, actions and strategies. And, in the end, no one wins (least of all the honor of the selling game) if you or anyone else gives sales a bad name.

Treat the selling game well and it will reciprocate.

# INTRODUCTION

**Thursday, January 26, 2012**

**734 days later.**

"And… he took me out. Fired me. After 9 years and three promotions with an exemplary record and sparkling appraisals. All over a personal issue he should never have known about and forced into the workplace that had nothing to do with the company whatsoever. And the worst part is I saw it coming; I knew what I was getting myself into when I testified against him in the investigation. Somehow, I trusted the company when they said he couldn't retaliate… and somehow I thought I was invincible because of everything I did for them. I did the right thing and believed in justice and we were all told he'd be removed for the horrible crimes he had committed…and I'm the one who got knocked out of there.

"I was going to retire from there – they told me I'd be the CEO someday. I had everything. And since I've been gone, my department alone has lost hundreds of millions of dollars in revenue, laid off three-quarters of the workforce and been sold off to a third party, after four straight years of crushing objectives and quadrupling the profits under me…but it didn't matter. It doesn't matter how profitable the machine; once you show you are not part of their cookie-cutter, unethical fortress of secrets and lies, you're expendable.

"No one that was supposed to uphold justice did anything. My team predicted I would be back in a matter of days or weeks, but my old bosses threatened everyone with various methods of retaliation if they stood up for me and told the truth. I lost all my so-called friends. I barely sleep, and – when I do – I dream about the place. Constantly.

"The lawsuit process is outrageous and long and certainly doesn't exist to support the victim. It's been over two years ago this week. 734 days. And – believe me – I've endured every single one of them like a nightmare… like slow, calculated torture.

"And as if all of that wasn't enough, my daughter's mom and I have been in and out of court 5 times; I've dropped tens of thousands of dollars to get the maximum time with Elizabeth possible… I live and breathe for her, do everything possible for her and fund far more than my fair share… and Abby and I have been off and on for 6 years and no matter how bad it's gotten for either of us, I've always been the only person who has come through for her every single time. She told me two weeks ago that she's in love with me and I'm the one for her. And I just find out from my daughter's mouth she's engaged to marry someone else."

The previous 734 days had been filled with agony and loss. They had been humbling, horrifying and harrowing; a life- and character-altering unforeseeable turn of events which had molded and scarred. And they had been experienced at an excruciatingly sluggish pace.

Day after day after uneventful day with no end in sight and no one in his corner, applying to jobs and being rejected and dejected all while his former kingdom crumbled and was dismantled. He had once been the king of his kingdom; after being unceremoniously discarded, he was completely alone. A leper and curse word in the department he had built.

Vincent Thomas Scott III now sat, contemplative, in a sandwich shop in downtown Minneapolis, Minnesota, across the street from his biggest failures – plainly visible through the window. Once a clean-cut pretty boy, his formerly close-cropped golden hair is much longer and not as thick, the twinkle in the steel-blue eyes not as bright and the flecks of grey-white in the temples and the beard that now adorns his face grow more profound. He had traded in his suit and tie and carefree act for black shirts, slacks and his black leather jacket over a much darker heart.

Now hardened, Vincent was barely held together physically by his caffeine, the numbing effects of alcohol and the excruciating workouts to keep him fit and preoccupied; spiritually his only salvation was the love for his daughter, Elizabeth. When Vincent was with her, his world was whole no matter the predicaments caving in from outside. When she was with her mother, Vincent tried to be as unconscious as possible.

At 33 years old, Vincent Scott was 11 years removed from his birth as a salesman. His belief in forever – in public and private facets of his life – was gone; stripped from him akin to a loss of innocence.

His quest to change the world had stalled. If he was not doing something of impact in any given moment, he felt lost.

There are not a lot of men like Vincent Scott; an old soul, a tortured type but romantic sentimentalist at heart. A man who sacrifices and genuinely cares about profoundly impacting the lives of others, who wants to contribute greatly to society but spends much of his time withdrawn in thought and solitude. A writer, a reader, an enthusiast of classic novels and films and music who sometimes says little and often disappears into his apartment but when he appears and speaks he captivates and motivates and drives others. A loner and introvert but an actor; he would transform himself into whatever the situation required – even extroverted, confident public-speaking sales leadership wizard – to achieve success through himself and others far above what anyone else could achieve. Many hated him for it. And – for now, at least – it seemed they had won a temporary victory.

Years of being relentlessly and mercilessly hammered and batted down by dictators of corporate America, deceived and betrayed by those he called friends and girlfriends he had trusted, and being forced to fight for everything and everyone he cares about in many losing battles have turned this man into a deadened, solitary man.

Over a decade removed from his status as an upstart phenom sales rep whose confidence and commanding presence earned him promotion after promotion, Vincent now loathes the selling game he is forced to play because his talents dictate it and growing attorney bills to wage the wars for his heart and soul and justice require it.

He was forced to the sidelines illegally and found out just how hard it was to resuscitate his career – mentally and physically. Merely having to do so through no fault of his own made him all the more bitter. Having to go at it all alone made him all the more independent and reclusive and untrusting.

He stared at the citadel fortress of his previous employer looming 45 stories tall on a street corner close enough he could have thrown a rock to it but that was seemingly surrounded by an invisible barrier; one constructed when he was deemed persona non grata 734 days ago in an unlawful move after Vincent assisted his managers in mutinying their dictator Director. The attempt failed because of dirty business politics and – when it went awry – Vincent alone suffered the consequences of standing up for justice.

His court battle against them had been slow and often uneventful, bogged down in bureaucracy and paperwork with government agencies failing to do their due diligence or even speak to the droves of witnesses or mull through the hundreds of pages of evidence Vincent provided them. There was no speedy trial process.

Vincent was now faced with the decision of having to come out of pocket $7,500 retainer facing potentially $40,000 or more in lawyer fees to take this all the way against an army of well-paid corporate attorneys hell-bent on keeping the corruption safe behind a potentially limitless bankroll.

Everyone told Vincent he was a fool to pursue it any further – even though they knew he was right. They could not fathom why he could not let it all go. People got fired every day – many of them for political reasons – why couldn't he just move on?

But they did not understand.  Vincent couldn't drop it and move on because he was living in the shadows of it every single day, unable to escape.  He needed vindication; he needed closure.  He needed to have his belief in justice rewarded.

In that building worked several people with whom Vincent was once very closely aligned – former employers, employees and lovers.  None were more significant than newly engaged-to-be-married Abby Winters, the mother of Vincent's beautiful, intelligent 4-year old daughter Elizabeth Scott.

Vincent and Abby had been off-and-on for 6 topsy-turvy, tumultuous years and now she was set to stroll to the altar with someone else – Chris Hurst, the occupier of her time during her "off" time with Vincent.  He was the antithesis of Vincent in nearly every way but filled the gap in Abby's life of being with someone who needed her, someone she felt superior to and had less drama with.

On the side of the street Vincent currently occupied and across from the fortress was an ironically placed Cellular Horizons store – one of 33 in his jurisdiction across the Midwest.  He was VP of Sales and Marketing now for their largest franchisee's largest franchise – Brink Management Company – and their business faced quite an uncertain future.

The title sounded grand but was glorified and designed to pacify an overqualified Vincent, who was pacing to make barely over 60% of his income from his previous best year with no company-provided insurance and questionable job security.

The fight it took to get Vincent just to this point had taken its toll, as he was facing this penance unjustifiably.  After a lengthy, torturous 13 months – 390 days – of doubts, second-guessing, working through hatred and bitterness and the betrayal from dozens of so-called former friends, days on end of applying to 1,627 jobs and being unwanted or toyed with before the rejection from all but one of them, he finally secured employment as division manager of a retail group of an authorized dealer for a top wireless provider.  On paper, it sounded promising and the CEO filled his head with grandiose hopes of $200,000 per year.

It was better than starting over.  It was better than drunken depression from his couch.  It got him back into the game.

In the most chaotic of times, with our backs against the wall and stuck between the rock and hard place, we define ourselves.  Vincent Scott's promising career had been destroyed out of malice and spite.  He had been forced to fight mightily for what he loved most – his daughter, his career, his sanity and soul – and his wonder at this point was how much fight was left.

But there would be no rest, as his leadership would be required more now than ever. The people once again turned to Vincent Scott for guidance and wanted him to go rogue as the future ownership of their little band and fates of all of their jobs were in question.

Flanking him at the restaurant table were Terry Bunche and Saul Porter, his two most trusted comrades in the Brink hierarchy. Both were initially dubbed Store Managers and Vincent was Regional Manager for Minneapolis yet through Vincent's ingenuity, direction and results he proved they could do more for the entire company. Vincent named Terry his Director of Marketing for Brink and Saul District Sales Manager for Minneapolis so he could assist in their additional markets in Missouri, Wisconsin and Texas. However, due to the shoestring budget of Brink, both also had to fulfill Store Manager duties for their home stores.

Pay was miniscule relative to others in this industry. Store managers had initially gotten a base salary of $1,200 a month plus a cut of store profits, which varied heavily. Vincent had scored Terry and Saul higher salaries due to additional responsibilities, but retention in this structure was difficult and everyone seemed to be looking. It was a daily struggle for Vincent and his Cabinet to keep their wits about them and hold the whole thing together.

Terry was in his late 40's and a journeyman sales manager and former business owner. He had three kids and had divorced their mother long ago; in need of little, Terry just wanted to contribute to something he had some say in. He had left a prior call center engagement where he made a little more money because he was tired of the lack of motivation and being under that level of micromanagement. A great talker and a constant conversationalist, Terry was very frustrated with the current state of affairs in Brink.

Saul was in his early 20's; a pup in the sales management game, but his raw sales tools and people skills had made him quite successful. Vincent had helped groom and polish him, and Saul was learning to harness his existing skills into a leadership pedigree. With many of their local Brink employees young and often misguided, they related well to Saul, who had plowed through and found accomplishment despite adversity in his life.

"And here I sit," Vincent continued. "Surrounded by my most significant failures in life."

"Come on, man," Terry interjected. "Don't beat yourself up – it's not that bad. We wouldn't be here right now if it wasn't for you."

"Exactly," Saul chimed in. "Nobody gave this market any chance at success until you came along."

Vincent took a sip of his diet cola.

"We have great service, solid products and a winning team, and we can't even make it work because we don't have the support to do it with," Vincent said. "It's so frustrating – not being able to carry out your role because of so many factors completely out of your control. For some reason, I just always thought we could somehow win. Hell, look at what we've accomplished with zero budget and zero leadership just up to this point."

"Absolutely," Terry responded. "We've come this far on your back."

"One way or another, we'll figure out our next move soon," Saul added.

"And then there's Abby. For whatever reason, I thought we would figure it out – that we had time, the door was open and we'd figure it out. We were engaged, we drove each other mad, cheated on each other, had restraining orders against each other, we've battled in court five times… I had her exactly where I wanted her in court and could have gotten full custody and all my money back, but couldn't bring myself to finish her off. She's like my kryptonite… and I can't stand the thought of her with someone else. I've always been the guy she's turned to when she needed anything and I've always been there for her. I've just always believed we would eventually grow into the people we wanted each other to be… the door was open and now she's closed it."

Vincent took another pensive sip of his drink.

"It's not over 'til it's over, man – you know that. On either front," Saul offered. Vincent shook his head.

"Every time we come back together and try, something happens and I run for the hills," Vincent continued. "Sometimes I look for excuses to run. Sometimes she hands me the reasons on a silver platter. But I run every time."

The conversation was interrupted with Vincent's phone ringing. He fished it from his pocket and looked at the Caller ID.

"This should be interesting," he observed.

\*       \*       \*       \*       \*

## "The Surviving Game" by Vincent Scott
## The Purpose to All

It may not help you to read about how many times Babe Ruth struck out or Michael Jordan missed a shot because – let's face it – these are mythical creatures we may have seen a glimpse of, read about or watched on a highlight reel.

To help your perspective, I've personally been rejected for 2,578 jobs I've applied to and my book was rejected by 953 publishers and agents before publication. Despite that – or, perhaps, better said in the face of that – people often consider me successful. I consider myself plugging along on a quest that is yet unfinished – who knows where it will go.

Success is relative; tied to a great many things. Most of all, it is relative to the definition of the beholder and their prioritization of love, family, money, fame and power in their lives. Some feel they need only one of the above while others constantly scramble to attain it all; someone with their priorities in order can find "success" with far less than others who are never satisfied.

Many types of success can be obtained and then lost; these fleeting achievements make finding spiritual success and gratification through your satisfaction with yourself, and/or through family and friends all the more important. Affiliating ourselves with long-term sources of joy and happiness can provide more lasting effects. Having people around you that have a positive impact on your life and who weather the storms with you is often the greatest success of all for many people. For others, finding peace and understanding in their solace provides this effect.

No matter your level of mastery of selling, management, leadership or life, you will be challenged tremendously over the duration of your personal journey for success. It is highly likely you will witness unfair practices, be a victim and struggle with losses that are completely out of your control – no matter how good you are at whatever you do. That is why – even more important than the selling game – there is the surviving game. Surviving whatever life throws at you and continuing to plow forward through it all leads to what many deem to be success.

If you are reading this, let me lead off by saying thank you.

After *The Selling Game* I felt accomplishment; I had summed up something I wanted to contribute to the world and managed to fill a book with said musings. The experience was (and is) a tremendous learning one. It also gave me a priceless opportunity: connecting with people all over the world that I could learn from and mold my experiences because of.

Writing this was much more difficult; I had to remind myself many times that I was not writing about finding prolonged senses of joy or happiness; I'm stumbling and falling along this voyage of life just like many of you may be. I chose to write about surviving: a topic I am well-schooled on.

Our lives are constantly in motion, continuously classified as works-in-progress and, regardless of circumstance we are faced daily with decisions that will craft our futures. This is why having a defined plan to reach your goals is so vital. This is why knowing what you want to achieve, recognizing what it takes to get there and checking things off the list in that quest as you tackle them is pivotal in following that road map.

Research shows that the people we deem as most successful in life do just that: make a long-term plan, divvy it up into daily checklists and tackle each one at a time. This ensures we are accomplishing the necessary tasks along the way but also shows us a concrete synopsis of where we've been, where we are and where we're going.

We cannot control many of the things life throws at us, and we will often be knocked several steps back…but we continue going forward where others stop cold in their tracks and we will eventually find the finish line.

If it was easy to be "successful," everyone would be doing it. We must continue where others would stop trying and especially when we are tempted to stop.

As we discussed in chapters regarding battling burnout and earning the promotion, keeping fresh challenges in our lives is paramount. In addition, living a life you can be proud of, making choices you can and will have the courage to stand by and operating without fear and regret are extremely tough to do. Sometimes they seem downright impossible.

It is often suggested that our chosen career path should coincide with our answer to the question of what we would do with our lives if money and privilege were no object. The thought behind this theory, of course, is that when we choose with our heart, we find career happiness. Of course, money very much does play a factor, but there is some merit to this point. Your talent matters, and it is often very much tied to the gifts we have to contribute to others. If you're great at something and passionate about doing it, your probability of success in that field is greater hence you can sometimes make a career out of it.

We all came into this world with something to contribute. The trouble is, we often get caught up on what we do not have or what is holding us back rather than making the choice to shine.

We are often our own worst enemies. It is not until we can train our mind to dismiss thoughts of negativity and doubt upon recognition of such thoughts that we can start to make a significant impact to our trajectory. Fleshing out the goals and the plan are part of the puzzle, but how you address and react to the perils along the way (both internal and external) will greatly affect your success in putting it all together.

We often wait for affirmation of some kind – someone to tell us that we are good. This is why many of us seek this in significant others or friends and become dependent on that "love" – such people feel they must have this confirmation to keep themselves going. Others find the drive and necessary mechanics internally. Some just cower in the corner as wallflowers, afraid of rejection or ridicule and choose to never put themselves out there.

But everyone has a gift, and it is our duty to share it with the world. It's why we're here.

We each have our talents and our shortcomings. A delicate trick of life is to keep balance to our focuses and not let the latter overcome or overshadow our ability to display the former. What we are passionate about or good at needs to shine through despite turmoil and in the face of uncertainty; often these are the very things that carry us through.

This is the very reason we are often told to count our blessings or remember what we should be thankful for. Perspective – again – is critical, as "it can always be worse" and "this too shall pass." These phrases have gotten many people through such dark times, as has prayer.

People rarely believe me when I describe myself as an introvert. I have reached out and expanded my horizons as necessary over the years, but specifically growing up I was quite private.

Speech class was something I dreaded, I did not proactively seek new relationships and I kept to myself. It takes time to pinpoint where solitude fits in your realm of solace.

Yet to achieve our goals, we must often transform ourselves – a necessity to gain the support and conjure the confidence to succeed. This is a step some choose to ignore – to their detriment. Only once we become who we must be to truly utilize our talents and share our gifts with the most people possible can we really experience life – and the taste of what success is for us.

We owe it to ourselves and others.

Many of us spend so much time worrying about negative outcomes that never come to fruition, but – unless we keep it under control – those doubts have a way of drowning out the positives.

A dear friend taught me years ago that we must immediately recognize the presence of a pessimistic thought or doubt and dismiss it from our consciousness. At first, this seems like taking on Goliath with a water pistol, but with concentrated practice over years, you can better control your thoughts and emotions and not let all of the potentially undesirable outcomes drown out your dreams of success.

You may be the best at something, or might be $10^{th}$ best. The Games are not open to just one participant; there is not just one sport, one team or one destination. Not just one politician, occupation, work of art. Success and purpose are interwoven throughout time and cultures – finding our niche, while sometimes difficult, should always involve following your instincts and heart, trusting in dreams, the occasional leap of faith and gambles, willingness to learn and make mistakes and living a life without regret.

What would you choose to contribute to the world if money was no object and failure was no option?

Of course, they very much play a factor – sometimes more than ever – but dare to dream and find a compromise in your balance of obligation and pursuing goals. Make time for pursuing your dream on the side while you work to pay the bills in the hopes someday the former outweighs the latter. Put yourself out there. Let the well-beings of those you care about and are responsible for temper your decisions but ensure that you are not turning a deaf ear to your calling.

A well-organized, strategic plan to reach your goals taking into consideration everything and everyone you are responsible for, preparation for and ability to react to downsides along the way and repeatedly revisiting the plan will lead you where you seek.

We get one crack at this thing called life; we have a gift, and it's a crime not to let others see it. Do what you love, hone in on your passions and decide carefully how you are going to express those gifts and enjoy the dividends you will receive by investing them in bettering the world.

What is the end result you want in each area of your life? Write it down, construct a step-by-step process to get you there and carry it out. What needs to be accomplished every step of the way? No long-term goal can be achieved quickly or overnight, but taking care of the steps that get us there will lead to the victory we seek.

Journal your experiences. You will learn from your choices that yielded good, bad and unpredictable results.

Sure – we're all faced with obstacles along the way but it is the carrying out of our initial plan and our breaking through the barriers of roadblocks along the journey that determine if we finally reach the Promised Land.

Every day, in every way, my mind continues to accept and process just how great and vast and wondrous this existence is and can be. Things that make no sense at first glance, things that confound and confuse many, are all revealed when we allow our true selves to come into focus.

So – what is the purpose to life, to our reality and to the things large and small that we encounter, experience and expect daily, monthly and over the annals of our years?

You may be a powerful person in the business or political world, or a cog in the wheel of the front lines working with customers. You could be the great-great-great grandmother to the doctor who cures a fatal illness, or you could be that doctor. You could write a song, play, movie, or television script that inspires someone to get off their couch and do something that touches someone else's life; you could be the person inspired to jump off that couch and make a difference.

You could be an athlete with motivating ability, or be a janitor whose handiwork prevents someone from falling and breaking their neck so they can go on to win an Olympic medal and inspire millions worldwide.

You could positively impact one other or one million others. Who is to say which act of inspiration was more or less worth it than the rest?

The point is that it all matters; that's the purpose to life. Our lives are all intricately intertwined and everyone has purpose – even if they don't know what it is right now or – like some great explorers or artists – don't have the profoundness of their impact known until after they leave this life.

The real challenges lie in finding our own purpose, committing to that destiny and staying on course, despite all obstacles that will inevitably present themselves in our paths over and over until the day we die. That is the surviving game – essential to the success game.

These obstacles can break your spirit, your physical body or your morale. But they only will completely stop you if you let them.

Believe me: you will face hardships and stumbling blocks and grief like you sometimes cannot even imagine. It may not let up. Your definition of happiness, your desires and your destinations may change, and often at that. At the core, however, the most vital attribute is staying true to yourself, your beliefs, your morals and what you hold dear.

And even if you have been crippled by the brutality that life can inflict on you, it makes you all the more valuable, versatile and viable in your quest of facing the trials that still lie ahead.

Those who allow life to keep them down will be kept down. Those who move past the hurdles, learn from them and challenge themselves to be great will be.

The most profound morsel from Napoleon Hill's revered work *Think And Grow Rich* is that the preponderance of those who have found what the general consensus deem to be success found it just after most people would have given up. The moral of the story? Keep taking steps towards your goals and your destiny, no matter how many steps you get knocked back. Weather the storm. You will eventually find the blue skies.

Is the aspiring actor who never becomes a household name, but keeps trying all while they are waiting tables to pay the bills, any less valuable to the world than those who broke through and made it against all odds? Who's to say that just because they were rejected the last 20 times, the 21$^{st}$ won't be the charm?

The people fighting who don't necessarily "make it" in the eyes of the public can still find what they need or want through their craft. The experience and the journey will lead to relationships and moments that define them. They also push those regarded as "the best" to be even better – which benefits everyone.

We all have our own preconceived notions about what "making it" is. Live a noble life that you can be proud of. Make a difference, one step at a time, one day at a time. Embrace each day you are fortunate enough to receive and own that day.

Only if one believes they are not valuable does that become true. Only if one fails to choose to put forth their best foot, best effort and their all will they find that rewarding life. As long as you have breath left in your body, it's never too late to start contributing positively.

The things that are easy to obtain come with less sense of reward and triumph. The best things we have – the accomplishments, the victories and successes – often came at a price or with extensive effort. At the end of the day, the people and things we have in our lives that truly add value are what we must be thankful for and we must spend our time treasuring.

Be proud of yourself, your transitions, your forward-thinking strategy, the steps you are taking and the person you know you will become. Other people can and will be obstructions, just the same, and often for their own jealous reasons. If it or they are not adding value to your life, that obstacle must be jettisoned immediately.

Life and pursuit of happiness and success in any goal are a process. You cannot achieve it all in one day or one year – it is an ongoing decision to continue along the path, doing what you know to be right by others and yourself. There will be unexpected events, but often they will enrich and better you. There will be failures along the way, but they will teach you. There will be times you doubt everything; they will simply determine how badly you really want what you claim to want.

It's not easy to find what you seek, but nothing worth anything is. You are exactly where you are supposed to be; revisit your plan, readjust your mentality when needed and keep moving.

A string of ten failures in a row does not mean the eleventh attempt will result in another one, so why do we ever stop trying? Athletes miss shots, lose games, but they keep conditioning and playing. Actors put out poorly-received films, but they keep cultivating new ones. We lose jobs, we have horrendous relationships – but do we stop working or trying to find a match that will fulfill and enrich us?

Think about the people you consider great. They are majestic in our minds because they never stopped when faced with adversity. If they inspire you, let that attitude inspire you more.

People love success stories, comeback stories and tales of greatness and grand ideas because, if even just for that moment, they believe or believe again that greatness can be achieved by all of us. It's why we rally behind stories of accomplishment in life and business and sports; it is why we lose ourselves in films for two hours and it is why we often seek escape from our lives in these other mediums. Find something when you escape in these other worlds, take it back and apply it to your life.

Life, business, politics, medicine, operations, sales – these are all processes that have been practiced and experimented with over the history of our world. Someone can have flash in the pan success and disappear from public consciousness. Someone can flounder around with the wrong course of action and never find success. Or, you can live a life that allows you to look back and know you did everything you could to squeeze out all the juice of life in every situation.

That choice is yours.

The most difficult part of life is actually living it. There is so much uncertainty and so many impediments. Happiness is often just a fleeting period of contentedness, interrupted regularly by roadblocks. If everyone could make it to the top of the mountain, they would, but most people stop somewhere along the way after multiple falls.

Through decisions, learning, falling, and getting back up, weathering storms and keeping your eyes on the prize, you can find reward.

We are not inventing or re-inventing any wheels here; the processes in the aforementioned walks of life have already been created and done a thousand times over. Our role is to contribute. Our role is to add to what has been done; to make our own invaluable entries in the ledger of life. Doing these things will prolong your periods of happiness and give you the reward and satisfaction you seek.

It is key to remember that everyone has at least one talent or gift they are here to contribute. Everyone has a part to play. Everyone has something to offer, and you cannot let anything stop you from making that contribution or helping others make theirs – even if you have no idea what the end result is. We are investing in future successes; we invest without assuredness of outcome, but with strategic, well-plotted investments we give ourselves the better probability of success and happiness.

Figuring out what you want can also be tricky, but without that goal to move towards we are just moving aimlessly. We wake up one day and realize we don't have what we want; but we're to blame for not figuring out what that is. And being able to commit to that, commit to a plan, commit to the process that matters and commit to staying away from the evils and obstacles is a very challenging task that will literally consume your entire life.

Are you satisfied with absolutely everything about your life right now? Figure out what you are not afraid to risk to get what you deem is happiness; if there is no satisfaction in your life, you can risk quite a bit. The positive change can yield positive results.

There is no such thing as a prescription of action that will handle or appropriately address anything you could possibly face. There is no road map to life. There are no-win scenarios. Your heart will be broken, your fears realized and your limits tested. Daily.

Just make sure that you focus your sights on what will truly give you the feeling of happiness, accomplishment and satisfaction; don't settle and do not let the knockdowns of life keep you down. Do not let fear prevent you from taking the necessary steps to sharing yourself with the world or taking the necessary risks to achieve something great.

Celebrate the wins when you get them. Relish the good times and people you are blessed to encounter. They make the dark times manageable.

Control what you can control and do not get lost in what you cannot; follow the same process in how you treat others and conduct yourself whether you're winning or losing. For every great thing you put out there into the world or for every group of people who loves you, there will be those who hate for no reason, condemn without justification or try to erode the confidence of you and those like you. They wish to bring you down to their level of misery or lack of success – don't let them. You cannot control others but you cannot let anything diminish your spirit or resolve; you owe it to the people you make a difference to who actually matter.

Take the hits. Absorb and learn from them and keep moving forward. Even if you do not understand the reasons now, you will in time; you will look back and the path makes sense. You will realize it was all worth it. And you'll have no regrets.

It is how we handle the setbacks and the choices we make in the face of them that define our legacy and mold our outcome.

We have all been there; staring down the barrel of the unbelievably difficult situation, not liking our choices and having no one to hold our hand while we have to take a leap of faith into an uncertain future. The sink or swim moment; you can allow the tides of life to wash you away, or you can stand, fight back with all your might and choose to survive.

The hardest part is the having to remind yourself that "it *can* always be worse," that "surely this will beget something else." We think no one else can understand our frustrations and fears. Some of us are forced to go at it alone; some of us choose to. We know that at this fateful moment we are such a far cry from the trajectory we thought we were on or where we hope to be.

We long for those days of innocence long gone; we look to children and envy their carefree days and ways.

When we were born, our life was a blank canvas; one to which we have added brushstrokes of brilliance at some points. Nevertheless, we all have our burdens to bear; the masterpiece will not paint itself and we must endure the dark as much as we enjoy the light.

A lot of poor souls are burdened with the absentee parent or parents or being born into an undesirable environment; they meddle through life with a lousy foundation and bad example having been set for them and find it difficult to trust and have no one to fall back on. It can be overcome, but that takes strength of character, resolve and commitment to the process that leads to overcoming such an environment.

Life is not easy for anyone. I think sometimes we look at celebrities and think they have it all; but the truth is so far from that perception. Their lives, missteps and problems are played out for the world to see. People take potshots at them every day, most of which they do not deserve, because it is easy to armchair quarterback someone you want to see fail because their failure makes you feel better about yours. They are also often slaves to the system that makes them famous.

Perception is reality and we all – for better or worse, fair or unfair, deserved or undeserved – are judged by it, even from the least credible of sources.

Our carefree days of youth give way to high school and sometimes college and the real world where it becomes all the more important to apply yourself and the innocence fades away. We become adults on life's timeline and there is no going back.

Nothing can prepare you for the awkwardness and complete and utter confusion of puberty, that first kiss, learning to drive, dating, wondering what the hell you are supposed to do with your life, declaring a major, getting a job, keeping a job and, then, on top of it, wondering every step of the way if you are doing the right things and dealing with your own set of unexpected circumstances.

But we – our fears, our minds, our worrying about things that will never come to pass – need to make sure we are helping ourselves rather than hurting.

We must adapt and become the people we have to be in order to be a success in the path we choose. Failure to do so leads to failure. And there will always be somebody there to take our place, pass us if we stand still, or deny us based on our hesitation. Figure out which fears are holding you back, dissect them and dismiss them as best you can. Find the validity in them and address them in your plan of attack.

Every day, I see or talk to people who wonder why they are getting passed over for jobs and they are in danger of getting lost in their own misery or uncertainty. Little do they know that the only way to succeed is to keep throwing yourself into the lion's den. Keep applying, keep looking for ways to set yourself apart from the hundreds of others who want the same spot you want. What have you done to prove you're the one and only? What are you doing or willing to do that they're not?

We obsess so much about these things that are far more trivial to those around us – our looks, how popular we are, how quickly we succeed. Many of us care so much about the superficial, about what these people who will abandon us in a heartbeat think about us, and about fitting in to cliques that only want something from us. Treat people the way you want to be treated. Treat people that take you for granted to the exit.

Learning matters, knowledge matters, health matters, and building meaningful relationships with people we can actually trust that help get us through the day matters. How you control what you can control matters; how you accept what you cannot matters.

Your greatest competition is against your own potential. No matter the potential or the prodigy, the game must be played. You do your best to control what you can. You get your heart broken, you break hearts. You either drink, smoke and experiment with mind-altering substances or you don't. You fit in, or you don't. You are alienated, or you alienate. Or, sometimes both. You take care of your body, or you don't. You go to college, or you don't.

You have to figure out what you love, what love is and what it is not.

You kiss, you get butterflies, you get physical.

You either have a social and professional network, or you don't. You try really hard to find a job you may very well hate, but might be a stepping stone to one you don't.

You learn that complaining accomplishes literally nothing, or you don't and you keep doing it.

And – on top of that – you deal with your own brand of unique circumstances, issues and problems.

It *is* all about who you know and not what you know, no matter how unfair that is. So get to know the people who will care about what you know.

You deal with loss, you cope with catastrophe.

You finally, eventually learn what really matters: family (be it biological or not), faith, true friends, work ethic, and always moving towards your goals no matter how many times you fall down or get knocked backwards.

Truth is, you cannot spend your life worrying about things that do not matter. The quicker you find that out and the earlier you learn that, the better.

You can't be afraid to lose, make waves or piss people off. You can't live outside your means, but you also cannot hold on to dear life to things that are worthless to you when you die.

Do what you love doing. Do what you can for you – as often as your life permits.

Seize good days and good moments and good friends while you can, for it can all be taken away in a moment, a day or a heartbeat.

Learn to pick your battles, but do not let worthwhile battles go unfought.

And always live without regret, for regret is one thing that can certainly not be erased.

The moment of truth – that sink or swim moment – will find all of us; sometimes our lives will afford us multiple forks in the road like this. The decisions we are faced with will sometimes surface in a haze of uncertainty; big weights will be on our minds and hearts and huge things at stake. But, through it all, do not forget that it will one day all make sense, even if it could not be farther from that place now.

Any activity in life if repeated numerous times can become monotonous and mundane, even in a fast-paced society or occupation. The challenges of learning and mastering a trade and discovering your talents and gifts to their potential notwithstanding, it is incumbent upon us to regularly resurface, reapply and reinvent ourselves. Keeping a few fundamentals near and dear to our hearts can greatly ease the process.

First, recognize that you will be dealt your fair share or more of rejection. Baseball players are fortunate to get a hit one-out-of-three times they march to the plate, hockey players may make less than one in ten shots on goal, and it is likely your conversion rates in things that your success is derived from is far less.

Hearing the word "no" over and over can be a blow to the ego, but it is certainly not personal and not uncommon. Get to the point where you can look back on every transaction or event in your life and career and know the specific reasons why it went the way it did. Learn from it. Utilize that knowledge in similar situations going forward. Go to school off your experiences.

Hark back to the best version of you; perhaps the person you were on the day you interviewed for a job or the day you made the decision to improve yourself. Recapture that vigor. We all lose sight of that energy from time to time; we sold ourselves or someone else on future activities we would carry out – a workout routine, an impeccable job performance or a better diet – and we will hit brick walls. That's normal. But when the walls are hit, we find ways to scale them, go around them or barrel through. Don't let them stop you.

We all lessen our intensity from time to time, but we must analyze ourselves and our performance. Be our own toughest critics. Be open to constructive criticism from others. Ultimately, do not let something that is not indicative of who you are and what your potential is become the perception of you… because it will shape your reality.

We can often control far more than we give ourselves credit for. Our effort and our reactions and our treatment of others and our activities fall under this jurisdiction.

Keep your personal life relatively personal; as a general rule, you can trust far fewer people than you may initially feel inclined to.

Keep finding what it takes to motivate you to continue your quest to the next level.

Pick yourself up, time and time again. Keep yourself grounded in reality, remind yourself who you are and what you're after and stay focused on the big picture – no matter how hard that becomes. Each day comes to a conclusion and God-willing we get another one with which to improve upon the last. Keep the past in the past, take the knowledge with you on the journey and make the most of each day you are fortunate enough to have.

We are on evolving, continuous quests to find something – knowledge, power or the elusive grail known as prolonged happiness – and, like many ordeals it is the trials, tribulations, wins and losses in the meantime that mold us into the people we become. The journey is the payoff; not the destination.

Our best lessons often lie in defeat. We are able to (and should not be afraid to) look back and realize what we gleaned from the endeavor and how we move forward more effectively. We decide to address the inadequacies we have uncovered about ourselves. We decide how to better apply our skills and traits and talents in the future to either avoid pitfalls or better arrive at the end results we desire.

Lessons are everywhere: in relationships both business and personal, in what we do and do not do and in the results from everyday choices. Learning is a large part of what we have; it is fundamental to growth and keeps things interesting at all times.

We get into situations where melancholy and misery make us miss the monotony life can provide, but it is during these times of tests and personal challenge that we figure out who we are and who we are destined to become.

These are all words – to be fair. It's trusting them and trusting ourselves that play a large part in determining the outcome.

Embrace the challenges. Look for the teachings and lessons in every little thing. Often, we are quick to dismiss other people's ways of thinking or opinions, but unless we are constantly looking for ways to improve ourselves and the world around us - what is the point? Why are we here? Because it sure as heck isn't for no reason. We are here to leave our mark, to contribute to the team that is the human race and to give of our talents and skills to help mankind.

A day without learning is a day without living. It is a day you can never get back. These are opportunities you may never see again so you must seize them as they enter your field of vision. Take the fruit you are given and squeeze every drop of juice from it you can before it spoils; only by taking life by the reins and directing your destiny can you truly live a life of no regrets.

Pain and suffering and tough lessons are a part of life. Who would we be without the break-up's, the betrayals and the beatings we have endured? We begin life as a blank canvas with limitless potential to become a masterpiece.

Look for the lesson and the moral and the meaning in everything you do. Challenge yourself to improve every day. And never stop that journey because the second you stand still, someone will pass you. The second you stop climbing, you inhibit your own chances of reaching your peak, your summit.

And a day without learning, challenging yourself, or doing whatever you can to make a difference is a day without taking full advantage of this gift of life that has been bestowed on us. Will you look that gift horse in the mouth? Or will you do everything you can to seek the answers of the world?

That power and that decision is always up to you.

We all came into the world a blank canvas. We had a beginning and a foundation – weak or strong. And I bet that each of us have easy excuses just laying around that we can use at any time to justify in our minds why we don't always do our best.

The success game has no place for such excuses. Those excuses will be what keep you from making the moves to get ahead in the game. Of course, even "winning" in the success game can be temporary and you have to keep playing and playing through more and more muck. But we all have a starting point, we all have the ability to stop and reassess and we all can ultimately turn our canvas into a stunning work of art.

When you get knocked down, do you play hurt, or do you call in sick? Do you make excuses, or do you accept literally no obstacles? What do you do in the no-win situation - call it a no-win situation, or die trying? Do you sit back and accept injustice, or do you fight? Do you risk lackluster results and tweak your process to get what you want?

Success has a million different definitions. Those society deem successful likely do not even view themselves as such.

It takes extreme courage. Life often requires you to take the flying cannonball leap into the deep end of the swimming pool to get what you want. Sitting back and wishing will lead you to look back years from now and say, "What if?" Instead, say, "Why not?"

Challenge the norm. Put yourself out there.

Bide your time, even if you just have to take a positive step in the right direction every day. You will eventually reach your destiny and you will become better every day.

Every day, every loss, every failure is a blip on the radar.

It takes heart, character, determination and courage to be successful - whatever your definition of the word is. Never take your eyes off the prize - that's the only way it can get away.

For, in the end, the real truth is that life and finding purpose and realizing personal success is nothing more or less than the surviving game. Surviving – and surviving well – in our endeavor to contribute our talents to the world lead to success – and that's the purpose to all.

\*     \*     \*     \*     \*

### Learning to Walk Again

In January 2010, Vincent Scott got his first true taste of the price of standing up to corporate corruption. His bright star was extinguished and world came crashing down.

He did not take it lightly; he pursued legal action and followed that slow, arduous process. He was applying to 50 or more jobs every week for months and months. He secured interviews within mere weeks for Director level positions and appeared poised to either be reinstated to his previous role or land a better one right out of the chute.

His relationship with Abby was sullied by her forced involvement in his recent downfall and they were – once again – at odds. She was reluctant to reach out to him because she knew he and everyone at work blamed her.

Vincent also could not reveal recent events to his parents. His whole life to this point had been spent fighting the insurmountable expectations of being an only child to flawless, well-respected and successful parents; he could still clearly recall the conversations about what he was going to do with his life and how every kid from Mankato that made something of themselves in dentistry or the medical field or as attorneys were so great and he felt so not. He had finally reached a status and income his parents could be proud of – only to have it taken away.

Vincent had been thrust into this capitalistic world and was hell bent on impressing everyone, taking the world by storm and marching quickly to the top. He craved money and power and a position where he could make a difference and protect and inspire the most people possible; he got there, and then had it illegally stripped away by the oppressors he fought.

In those early days, Vincent was very determined. In the days to come, rejection letters for jobs came in droves. News from his former co-workers became grimmer and less frequent due to allies leaving his camp to prevent being targeted and terminated. He learned just how broad the conspiracy had been, how many people knew about it, were in on it and what was being done to cover it up. The determination morphed into discouragement over the months to come.

Vincent went days without shaving and sometimes without showering; his workouts became less frequent with his sometimes-waning motivation, and alcohol consumption more so. Thanks to the final court battle with Abby, he had majority physical custody of Elizabeth so he was able to spend far more time with his pre-schooling sweetheart than before but when she was with Abby, Vincent's life was adrift in a sea of sorrow with no companion and no raft.

A man who formerly bounced out of bed at 5 AM on a mission and was the first to the office was now unshaven, unkempt and barely able to pry himself from the couch. His days were spent applying to jobs he would not get, getting nothing but bad news on business and personal fronts and drinking himself to oblivion. Day after day after day after day after day after day…

390 consecutive days, in fact. 13 months can seem like a relative blip on the radar versus a lifespan of 70-100+ years but when you are caught in the midst of an undeserved prison sentence it plagues every fiber of your being. Vincent hated his existence and cursed everyone who had a hand in putting him there. He was consumed with anger and rage, and was completely unable and unwilling to see past it.

He second-guessed himself, but realized it was inevitable: the only way he could have avoided this was continuing to indulge in the corporate Kool-Aid and turning a blind eye to fraud, commission scams, illegal backroom deals, nepotism, racism, sexual discrimination, retaliation and every other illegal act he had witnessed in his management career. He didn't have it in him and wouldn't have changed a thing. Unfortunately, he had tried to escape, but was fired on the day he had an interview scheduled for promotion into another department.

It was sobering to learn how worthless his seemingly solid résumé was. It was humbling to make the march in the cold and snow each four weeks to the unemployment office for his monthly check-in realizing he was among these multitudes of people who were at varying levels of despair. Vincent Scott – a man who had been responsible for driving literally millions of dollars in revenue and inspiring hundreds of people through his words and actions was now lost and alone with destination unknown.

He went from six-figure paydays and standing ovations to excommunication and desolation.

Partly to blame was Vincent's affinity for literature and film and television that supported this belief in justice and happily ever after that could be achieved within a 30-to-60 minute timeframe plus commercials. It was a rude awakening that people he had sacrificed everything for would choose their careers and families over a man who did the right thing. It was harsh reality to see that he was getting an interview for about every 100 jobs he would apply to, and the financial figures he was being quoted were a fraction of previous earnings at a first-level management or sales representative level.

It appeared likely Vincent was going to have to start all over or take a significant step back – again, through no fault of his own – and he despised everything and everyone involved in the massacre even more. He was blinded by hate and wanted vengeance by any means necessary as soon as he could obtain it. Much of his time was spent painstakingly obsessing over compiling hundreds of pages of documentation for his pending lawsuit and pleading his case via elaborate e-mails to those who could overturn his termination, to no avail.

His forced sabbatical was not for naught. In recent months prior to termination he had begun penning a book – *The Selling Game* – to tie together lessons he had learned during his career and his unique way of building relationships, closing and overcoming, and finding success in sales. With no job taking up the bulk of his waking hours he had more time to devote to and complete it.

He spent a lot of time commiserating over the state of the business world with close pal and former co-worker Jeff Mason, who shared his disdain for the bullying and thankless nature of the working world. They had worked together across two departments, knew the same heroes and villains and had seen firsthand just how much hard-working, honest laborers were up against in this politically-charged world.

And – of course – he spent every second he could with Elizabeth. For whatever torture of his soul he was undergoing, she kept it at bay. The breakfasts, the trips to the park or zoo, the cuddle sessions and stories and hide-and-seek and tea parties and Barbie-doll gatherings (with occasional cameo appearances from DC or Marvel superheroes and He-Man figures from Vincent's youth) and going for walks and ice cream kept him hanging on. That and his belief that – at some point – all would become right with the world again. It had to.

February brought interviews with a "marketing firm" that turned out to be a life insurance lure and a Director call center position Vincent would have run circles around that went to the hiring manager's friend.

He couldn't get his hopes up about any of these prospects because no matter how qualified or how good they sounded, something was amiss every time. Coaxed to the marketing firm, he wasn't told until the third interview with them that the $100,000+ he could expect came with no salary; "Oh, there's no free rides here!" the interviewer bellowed, after previous interviewers had cagily dodged the question.

And no Vincent Scott here, either.

An interview the following week was Director of Sales for the radio station selling multimedia – right up his alley! He had done this previously to much acclaim.

Of course, upon arrival he learned that position had been filled and they used the leftover résumés for perusal in their search for commission-only sales reps.

The letdowns were fast and furious and they continued to strike hard and direct against Vincent's once unflappable confidence.

Vincent's love life was just as haphazard. Through social media he reconnected with Carrie from high school; through a party with friends he came back in contact with now-divorced Tracy; through another get-together he became reacquainted with friend-of-a-friend Emily and one weekend in Mankato he ran into Casey. Each of these pairings would be forged with the guideline that it would be anti-relationship, which would last anywhere from a weekend to a few months before they realized he really meant it.

The only way Vincent could wipe out constantly missing being the star attraction, being the leader, running the show, being in love and climbing the ladder when he was not with his Elizabeth was through mindless antics; his writing and purging his mind and attempting to suppress every detail of his previous life – wading through pointless associations with females that could heal some of his ego, medicating with his vodka and finding any way possible to make it through each day in hopes the next would bring something he could cling to. He had committed too hard to people and places; now he was training himself to do the opposite.

Tensions with Abby did not help matters. Vincent was miffed that she had never reached out to him with concern after his downfall. Abby was having financial issues due to their many trips to court and was living with Chris Hurst – her other on-again off-again lover in Vincent's stead since early 2009. Vincent would give readily of his finances when he knew they went directly to Elizabeth, yet when Chris was unemployed and living in Abby's expensive condominium rent-free he had considerably less sympathy.

Their dynamic was difficult to decipher. Having met in 2006 when Vincent hired her as a sales representative in his quickly-growing call center, they had a secret workplace affair that lasted a couple of months before Vincent distanced himself. She was getting too close, he reasoned, and it was certainly not good for his career. Married to his work, Vincent rarely dated outside his area of business and for that he regularly paid dearly.

Despite being in a new relationship he had been wanting for nearly a year upon hearing the news of her pregnancy, Vincent jettisoned his new Gal Friday and attempted to make things work with Abby. They soon moved forward with shared living and engagement… and then the wheels fell off.

The years since were plagued with constant immature attempts to one-up or outpace the other in the race to be the better parent or the quicker one to move on or the points leader in the court proceedings. Still, Vincent couldn't find anyone with whom he shared the chemistry and passion he and Abby had, despite their straddling of the line between love and hate. Abby sought out men who made her feel needed and secure and superior, but they failed her every time the chips were down and she ran right back to Vincent.

It was quite the cold war – but both sides intensely longed for a day they would get along and resolve this thing one way or another.

Vincent would dread the times he couldn't drop Elizabeth off at the sitter's and had to see Abby and hide his pain. Abby would find her relationship missing what she had with Vincent and send him the occasional e-mail about how co-workers thought they were meant to be or would try to engage him in unexpected friendly conversation that lingered too long in the hallway after drop-offs. For years, it was a yo-yo – drastic ends of the spectrum between hating one another and in each others' beds, culminating in catastrophic conclusions.

For 390 days, Vincent spent his days miserable and his nights plagued by dreams of his enemies when he was actually able to fall asleep.

Of the aforementioned, the only person Vincent let into his inner sanctum during this time was Casey Carnes.

Casey had attended the same high school and had been in some plays with Vincent in their teens. Aside from that, they had little interaction but they ran into one another at Cooke's Grocery store in Mankato and started chatting online shortly thereafter. She had been to hell and back with the father of her two children and they bonded over shared horror stories, both under the pretense that they would have the anti-relationship relationship. They talked when they wanted to – sometimes for 4+ hours on the phone or through countless Internet messages – and, without the pressure, Vincent shared his heartbreaks and even let Casey see his book in the works.

They both needed an outlet and someone they could let in, and found that in each other.

It was enough to pull him slightly from his funk; he was still the charmer and they had a most epic first date. Vincent had Casey list her top five date activities and he fulfilled every one of them – miniature golf, dinner, a movie, a walk through the park at midnight and people-watching near the Minnesota River – all on date #1. It aided both that they were separated in distance between Minneapolis and Mankato by 85 miles, giving them the buffer and space both required but enabling them to speak and see one another relatively often.

Thanks to her, his vodka-fueled binges slowed and his rage subsided to the point where he could start to work on healing. Her presence in his life also served to curb any chance Vincent in his weakened state would accept the occasional dinner invitation from Abby or flirtatious message when she was in a rough spot with Chris. In turn, when he decided to get her an overly thoughtful Mother's Day card and gift that he put in Elizabeth's bag for her, she was doing well enough in her relationship to not let it coax her back in either.

Vincent's interview persona and presentation was stellar; borrowing an idea from his friends Ted Benton and Jeff Mason he had constructed a "brag book" – a compilation of successes from the prior years. It contained articles he had written, countless awards for sales, service and leadership, pictures of him with high-ranking officers accepting said awards and the like. He would blow away every interview, focusing on real results that illustrated his philosophies, specific actions he had taken to generate those results and what he had learned from his experiences.

But each job went to an internal candidate (whose "skills are more closely aligned with the position," the carefully concocted HR-speak would say) or a buddy of the hiring manager. Every single time.

It was not for his lack of effort. Thousands of job applications yielded the one end result of Brink Management Company, and getting there was a lot of frustration and work…only to yield a lot more of both, albeit a different flavor. Nevertheless, Vincent realized he was missing something here and could not quite pinpoint what it was. He could control where he applied, how many places he applied to, where he looked and what he put out there, but he could not control this intangible force field keeping him from landing a role in line with his skill set.

He also refused to start all over unless he absolutely had to. He had not advanced in his career multiple times over 9 years only to retreat to an entry-level role. Not unless his search remained fruitless for years. There certainly was not anything wrong with those who did, but he had earned the escape from the front lines and knew his impact would be more significant and talents better utilized if he was leading teams.

With Casey as his affirmation on *The Selling Game*, Vincent started the process of penning query letters to publishers and agents he found via textbook and online resources. Vincent was passionate about his book project and it was a welcome escape from the thankless duty of applying to jobs he would be rejected for. However, between the two endeavors, he was rejected thousands of times in his quests for greatness.

The commitment bug reared its head with Vincent and Casey; her son asked Casey if Vincent could be their new Daddy and they had shared pain, out-of-town trips and spent considerable time together or talking. Vincent, in true Vincent style, found every reason to convince himself this was not the sacred "one" and started shying away from her touch, her call and her company. He silently goaded her into starting the conversation about ending their relationship because she was falling for him and he was detaching from her.

Vincent then accepted a couple of dinner invitations from Abby against his better judgment; he had the hardest time turning away chances to see Elizabeth and attention without commitment. There was always something that pulled these two together even if something just as forceful would drive them apart.

Vincent's lack of confidence and despair were at all-time highs: rejection after rejection was pouring in between his job hunt and his book. Nevertheless, he became so attached and accustomed to his pain and solitude that he seemed to throw himself into it every chance he got.

Another interview would pop up that he was ripe for only to result in rejection. A meeting would come about as a result of Vincent's network and he would be in talks to come on board as a consultant or special project manager…only to have the talks collapse for whatever reason. Whether overqualified or underqualified, he was never right on the money. A publisher would show interest in the concept of his book only to decline after reading a sample. His 9-year winning streak had not only ended, but he couldn't buy a win.

He contacted 968 publishers and agents in all. 15 offered to read his work, 6 offered to publish it. One company wanted *him* to pay $20,000 for a distribution deal. Another was going to give him an advance of $1 with a miniscule royalty. Others also insisted he fork up money upfront to enter into a relationship.

He chose the one he felt had the best distribution with no fee on his part and a respectable commission. For a first-time author, he was realizing the options were slim – it was this or self-publishing and he wanted his first book to find a home for the mere sake of having had a real publisher.

Vincent signed on the dotted line for publication on July 2, 2010. *The Selling Game* was being published and would be out on Elizabeth's third birthday.

As part of the marketing for the book, Vincent did some radio and television spots in Mankato and appeared in the local paper a few times as a result of writing and distributing press releases anywhere he could think of. He also developed a YouTube channel whereby he would tease the book and cover sales and leadership topics in each video. It was yet another welcome distraction from the daily grind of applying to jobs and feeling hopeless.

His first teaser video aired July 13 and elicited over 500 views within the first few hours. Vincent spoke of corporate vampires and zombies (capitalizing on icons of the times while taking veiled potshots at previous co-workers and bosses) while sprinkling in a few sales morsels as appetizers for *The Selling Game*. It was a riot.

Doing the videos forced Vincent to shave his beard and they got him back into the familiar suit and tie and dress shoes he had actually come to miss. Being on the sidelines made him doubt if he could still deliver the hard-hitting sales message and inspire others; if he couldn't do it in his old playing field, he'd find a new arena. And – in this one – there was no limit to the number of people he could touch. His video views would count in the tens of thousands while he had previously only spoken to hundreds at one given moment in a room.

The same ego, the same swagger and the same super sales tips were all there, with the wink, the smirk and the pointing; the verbiage, the confidence and the ultimate closing techniques all intact and in full glory.

Criticism came harshly, though, and anonymously – through responses in posts on his videos or through his website. They would even out with those who called to praise him, but he always took the hatred so personally – specifically when someone told him they wished he and his family would die in a fire or when they would attack him based on his previous job. Vincent wanted nothing more than to have a positive influence on others and give to them while taking nothing; his intentions were always pure even if execution had occasionally been misguided. The trouble with playing Superman is you can only save so many; the ones who disagree with your decisions or that you don't save will resent you.

People did not understand Vincent and were jealous of him; he realized that. Heck, no one knew the real him. He used fake arrogance to hide his insecurities and let very few see his true self, but that did not make taking the flak any easier for naturally introverted Vincent.

However, he plowed forward. He would take the potshots in stride as much as he could, escaping into his vodka and doubt only to come back the next day and plant more seeds. More job applications. More social media sites touting his book or quotes from it. More videos. More articles he wrote or destinations for his press releases.

While his termination was a death blow in many ways, it was a window of time and opportunity to be with Elizabeth more and to pursue a goal of being an author while he attempted to find a career home where he was not pummeled into submission by corporate dictators. Hopefully.

Support and criticism also found him in poignant ways on August 22. It was that day he finally revealed to his parents the story of what happened to his career but that he was not resting on his laurels. Knowing that the flap of his book would reveal him no longer at his previous employer, he had no choice. They pleasantly surprised Vincent and were nothing but behind him and his plight for justice 100%.

Furthermore, he had a detractor when he dropped Elizabeth off at Abby's condo.

After the usual pleasantries upon seeing her mother for the first time in days, Elizabeth started playing with her dog in the parking lot.

"So – how's the job hunt?" Abby inquired.

Vincent, always suspicious of Abby's motives whether he had a reason to be or not, responded, "It's going fine."

"You're quite the stir at work."

"I hadn't noticed," Vincent lied, fully aware that his latest moves were the talk of his former stomping grounds.

"Everybody's talking about your videos. They are watching them on the floor throughout the day."

"Good for them. I can use the book sales."

"So when are you going to get off YouTube and get a job?"

"Get a job?!? Abby, last I checked, being a published author IS a job," Vincent retorted. "I've applied to 800 jobs in 7 months, written a book, got it published and you're going to attack me because my publisher wants me to market my work with these videos?"

"I just—"

"No. You just have to kick me when I'm down."

Vincent made a motion to Elizabeth and went to hug her.

"Baby, I love you," Vincent said, embracing his daughter one last time.

"I love you, Daddy," Elizabeth responded, smiling and kissing her Dad.

He opened his car door and moved to get inside. Abby – frustrated and flustered – softened her facial expression and tone.

"Vincent… Vincent, let's talk."

"You've said enough."

And for the umpteenth time in their sordid relationship, a conversation concluded with one of their vehicles tearing off and away.

With Vincent getting distance from Casey, he soon found himself chatting online and via text message more with Emily Nance; the bridesmaid he walked down the aisle at his close friend Jack Johnson's wedding. They discussed spending time together. Vincent spent time with Carrie Garner again. He also got a call from Julie Lansing – his previous most infamous girlfriend – who had pre-ordered his book and become his first sale. She was newly single and indicated interest in obtaining an autographed copy, asking about the chances for a book party.

So many potential prospects, between jobs and girls, yet Vincent had no idea where he was headed. This was part of the dilemma, for everything had seemingly been laid out so nice and neat by his parents: grow up, go to college, get a job, get married and have kids. Unfortunately, Vincent had no idea what he wanted to do in his life so he didn't care much for college, he found a skill in sales and management but not in dealing with the politics, had a child out of wedlock with a co-worker because he was so devoted to his job, the relationship imploded and now he couldn't even commit to good song on the radio for fear he was missing out on a better one, much less a career path or romantic relationship.

Vincent had not seen Julie in 8 years and they had ended poorly, but both had learned a lot from this youthful relationship and there was never any closure. Julie missed Mankato after the two moved to Minneapolis together and she left while he stayed. Now she was back in Minneapolis, single and 8 years older.

In late August with the book release nearing and a book signing announced, Julie and Vincent spoke more frequently.

At heart – despite his everyday attempts to stifle it – Vincent was a romantic. It was why he built dream dates for Casey. It was why he had made grand gestures for Abby. It was why he held out hope there was a soul mate. Why was Julie Lansing reentering his life at a time like this?

And there was Emily Nance – she happened to be going through a divorce and she and Vincent (like Vincent and Casey) bonded over their shared romantic and single parent woes. Furthermore, her connection to Vincent's oft-spiritual guide Jack Johnson made this seem even more like an intriguing connection.

There was also the bizarre chemistry and connection with Abby; it wasn't just Elizabeth that existed between them, but there was still too much toxicity in the water.

It was at this point in time in the sabbatical that Vincent could take no more. He could not sit at home in his solitude and anger any longer. He could not tolerate his rage toward former employer and daughter's mother. He had all of these balls in the air and no idea where to go.

He reached out to a career counseling service and set a meeting. He turned up the heat on his job search and started exploring new ways to reach out. Vincent was going to figure this thing out – one way or another.

He even called a psychic after too much vodka, too little sleep and a late night infomercial. It didn't help that she told him he would find success in business and that he had already met his soul mate.

Vincent was getting closer to a conclusion to this debacle, but it would not end as soon as he would have liked or in any type of way he could anticipate.

## "The Surviving Game" by Vincent Scott
### Coping With Catastrophe

Whether you are born into poverty or the penthouse, you will face catastrophe. It strikes the poor and rich alike and does not discriminate based on any factors. You can try to stave it off, but it will creep up on you. You can conquer one, but another will eventually take its place. It's how you handle these catastrophes along your road to happiness and success that determines how quickly and if you reach your desired destiny. It is how we persevere and endure in times of loss and strife that will forge our legacy and our ultimate success.

Catastrophe comes in many forms, but the common theme is that of loss; losing something or someone you hold dear that you may never see or feel or have again. Or even if you have the chance of experiencing it again, you are having the initial difficulty of looking past the grief and anguish and uncertainty you now face.

We can face catastrophe through our own doing, forcing us to shoulder the responsibility of making amends and making it right. We can face catastrophe through no fault of our own, which makes it all the more difficult to bear.

Caring or loving or investing any part of yourself in anything opens you up to potential loss, which is why we must be so selective and guarded about such an investment. You do not gamble your life savings in the lottery or casino, much like you do not give all of your heart or soul to something or someone undeserving, lest they use it, abuse it or diffuse it.

We spend a lot of our time on this earth clawing and scratching and scraping to get back to the state we were in before loss: feelings, a partner, dignity or respect. Life will eventually strip you of much of what you have and accumulate; sometimes through no fault or involvement of ours whatsoever.

It is important that we do not lose sight of what value the lost element brought to our lives and that we incorporate the lessons obtained going forward – whether we can have that element again or not. We will also often take on new acquisitions – both relationships and items – that will hold a similar place and perhaps better esteem in our lives as we continue.

Live in the moment and do your best to bask in what you do have. Invest for the future – spiritually through the relationships you form and financially plan for potential downside. Be mindful of how everything you do affects yourself and others. And cherish the great things and the happiness you have while they are in your life.

All too often, nothing can prepare you for the losses you will have and the havoc they wreak on your life. Sudden deaths, unforeseen circumstances, or reversals of fortune happen all the time. You can worry or try to prepare for something, only to have something else altogether sneak up on you. We spend much of our lives worrying about things completely out of our control; the best thing to do is always to do the best we can. The best thing to do is prepare as well as possible and handle things as they come.

These losses, the pain they inflict on us and the lessons to be learned from them are our trials. No one ever claimed life was easy, and many people have few facets of their lives that are. The way you handle these setbacks, the way you grieve for those who no longer walk with you and the method by which you manage your emotions will evolve and grow.

As you tackle more loss and more severe circumstances, you will grow more accustomed to following the grieving process. Your ability to acknowledge the negative forces, address your emotions and move forward effectively will grow.

My first true romantic breakup stung. I had been over the relationship for months and longed for my solitude, and even did the breaking myself; but it was the initial sense of loss, the loneliness in the night and not getting the anticipated response of being chased that triggered the emotion in me. In fact, that breakup – over 11 years ago – was the most significant of my life even if I believed more in relationships since.

We go through pain so we can withstand more in the future.

We experience these feelings so we know what to do if they strike again. Like building immunity to an illness, our tolerance for these feelings of heartbreak strengthens. That, or it prevents us from investing of ourselves much again and being more selective in whom we allow into our lives.

What we cannot allow it to do is to shut ourselves off completely; try as we might, we will always need people in our lives. Failure to trust anyone, have or seek outlets of some sort or to expunge our demons will leave you hollow.

In our social media-drenched society, we think the more friends the better. As we age and gain experiences, our list of true friends will become very short but more significant.

The fear of losing someone we love to death follows many of us; when it strikes we are forced to realize that the story between us and that person has concluded. Finding the way to deal with that grief depends on a variety of factors:

knowing their pain – if any – has ended, relishing the time we did have together, and looking back fondly on the investment we gave that person.

Celebrate their life and the contributions they made to yours and to others'. If they made a meaningful impact on your life, try to pay it forward and make a similar impact on another. There are many ways to honor the memory of those we lose; their loss was certainly not for naught if we find admirable ways by which to remember them.

Some of us work through our pain alone. Some are fortunate to have others who will carry us along the way.

But the recurring theme of pain is that it will eventually end. "This too, shall pass."

It is so important that we never lose hope, we never lose sight on the big picture and on the full scope of our existence.

In the moment – or moments – of coping with catastrophe, it is extremely easy to find ourselves feeling hopeless or distraught. We often fail to see any light at the end of our tunnel of sorrow because we are so lost in the hurt or the fear or the anger we face. To survive, not only do we have to acknowledge the pain and suffering, realize the good things we still have and plot a course of action to get back on track, but we must recognize that all things – good and bad – come to an end.

The ending of suffering may not occur on our timetable, but the sooner we are able to address our emotions and work on healing though all methods available to us, the sooner we will reach peace.

There is no way I could pen this chapter without quoting the old faithful, "what does not kill us makes us stronger," but, in reality, how strong must we get? How can we ever truly prepare ourselves for what lies ahead? Or should we even get caught up in worrying about things that – most often – never come to fruition?

Coping with catastrophe is about acknowledging the presence of the negative thoughts, feelings and emotions, trying as hard as we can to dispassionately choose our course of action and moving forward. We will get knocked several steps back through our lives – sometimes through particular days – but we have to trudge forward one step extra. That is the only way we can stay ahead of the steamroll that negative emotions can often be.

The toughest pills to swallow are the ones we are forced to without our consent or without fairness, but we all face that predicament. The heroes in life are not heroes because they folded when things got unfair. And we cannot just cry foul and expect life to give us a mulligan or do-over. We cannot sit around waiting on the referee to call a penalty and give us a free throw shot. We cannot act injured or lay down or retire; the game of life keeps going and we have to keep going with it. Bills don't stop, the needs of others don't stop and life doesn't stop; it may be challenging to remain focused on the day-to-day grind, but we focus on what must be done, we focus on the positives and we carry on.

There are few better ways to remind ourselves of the positive blessings in our lives than to write them down; make them tangible. Keep a log of the things in your life that you want to remind yourself of on a regular basis and review them often. If you find comfort through prayer or talking to a friend or even just leaving your surroundings and escaping to new ones for a while, utilize these methods to aid your coping and healing.

Whether it is for our pride, our dignity, leading by example for all eyes that are upon us and depend on us, or showing our kids how they need to act through such things, how we hold ourselves up in the face of adversity goes a long way in determining how high up the mountain we can climb. In essence, we are controlling how many steps back life can push us in our journey. It is far easier to move forward when we do not allow ourselves to be pushed back any farther than necessary.

Everyone wants to reach the summit of the mountain, but many of us stop after several falls. Those who reach the top are simply those who keep getting up, keep climbing and never let catastrophe keep them down for too long.

And know that no matter how horrible you feel, how hopeless you think your situation is or how hurt you are, someone is less fortunate. Someone (and likely many someone's) is worse off: they lack food, they lack clothing or the money to even buy the book you are reading. Some are unwanted and unloved; some are without any education or a chance.

Hopefully you can muster up the strength and courage and will and faith to plow through; if you fail to do so, you, those you love, those who depend on you and anyone you will positively affect in the future all lose. Think about that. You matter, and a visit to the big picture can help alleviate the suffering you face.

In the wake of a wave of overwhelming emotion, we sometimes make our worst decisions. We can make uncharacteristic decisions that prove to be our biggest mistakes. We must always bring ourselves back to who we are, what we value and what we know to be right. No better way to cope with catastrophe than to set it against the backdrop of the big picture; take the lessons, celebrate the good that you had… and go on.

Tragedy will strike you and those you love. After all, we will not make it out of life alive. You will lose abilities, friends, loved ones, and battles, but don't lose the war. Don't lose hope. Don't lose you.

How you cope with the catastrophe that will befall you is the footing you have scaling that mountain. Get your bearings, keep your wits about you and make good decisions. You have no other choice, and a lot is riding on it.

Things can always be worse; in fact, you can make them worse through your missteps or misguided actions. Controlling what you can control in this case means controlling your willingness to grieve, your actions in the face of loss and how you take with you the important pieces of what you've learned.

Losing and being humbled builds our character. It forces us to alter our course. It hones our skills and makes us more effective. It also makes us realize what really matters in life – what and who we can and cannot live without. It shows us who is there for us during the trying times. It breaks us down so we can build ourselves up better than we were before.

Survival is an attitude. It is defiance in the face of life's many challenges. Life can continue to throw obstacles your way and knock you down, but the fight isn't called at three knockdowns and the bell doesn't ring to end it. Don't give anything – life included – the satisfaction of getting the better of you.

No one is worth your self-destruction. Your enemies want to see you implode and fail; why would you give them that satisfaction? Know and have faith that they will reap what they sow; the way they treat people will get them in the end when no one is there to cushion their fall.

Rely on your resources, be it your strength and ability to overcome, or the support system who wants to take an active role in your recovery.

A key mechanism to cope with catastrophe is living a regret-free life: basking in the joys you have while you have them, enjoying the people in your world while they reside there and continuing to plant positive seeds in all facets of your life. They will blossom and take the place of anything and everything you lose.

When a pet dies, we grieve and remember all of the unconditional love they brought to our lives. We can buy another pet who will never replace the first but will bestow new memories, new love and more joy on our lives.

All we can do is the best we can do, whether the skies are blue or we are mired in the storm. As challenging as it is, take ahold of yourself in these moments of setbacks and loss and fight to stay centered and in control. Find people and things you love, and you can survive any storm no matter the severity or duration. There will always be blue skies ahead. Even in the wake of inevitable catastrophe.

## "The Surviving Game" by Vincent Scott
## Mastery of the Job Market Game

At some point or another, in all likelihood unless you're blessed with more money than you know what to do with, you will seek employment. When you do, there are many steps you can take to enhance your chances at success. There are common misconceptions and missteps that prolong this process far more than necessary. It pays considerably to know how to play this game.

There are few greater frustrations on the job hunt than the constant rejection – especially for jobs that you are perfectly qualified for and get your heart set on. How many times have you read a job description and said, "This job would be perfect for me!" only to get the rejection notice in your e-mail just hours or days – or even months – later. While they were impressed by your credentials, they went with someone more closely aligned. "How is that possible?"

First, there is a reason they say, "it's not what you know, but who you know," because the most valuable resource in your career path is not talent, not ability, but network.

This chapter will not only delve into utilization of your own network, but how to branch out and forge new additions – even if you are an introvert.

Construction of a résumé is crucial to the process, but realization that you are up against dozens – if not hundreds – of other candidates in your quest is even more so. What sets you apart? This is the most important question to ask yourself as you set sail on a new career path. Those differences are what you must expound upon and advertise as you target the next stop on your career path.

Playing the job market game is like gambling; the odds are against you. They could be 10-to-1 but are likely closer to 100-to-1 or worse for every single job you apply to. With the ease of Internet applications in this day and age, anyone can apply to any job that is showcased for all to see on the web. That is why you must also utilize other methods by which to get yourself in front of decision-making parties. You also must temper your expectations and not get down when you are rejected for one or two jobs; if you decide to just apply to a few jobs or decide to stop looking because of rejection, you will destroy your search before you even get started.

There are many schools of thought on résumé construction and applying to jobs; personally, my philosophy in building network and seeking careers is akin to my sales philosophy: do not discriminate against any potential lead sources. You never know which one will yield the golden ticket.

Let me liken your job hunt to putting together a marketing campaign, for this is exactly what you are engaging in. You are marketing yourself. This is why – just as companies do for themselves – you must figure out how to differentiate yourself from the rest and emerge the best. Why would a potential employer select you and your résumé over the hundreds of others they received?

Fair or not, not every résumé sees human eyes after being dropped into the job application well. In essence, it falls into a system; a system that is designed to eliminate as many résumés as possible. The last one standing is the one who takes the job.

And you may feel very proud of your résumé; but the majority of the other 100 people who applied may very well be, too. This is why finding and employing every mechanism possible to market yourself is the best way to increase your chances at landing a job.

It starts with presentation. I've actually received résumés scrawled in pencil on a piece of loose leaf paper. I've gotten the fancy paper, seen one-sheets and several sheets. Truth is, as a hiring manager, I don't look at résumés much, but they are important when it comes to getting you through the gates.

Initially, your résumé will be run against keywords that the employer may be looking to find or avoid. Companies and employers are looking for different things for different roles, which is why many people will tell you to use a different résumé for different types of positions you are applying to; there is merit in that statement. The secret sauce changes all the time, but you should make certain your résumé is tailored to the role and type of role you are seeking.

As a general theme, what most résumés are missing is real results. As a candidate attempting to attract a company, your goal is to show them what you've done in a way they can visualize you doing it for them.

In other words, it is far too common for a résumé to read: "Answered phone calls and sold plans to customers." What does this even mean? Does this make an employer fall all over themselves trying to sign you? Or does this sound like something anyone can do?

The burden of proof is on you to show that you are uniquely qualified for the position; that you will bring something to it no one else can. Rather than stating a simple fact of what your job function entails, post, "Exceeded 125% to sales goal all 15 months in inbound call center position. Averaged 95$^{th}$ percentile in call efficiency. Earned customer service award 6 months for top service surveys. Mentored fellow team members and increased their output 45% within 3 months."

Your résumé is your key to the kingdom. Once you get in, you have to perform for the royalty but before that, you have to gain entrance by showing you bring something of interest. Otherwise, they will not waste anyone's time – least of all their own.

Should you apply to online openings? Yes. However, you should certainly not make this the chief method of search; in fact, it is not even secondary. But you never know who will see your résumé – whether you are networking, reaching out to existing network or dropping your résumé off door to door – so you must ensure it is indicative of what you bring to the table.

Each résumé should lead off with contact information and roll into a summary, highlighting your claim(s) to fame. "#1 Account Executive." "Top 5% in Sales Leadership." "Recognized for training and mentoring peers and construction of process improvement plan that increased office efficiency by 25%." This is where you trumpet your talents and what you have accomplished for – remember – an employer is asking, "Can they do this for me?"

What areas do you have talents in? "Extensive experience in account management, sales leadership, retail, inbound and outbound call center, customer service, conflict resolution, escalations…" You get the picture. If you have any accolades, significant achievements that you can show through results and unique accomplishments that set you apart from the pack, point them out here.

From here, it is time to summarize your work history. The more distinguished your experience and/or the higher you are attempting to climb the ladder, the more important it becomes to have consistency in your work history. This can be any number of things: first, consistency in dependability for a company and a reason behind any lapses in working. Second, this could consist of an undertaking you have on the side, be it consulting, real estate, writing, or any other entrepreneurial effort. It shows that you have been actively working, have always been trying to work and it lessens questions your potential employer might have about your work history and ethic.

Many of us will have circumstances from our work history that ended a particular job; your explanation as to why it ended should never have anything to do with not liking your boss or employer. Just like in sales, you quickly acknowledge and are prepared for the question, you address it and bring it back to the matter at hand: you see this as the opportunity for you based on your skill set and the job description, and you point out specific items that line up between you and what the employer is looking for.

"Absolutely, I chose to leave that position because it was not in my chief area of interest and I wanted to devote the necessary time to finding my calling. I'm currently only exploring roles in that area, which is what brought me here, and based on the job description and what I have accomplished (such as…), this would be a great fit."

You might have hated your job and your supervisor, disagreed with their policies and disliked illegal activity they performed, but anything you say disparaging about your previous employer will only make your new prospective one wonder: "Will they talk this way about us?"

You may have been terminated for a job, but you can answer this away by making sure to take the focus off the objection: "Yes, that job ended in termination of employment. My customer service statistics and efficiency were exemplary, however my sales numbers were not. That is why I am seeking a role that will focus on my areas of excellence. Since this role we are discussing does not entail sales, but does involve service and efficiency, it would be right in my wheelhouse."

Remember: your new prospective employers have seen a lot, talked with countless numbers of candidates previously and they know what they want and do not want. In fact, you may be doing a job that has been done many times before or is being done now and they want to visualize you coming in, doing the job well, performing, and co-existing with their team. Everything you can do in your presentation, your résumé and your interview process to convey those attributes and sell that persona will again enhance your likelihood of joining their team.

That said, stay away from generic jargon on your résumé like "team player" or "strong work ethic" or "trustworthy" or "excellent customer service skills"; they are not tangible and therefore they do nothing to further your cause. These are attributes you want to illustrate through actual examples of excellence, both in your résumé and interviews.

How were you a team player? Did you form or contribute to any committees to ascertain people's opinions and foster collaboration? Did you survey your team to determine how you could best serve them? Were you part of any collaborative groups or sessions to improve the overall team performance?

How do you know you had excellent customer service skills? Did you receive commendations or awards? Did you employ a way to gauge your customers' satisfaction? Are there any measurements of work or statistics that gauge your performance in this area?

Another valuable item that can set you apart from other candidates vying for the same job is a "brag book"; this is a compilation of your certificates and any other proof of your achievements. It can contain articles you have written, results, letters from supervisors, and anything and everything substantiating your superiority as an employee. When potential employers see this, it serves as evidence of your good standing. It makes the leap of faith any employer makes when they take a new hire at their word easier to make. It's also something not a lot of folks do, meaning you have done something to stand apart.

For, this is the goal of a job-seeker: take as many steps as possible to eliminate the obstacles in your way and tip the odds more in your favor, cast as wide a net as possible and make yourself stand out above the other candidates you are up against.

Many candidates in this day and age also construct a video résumé, whose web address can be attached to your physical résumé, sent via e-mail and through social media sites. It does not even have to be professionally compiled or edited; it is you selling a potential viewer on why you are a candidate worth paying attention to. Whereas I do not believe the "objective" segment of a physical résumé is vital, here it can be inserted. "I am looking for an innovative corporation who recognizes hard work, wants to grow and will be the company I retire from."

The trick of job hunting is that there is no silver bullet; you have to reach out to as many places and people as you can with the best presentation possible. Sadly, it's as if they are looking for a way to eliminate you and – honestly – who can blame them? From their vantage point, they receive 100 or more applicants for one position, all touting the same things – greatness. How do you pick just one person? Even if you're seeking placement as one of 10 in a new training class, you are still grappling with 10% odds or less in some cases.

This is the very reason why you are rejected for the positions you fall in love with and think you would be perfect for; because 99 other folks are thinking the same thing. Especially if it's a job that is remarkably easy to apply for, like a one-click job or something that is just "attach your CV here" – if it's that easy, you're up against even more folks who took this easy path!

We are less-than-thrilled when businesses we work for bring in somebody else's buddy, right? But if they have someone they know vouching for them, it makes the decision to take the aforementioned leap of faith an easier one. Why take a chance on someone they don't know when they can hire Jim's buddy who has done something similar before and who Jim is vouching for? You're an unknown; a risk and a gamble. Your job search goal is convincing an employer that the risk of hiring you is minimal and the reward will be great. You know you'd be better than so-and-so's buddy, but they don't.

Of course, these words serve as no consolation when you are suffering through a drought of unemployment – I know this. Nevertheless, it is what we are up against, so to give ourselves a fighting chance, we have to network. We have to become Jim's buddy. Since not enough people care about what we know, we have to get to know the people who will.

Look at your network. This could be your address list in your phone. It could be your LinkedIn network, or Facebook or e-mail addresses. Your network is people you feel comfortable with reaching out and sticking out job market feelers to.

Let me tell you – there's no pride when it comes to job searching. You are talking about feeding your family and taking care of your livelihood; people are not going to look down on you because you reach out to them to see if they know of anything that might align with your skills. Frankly, this is why you should keep in touch with your network even in times of feast; if you're only hitting them up in famine, they'll be less likely to consider you a close enough friend or contact.

In fact, you may also find that you are doing them a favor. Many of your contacts may be compensated for referring high quality people to a position, so this could be mutually beneficial. Furthermore, ask what would you do or have you done when someone has reached out for your help under similar circumstances in the past?

Hard times hit us all. We can prepare against the downside, but it does not mean we will not find ourselves unemployed or even working in a stepping-stone job. The older we get, the more likely this will be the case. Unfortunately, for a variety of reasons, it is not as likely that we will work our entire careers with one company – or even two – as many of our ancestors did. Because of this, it is probable we will be forced to learn the job market game.

Many people reach out to their network and quickly latch on to something – even something that might be less than what they had intended or are qualified to do. This happens, and we do what we have to do to keep the lights on. But just like our actions in our jobs qualify as constantly "interviewing" for the next level, our actions networking – even while we are employed – should be constantly planning against that downside.

Networking can be free, easy and very valuable for a variety of reasons personally and professionally. Thanks to the Internet, some of the best networking can be done either online or by acquiring contact information online. Some simple company research on a wide variety of sites can yield names of those you want to network with, their contact information and methods of contact.

Many people are very open to networking with you for this very reason;

they know the value of networking and that there is no telling when a relationship will pay mutual dividends. Ask yourself: if you were in the position for someone to reach out to you and ask for some advice, would you give it to them if you could help? That is the same mentality many others have.

What is your preferred method of reaching out to your existing network? It may be the phone for some individuals; e-mail or social media for others. Remember that when you ask someone for assistance in your job search, it is vital not to be pushy, desperate or demanding. This is a passive, relationship-building process and – like any other part of the job market game – there is strength in numbers.

You get more flies with honey – this is key to networking of any kind. Growing your network also assists in you having more numbers of people on which to rely.

Call the people you feel comfortable calling. Contact the others in the way you see fit so they have the ability to absorb the information and see where you may be of use at their company.

Another reason it is important to constantly network and stay in touch with people is someone may feel opposed to helping you if the only time they ever hear from you is when you want help. This is another reason why social media can be so valuable, because it gives you the opportunity to engage them daily whether it is commenting or "liking" a status or post or sending them a quick message.

Your message to any potential networking source should be complimentary and to the point. Also, you should never ask for the desired end result – a job. This is skipping steps and will often result in no response or in the other person shying away from your request with a cordial rejection of sorts. You also have to realize that not everyone you reach out to is going to be in a position to help you – right now. You never know when they might be, so burn no bridges that may later bring value.

"Jane: How have you been? I hope this note finds you and your family well. I've recently begun exploring new career opportunities and was looking for your advice on where I might be able to transition my sales and customer service skills into XYZ Marketing. I'd love to chat for 5-to-10 minutes and get your guidance. If there is anyone else you can think of I should also talk to, I'd appreciate you pointing me in their direction, too. Also, if my network or I can ever be of service, please do not hesitate to ask. Thank you! Vincent."

Here we have expressed our desire for their well-being, which is always a classic. We've announced an interest in looking for a new career opportunity without coming across as desperate (I got fired, I got laid off) and even without spelling out circumstances. Remember: everyone on the other end is always on a need-to-know basis, whether you dislike your current job and are passively looking, or you just got canned and you are trying to get back in the game.

Asking for advice is far better than, "Do you guys have any jobs?" or "are you hiring?" because – again – you have to set yourself apart. People ask people all the time if they have jobs where they are – stand apart! Flatter them with a request for their advice; it shows you respect them and will break down any barriers they may have against such requests.

You have also planted the seed that you would love to talk to anyone else they know, which can assist in your exploration and open new doors.

Finally, you have offered your own network to them in a gesture that makes them aware that if they ever need you for anything, they can feel free to contact you.

Like anything else in sales or business, your #1 goal is getting the person on the other side to put down their walls, let you in and build a relationship. That is what improves your probability at achievement; it's the "presentation" piece of the job market game.

Be patient and be gracious; you need them now and that's why it is important to do this on their timetable with what they feel comfortable without being pushy.

Our networks start out at varying sizes but – specifically as we advance in our career or wish to branch out to new fields, it is imperative we add to them. Some prefer networking events and like working the room, meeting new faces and trading business cards like baseball cards. Others prefer a more passive approach, which is why they are often found trolling the Internet job boards to no avail. There is a way, however, to have success right there from the comfort of your home – to start. It is also very effective if done properly.

Networking events can be promising, however you are contending with several others – financial advisors, insurance agents and the like – who are working to get leads. The reason I prefer utilization of LinkedIn and online mediums to locate leads is because it is convenient, effective and highly targeted. You cannot control who shows up to a networking event, but you certainly can control how you geographically target individuals from companies or industries you are interested in.

Another thing to remember is you are not necessarily looking to connect with a recruiter or just a random person at a company of interest. Recruiters are already up to their eyeballs in résumés and will typically direct you back into their funnel by telling you to apply on the site. It does not mean to leave them out of your search; your best bet is to reach out to someone in a position above what role you are looking to fill.

The reason I led off with the résumé is because you must have one in order to start playing this game. LinkedIn is a phenomenal site that has been very lucrative in many job searches; the LinkedIn journey begins with your profile.

Like with anything else, standing out for positive reasons will help you catch the eye of a potential employer. Your LinkedIn profile should mirror your résumé structure and the nice thing about LinkedIn is that it will prompt you to soup it up quite a bit.

Once you have a strong profile, your next move is to join groups. My recommendation is to join the ones that are geographically and topically conducive to your job search. If you are looking for any industry or geography, your target can be a lot broader or you can even join the groups that your target contacts reside in. The reason for this is that you can connect with anyone in the same group as you, utilizing the shared group as the reason for your connection request. It is another aid in increasing the likelihood of their acceptance.

For, from this point, your entire goal is to build a network of people that can conceivably help you – one way or another.

When it comes to groups, there are some that begin with the title LinkedWorking followed by a geographical area or city name; if there is one near you, it would be advisable to join. There will likely be several others that bear the name of nearby cities – join them. The more of these groups you join, the better chance you have of sharing groups with some of the people you will want to meet.

Once you have joined groups (you have a limit of 50, and should leave some room to join groups that desired contacts are in) it is time to start making connections. Pick a company, or several. Pick an industry. It helps to keep a running list of both to help you log where you have looked.

Search for it in the search bar at the top of your screen and throw in a job title that is higher than the one you seek. If you wish to be a sales rep, pick Manager, Area Manager, Director, VP of Sales. If you wish to be a Manager, pick Area Manager, Director, VP of Sales. If you want to work for a small business, connect with the Director or VP or CEO or owner.

Reach out to the person whose decision it may ultimately be to hire you, or to someone above them. If the VP of Sales calls down to their Director and says, "Hey, take a look at this candidate I'm sending you," it goes a lot longer way than dropping your résumé into the black hole of online applications hoping to make its way upward. If you start at the top, you have a better chance of winding up in front of who you want to meet.

After the results of your search are populated, you can narrow them down to your liking; geographically and by current company, to ensure they are still at the company you are looking at. Of course, there is much merit for the other companies you may find high-ranking officials at. There is much merit to the small businesses that are out there, whose CEO's are much more available to you than the CEO at a Fortune 500 company.

As prominent as LinkedIn is and is becoming, no one is really off limits. Find someone you wish to connect with, select connect, and it is time to fashion another flattering welcome that gets you in the door.

Again, where many make their mistake is they ask for the end result rather than taking the steps to get there. At this point, we should not ask for jobs or even an interview. Initially, we just want to become part of their network, and they a part of ours.

The request is simple enough; select how you "know" them – often through the same group (you can even change search parameters to only show you people in your groups) and move to the field where you can personalize the request.

"Good morning/afternoon, Tony. It is my sincere hope this note finds you well. Our mutual interests and shared group led me to believe you would be a great person to share ideas with and learn from. I would be honored to be a part of your network. Much appreciated – Vincent."

You have stated your name and case, flattered them and sought only the connection. From your target connection's viewpoint, the risk is minimized and they really have no reason to reject your request. This first step has a 50/50 chance of working depending on their frequency of checking LinkedIn and interest in broadening their connections. Many of them will view your profile as well (which you can also monitor), making it all the more important that you make the right first impression with a strong, attractive profile.

Timing from this point is also important; rather than come across as an opportunistic weasel by pouncing on them the moment they accept your request, wait a few days. It reminds me of the movie *Swingers* when the minimum wait time to call a new potential date is 3 days (or, as Vince Vaughn warns, "You might scare off a nice baby who's ready to party"). Apply the same wait time here and let the dust settle on the acceptance prior to making next contact.

From here, your odds will diminish further, which is the very reason you again cast a wide net, you have your online applications you fill out and you reach out to your existing network, enhance your résumé and even film a video résumé.

Pull out all the stops. It's your career, after all. The end result will mirror the efforts put into it.

In fact, using this in unison with your online applications can only bolster your attack. Did you find a job you feel you're perfect for online, as we discussed earlier? Perfect! Target leaders in that company via this method. Reference the job title and requisition ID, quickly outline your relevant experience and request guidance on where you may fit in the business. Chances are, they will point you in the direction of the hiring manager or get you closer to standing out in the way that gets you noticed. These are also the "hustle stats" – the little things you are doing that those you are competing with are not.

When you have waited a few days, reach back out to the new contact with a quick message. The easiest way to keep up with who you need to touch base with is by saving the e-mails from LinkedIn regarding those who have accepted your request. Keep them marked as unread until you have reached back out to them.

"Good morning/afternoon, Tony – I hope this note finds you well. Thank you for connecting! The intent of my note is to seek your advice as I am exploring transitioning my skills in sales and management into the pharmaceutical industry. It would be an honor if we could sit down and chat for 15-to-20 minutes so I could obtain your guidance on where I may fit in your business. Please let me know what times this week work best for you, and I will happily make myself available. I look forward to meeting you. Much appreciated – Vincent."

There are a few ways of doing this; sending messages out like this early in the week leave plenty of time for your new contact to put you on their schedule for the week. A mix of connecting with new people and sending out messages like this is what you are ultimately driving toward; managing your schedule between allotting time to seek out new contacts while actually having advice meetings with those who accept is a dream scenario.

This is a continuing process – often even when you are currently working! Never pin all your hopes on one job or job opportunity; what will you do if it does not pan out? Until you have a job offer for your next opportunity, you are in transition. Even if you are employed and content in this day and age, there is no telling when changes will occur that could put your role in peril. Having a network, building a network in your field or others that interest you and keeping in contact with them is always of benefit.

A smaller number than those who accepted your LinkedIn invitation will take you up on the offer for a meeting in their office or over coffee. Nevertheless, this is what you were after to begin with: a chance to showcase your skills to a live person.

Sometimes, they will suggest a phone call; do not be discouraged. Ultimately, you want to talk to this person to gain insight into the business unit you are interested in; they may give you information, call you in for a meeting or point you in the direction of someone you should talk to. There is no bad discussion here.

Chief to the discussion is to prepare yourself similarly to an interview, but know that you will be doing the driving. You requested the meeting – not the other way around – so you need to come prepared to lead the discussion with questions and commentary on what you bring to the table. This can be daunting for some initially, but once you do a few of these they will come more naturally.

Fashion your pitch like a sale or precisely like the communications you have branded up to this point; thank them, state your business and launch into questions designed to elicit the desired responses. Arm yourself with some knowledge of the industry and their company gleaned from their site or articles. Ask questions and be prepared to answer some.

"Hi, Tony, this is Vincent Scott. We met through LinkedIn – how are you today? Great! First off, thank you so much for taking some time out for me today. I'm currently looking at ways to transition my sales and leadership talents into the pharmaceutical industry and took a specific interest in XYZ Pharmaceuticals because of your prominence in Minneapolis and some of the strategic acquisitions you've made. What advice or guidance could you give me on potentially making that transition?" "I see that such-and-such has recently been a challenge in the industry; how are you addressing that?"

From here, listen and ask additional probing questions. What they tell you may be that you have to start from scratch in their business, it may be changes going on in alignment and it might be in new divisions that are being built and not even advertised via online listings. It's like you are getting the inside scoop.

Ask if there is anyone else you should speak to. Be ready to answer questions they may likely have about your background, experience, skills and accomplishments. They have likely checked your profile and know a little of your background – these conversations can turn into interviews if they like you.

If the meeting is in person, it is another good opportunity to bring along your brag book. Remember – do not force your résumé on them and do not solicit an interview. Just cast the wide net of asking for advice and see where it goes.

Some of these meetings will seem utterly unsuccessful. However, if they do nothing more than get you in front of someone new who is prominent in the field who knows you going forward wherever they go in their career and it hones your ability to conduct these meetings, it was a worthwhile investment of your time. Investments do not always pay immediate dividends. Contacts you make today may pay off years down the road. Plus, keeping your networking or interview skills sharp is never a bad thing.

Just like following a job interview, follow this up with a brief, succinct thank you note showing appreciation for their time and guidance. If they have instructed you to do any follow up activities, do them quickly to reinforce your interest and seriousness.

And remember – your goal is planting as many seeds as you can with the best presentation, best approach and best follow-up possible. There are literally no guarantees in the job hunt, but the fewer gaps you leave in your search, the better your approach. If and when you find yourself in need of a new career path, you will already know how to best play the job market game.

\*     \*     \*     \*     \*

# THE SALESMAN RETURNS

## A New Horizon

Starting the Accord and embarking on a new adventure, Vincent Scott checked his mirrors, backed up and shifted into drive.

When Vincent had begun his sales career on September 17, 2001, he had been 22 years old, nervous and naïve; unsure of himself or of his talents. Now, on February 7, 2011, he was 32, a single Dad and a very different version of himself.

To prepare himself for the day ahead, Vincent always set his phone alarm clock to begin trumpeting daybreak two hours prior to the time he needed to depart. Pressing snooze to initiate several additional ten minute intervals of sleep or rest would typically ensue. On this day, however, Vincent Scott sprung forth from bed, ready to begin anew.

Would he be able to shake off the dust from his forced year-long sabbatical? Did he still have the ability to inspire the masses and drive unparalleled results?

Vincent was making the relatively brief drive this morning to Golden Valley, Minnesota, to a Cellular Horizons store owned by his new boss, Jordan Wallace.

Wallace had entered Vincent's life as more or less a fluke. Since his unexpected bout with unemployment, Vincent had applied for 1,627 jobs, scored a scant 15 interviews and – after his latest official rejection notice, from financial organization Bank Institute to run their local call center after three interviews and getting to the final two – he had decided on a whim to return Wallace's week old voice message.

On the message, Wallace had introduced himself as CEO of Brink Management Company, LLC and had referenced a Regional Manager position in the Minneapolis area. One thing Vincent had certainly learned through his year in unemployment purgatory was how these positions and titles were just as much a sales job as anything else. He really wanted to be affiliated with a name company.

However, after being dealt yet another blow to his career and ego after two rounds of interviews with Bank Institute for a job he felt he could have done in his sleep that went to someone in the banking industry, Vincent placed the call to Wallace.

"Hello?"

"Yes, this is Vincent Scott. I was returning your call regarding the Regional Manager position in Minneapolis for Brink Management Company. Is this Jordan Wallace?"

"Yes, hey, thanks for getting back to me," came the reply. "I actually am in town from Madison, Wisconsin, for one more day. Would you be able to meet for an interview?"

"Absolutely," Vincent responded. "What works best for you?"

"Let me see," Wallace responded, clearly checking his scheduling. "It's looking like tomorrow at 2 PM is available. Does that work for you?"

Vincent had no scheduling to check, but feigned a pause as if he did. "Yes, that sounds good."

"Great. Let's plan on meeting at the coffee shop at 34th and 50th. I am actually replacing the current Regional Manager, so it is important I do not draw attention to these interviews," Wallace stated. "Let me tell you a little about the position. This would be a Regional Manager position over 11 stores throughout Minnesota – mostly Greater Minneapolis-St. Paul – running Cellular Horizons stores."

*Interesting,* Vincent thought. *If only he had said that on the message the first time –* Cellular Horizons was an "it" company when it came to wireless technology. They boasted a strong network and top-tier products.

"I am very interested, and I appreciate you reaching out to me," Vincent responded, with the hint of hesitant excitement and anticipation that arose anytime a new potential opportunity presented itself. "I will plan on meeting you at 2 PM tomorrow."

"Great, sounds good, Vincent, thank you. I look forward to meeting you."

"Likewise. See you then."

Vincent's interview ritual was typically calling it a relatively early night, setting the alarm for hours in advance, hitting snooze until he was ready to rise, showering and entering the coordinates of the interview site into some trusty directions website.

Nerves no longer really impacted the man. He knew what he was capable of, knew what he could handle and, at this point, was not getting his hopes up about any position. He could only go in, say his piece and know that if he was not going to get this job, that it would be the next one, or the next one, or the next one. Eventually, one of them would pan out – right?

He was meeting Wallace at a coffee shop and it was fascination at first sight.

Jordan Wallace, 29 years young, walked in with a sport jacket covering a t-shirt, sporting skinny jeans and spiked black hair. He carried a laptop bag and an air of confidence about him the likes Vincent Scott saw in few people outside of his former self.

While Vincent was an attractive male specimen, he was always plagued with the insecurities of wanting everything to look just perfect; while he stood there in a charcoal grey suit and tie with his perfectly coiffed slicked back hair, he still felt inferior to this uber-confident business owner.

Wallace introduced himself, grabbed coffee and started talking shop. He had started out as a rep, working at a kiosk selling 800 boxes per month and then as the top manager in the country for Cellular Horizons, all by the age of 25. It was then that he latched on with his buddy Lyle Caminiti in their pursuit of running their own business and answering to no one.

There were a lot of standard interview questions: how would Vincent respond to taking over this struggling territory, what would he look for in recruits, and how would he communicate with his new team? How would he transition into a basically new industry? How would he mend any damaged relationships in this territory?

The regional manager in this business would not only manage stores that Wallace and his investors owned, but would also serve as liaison to stores owned and operated under his management umbrella. Wallace and his contemporaries not only owned 5 stores in Minnesota, 7 in Wisconsin and 3 in Texas with plans to open 4 more, but they also were the management company for several stores throughout Missouri and Minnesota.

The management responsibilities included handling all inventory and ordering processes plus providing the regional manager as a service: the recruiting, hiring, training, best practices and inclusion in all correspondence and communication.

Were Vincent selected to helm this region, he would have 6 additional stores reporting in to his structure, through three different owners aside from Wallace.

Vincent was calm, cool and collected throughout; Wallace would later recount to his business partners that Vincent Scott was the best interview of his career.

Weeks typically pass in the interview and hiring process; subsequently, Vincent got on a phone conference call with the power players in the decision-making process on the afternoon of Friday, January 28.

On the call with Vincent and Jordan Wallace: there was Lyle Caminiti, the Chief Financial Officer of the business, Paul Gemini (a heavy hitting investor, who also happened to be the father of the currently failing regional manager, Jeff Gemini, in an awkward tale of fathers and sons), who was taking the call from the deck of his Florida winter home with a cigar and scotch in hand, Derek Brink (the other primary investor in the business) and Doug Wilson, the Regional Manager for Brink's master agent, Moriarty Wireless.

When an aspiring ownership group endeavors to enter the world of wireless, it is required to enlist with a master agent to "ensure the path of success" for their business. While there are several to choose from, there are certainly some power players in this business; Moriarty Wireless was the premier such group in the Midwest and among the largest in the country, with hundreds of storefronts in their family of companies. Many of their dealers had one or two doors, but, with 33 in the unit, Brink was the biggest dealer in the Moriarty family.

The call showcased the tried and true method of Vincent Scott: give them far more than they could ever expect. A 15-slide PowerPoint presentation painted in the colors of Cellular Horizons and outlining a detailed plan of attack on how to mend fences in a struggling market, grow foot traffic through outreach and social media, communicate to the business regularly, galvanize the team and grow the organization, was what these folks received.

A well-laid out plan of attack, overcoming objections before they are even thrown at you, and a solid game plan that answers and addresses all questions not only adequately but exceptionally is the winning plan. Vincent Scott provided that this day.

Shortly into his employment with Brink Management Company and Cellular Horizons as Regional Manager, Vincent spent time with Jordan Wallace, driving to various stores, meeting managers, doing secret shops and the like, but during their drive time together, Vincent pressed Wallace on what the candidate playing field had looked like for the position he had now secured.

There had been over 300 applicants to his job. 42 résumés were selected from those for initial screening and 20 were interviewed. Wallace revealed that the reason Vincent's résumé had been picked – in fact, the only reason – was because he had written a book and his wife had brought it to his attention while helping him peruse applicants.

From there, Vincent gave the best interview and was among 3 who were selected to give a presentation. Vincent's was the best.

Vincent was in want and need of a mentor, a coach, an inspiring figurehead who could show him the path to hone and master his skills and greatness. He needed polish, but he needed someone to help bring it to him.

Jordan Wallace, a successful sales manager who now answered to very few people – if any – outside of investors and the guidelines of the Moriarty Wireless and Cellular Horizons dealer framework, could be that mentor. He had the freedom and lifestyle Vincent believed he wanted.

He certainly walked around like he owned the world and had it by the balls.

More time went by, however, this time, and Vincent assumed that, like the other jobs he had applied to, this organization, too, would move on without him for whatever reason they felt inclined to.

It was not until Thursday, February 3 that Wallace reached out to some of Vincent's résumé contacts; Later that day, Wallace's number flashed on Vincent's caller ID and Vincent answered the phone.

"Hello?"

"Vincent – it's Jordan Wallace, with Brink Management Company. How are you?"

"Doing very well, Jordan. Thank you. How are you?"

"Great. Hey, I wanted to give you a call and make it official and offer you this job. Are you ready to come on board?"

"Absolutely."

From there, Wallace went over the other specifics.

First, there was pay. Vincent was not necessarily expecting the $125,000 payday he had gotten in his last year of employment, but the capability to quickly make $100,000 again was certainly his goal.

The base was $50,000 with a $6,000 allowance for travel, meals and vehicle necessities, plus commissions.

"OK...what about the benefits?" Vincent asked, not thrilled with the initial figures.

"Well...there are no health benefits at this time," Wallace responded. "That's something we are working on being able to offer through Moriarty Wireless."

"OK," Vincent responded, processing this information in his head. He knew he would have to take a hit most likely, but seriously? How much of a hit was too much? He had turned down a job with similar pay not long ago. But he had also been toiling in the agony and misery of unemployment for over a year.

"I'm going to forward you over how the compensation structure works," Wallace said. "Basically, you've got 11 stores in your jurisdiction. The way it works is the average store requires about $12,500 in gross profit to break even and make net profit after all overhead; that includes rent, employee salaries, utilities and all other expenditures that we spend on a per-location basis. An average unit sold, a new acquisition or an upgrade, is about $200 in gross profit, and our minimum expectation per store is $20,000 in gross profit per month. That's just 100 boxes sold per month. We've got some stores who double that, and my goal is to get every store to $30,000 in gross profit."

"That makes sense," Vincent responded, soaking it all in. "What did my predecessor take home last year?"

Wallace contemplated the question for a moment. "Probably around $72,000," he responded. "And, keep in mind, he was struggling big time. It will be a draw against commissions. Let's say you have a store doing $30,000 in gross profits in a month. The maximum payout would be 5% of gross profit, so you would make $1,500 on a store like that. Let's say you get all 11 stores in your region to $30,000; that's $16,500 per month you would take home. That's…$198,000 per year."

Wallace was like a human calculator, quickly spitting out these astronomical numbers in seconds flat. He did not stop.

"In addition, we give you a car allowance of $500 per month on a company card. There's another $6,000 per year. So, ideally, this is a $200,000 per year job for you."

Jordan Wallace was definitely a quick and accurate mathematician in his head, and this was certainly a strong attribute in his sales acumen. The "return on investment" phase of the sale.

But Wallace did not stop there.

"The other thing, too, Vincent, is you're basically the owner. This is your business. You have a lot of freedom to run this thing the way you see fit, and once you get some established results here, we will add some more stores. I have three more locations in mind already. Once you get some tangible results, we are talking about adding more spots. That's just more money for you; in no time, you could be making a quarter of a million dollars per year."

"So what happens if any stores drop out of our unit? Does that mean I lose that revenue?" Vincent asked.

"That's never happened," Wallace was quick to counter. "We only plan on adding locations to our management company. I envision eventually selling the management portion of our business all across the country. Can you imagine having our management company sold to 1,000 different owners across the United States?"

"Yes, I can certainly imagine it."

Wallace sensed Vincent's hesitation but smelled blood.

"We're constantly growing," Jordan reminded him. "We started out with 1 store in Wisconsin. Now we have 7 in Wisconsin, 11 in Minnesota and are moving into Missouri and opening more stores in Texas. We sacrifice and bust our asses for a little bit, and we're all millionaires in 2 years."

There was something about Jordan Wallace that Vincent liked. He was a bit younger – just three years – and he just had this pride and confidence about him. He also had the benefit of having privilege and investors around him to pump money his way.

"Why do you think the previous Regional Manager was unsuccessful?"

"Frankly, he's not a motivator. I met with some of the employees here and he basically camps out at the Golden Valley store – that's like his baby," Wallace responded. "He had met with his store managers in person collectively just once in the last year. There's just not enough communication and team-building, in my opinion."

"That makes sense," Vincent continued. "I'd imagine – specifically with the close proximity of most of these stores – that we should meet as a group at least once per month. I'd have a couple conference calls every week but I think a big meeting would be a little less frequent."

"You read my mind," Wallace agreed. "See – you're figuring it out already."

"When do I need to let you know by?" Vincent asked.

"The sooner the better. We're ready to move forward with you in place. I am letting the current Regional Manager go today, and Lyle and I will be in Minneapolis; we'd like to take you to dinner."

"OK," Vincent responded. "Let me review the comp structure, see how this will work out and I'll call you back shortly."

"Sounds good," Wallace responded.

"Thank you," Vincent concluded.

After looking at the numbers, discussing the variables with his parents, and the realization that even if he only made a dollar more than unemployment was paying that this was a no-brainer, Vincent Scott accepted.

He was back in the game.

He was partnering up with Cellular Horizons – a company hopefully better than the monopolistic one that had dominated his previous life. He was going to have a good title, opportunity to make a lot of money and, most importantly, the chance to be a part of something that could give him a lot of impact, face time, and chance to make a real difference in a business.

Over the weekend, Vincent got his long hair cut off, going back to the inch-long crop of blond that had been his trademark. Facebook posts about his ascension to a third-line management position with a major company garnered a lot of curiosity and comments from former business and personal contemporaries.

The word spread like wildfire amongst former friends and foes alike: Vincent Scott was now a major player with Cellular Horizons.

It was the return of the salesman.

# "The Surviving Game" by Vincent Scott
## The Commandments of Sales, According to This Disciple

Sales is a psychology; a profitable arena where we engage clients, build relationships and seek the perfect balance for the holy sales trinity: customer, company and you. Without all of these entities in mind, the transaction and long-term stability of the relationship suffers.

That said, there are fundamentals we must ingrain in each and every leg of the process; without them, our method is defunct and the results will tell that story. Remember: *results do not define us, but they do not lie*. If there is a breakdown in your process, your results will be broken, too. It is imperative we use results as a guide when we tweak and ensure consistent execution of the right process.

**BE PROACTIVE AND THINK OUTSIDE THE BOX.** A major area of opportunity of many salespeople is their predisposition of wanting to follow the leaders or be like others; fit in, follow the beaten path. But why be like everyone else? That makes one average. Blaze your own trail. Stand out. Reach out for more customers; do not just accept the low-hanging, less challenging fruit. Don't get me wrong: you pick up every bit of fruit you can find – small or big. Nevertheless, always think of innovative ways to put yourself in front of new clients.

Like a billboard on a busy freeway, be where your customers are looking and show them why you're the one they need to pay attention to. Doing so puts you in position to guide the process. Not doing so puts the customer in control and your paycheck and career are in their hands instead of yours.

**LISTEN.** Salespeople often ask me how to overcome certain objections, but they fail to realize that if they had set the right foundation they would be using the customers' own words in the presentation, the close and any necessary overcomes. Your words and philosophies pale in comparison in the customers' minds to their own; listen and learn their language so you can speak it. Find out what you need to know from the customer so you can diagnose their situation; where do the gaps lie? How can you plug those gaps? How are you going to make them realize that jettisoning their comfortable, familiar ways of doing business and going with you is going to be better? You can't get there unless your ears perk up and you get them doing the talking.

**REACT.** React to everything, and know when to use your information. You can be the smartest person in the room – great. However, if you are simply unloading jargon and facts on your potential client, are you showing them why your way of doing business is better?

Knowledge is power, but knowing when and how to use it makes you powerful. Improve your pitch, but perfect your reaction. If you role play, don't practice improbable scenarios; get used to setting the right foundation and knowing how to react to every objection your client throws at you. See objections before they happen and address potential hitches before your customer even can. You will see many customers, but only a few themes; master those themes and there's no slipping one by you.

**FOLLOW UP**. Unfortunately, no matter how effective a closer you are, the sale will not always happen on your timetable. Don't get me wrong: you need to do everything you can to build trust and determine why specifically the customer is not doing business today. But if they leave the table for a viable reason, you must have an organized, prompt and thorough follow up process in place.

Customers will "browse" or "do research" and finally get tired enough to do business and pay more elsewhere if you do not stay front and center in their universe. Follow up within 24 hours to a week and reignite the lead. You cannot win them all, but you can nurture them all to as close to completion as possible. That's your job. If you can look back on every transaction and know you did everything you could to earn the business, you did your job. Congratulations.

**MASTER THE GAME**. There are ups and downs; when you're up, ride the wave. When you're down, make sure you behave – according to process, that is. You may get the shanks in your golf game, but do you drastically change your swing to get back to desired results? Of course not. You have to envelop yourself in the process and get back to the basics for the previous successful results to reappear. You also must learn the playing field – how can you make money where you currently are not? What best practices are others using? Steal them shamelessly; those who execute best are the best.

Finally, refresh and recharge often. You need to make sure you are the person you were on interview day. Play for the love of the game, win the crowd and act to the benefit of the customer and you will be victorious.


There are many points in the sales call or meeting where the balance of power is potentially in jeopardy. Once we as the salesperson lose control, all heck breaks loose and the rest of it spirals out of control like a weekend with Charlie Sheen.

One of these such moments is the "OK, let's cut to the chase; how much does it cost?" moment; it can stop even the most seasoned sales professional in his/her tracks and it attempts to derail your momentum train. However, like any obstacle - the "initial shutdown", the objections or the inevitable short attention span of your potential clients - you must anticipate, diffuse and bat away this statement to move forward in your sales process.

Let's call it what it is: the "how much does it cost?" moment is an attempt by your client to bottom-line it; the lure you have cast has yet to catch onto something and spark interest in the customer. At least, that is partially true.

If the customer has stayed with you to this point, and they are asking this question, it means the idea has not repulsed them and they are on the verge between hanging in there and dropping out.

You've heard it before and I shall say it again: everything is selling. Every facet of the sales call or visit is selling through process points until you reach the climax. In this event, you are called upon to sell your customer on why they should divert their attention from the price, and pay no attention to that man behind the curtain.

You have an agenda. Your customer has an agenda. To keep on yours, you must often pacify them into thinking they are still on theirs; by that, I mean you will acknowledge their statement, put it in its proper place with a little salesmanship and you will continue on your process without typically drawing so much as a breath.

"Mr./Mrs. Customer, absolutely - I understand price is a concern and I appreciate your enthusiasm. Fact of the matter is, I don't make the same program for the butcher, the baker and the candlestick maker. If I'm making a building, I need to know if I'm making a treehouse or the Sears Tower. I need to know a few more specifics so I can tailor-make a recommendation, personalized just for you and your situation. If I create something that works for someone else but not for you, our relationship suffers and so does your business. Where specifically do you need to market yourself geographically?"

Of course, not every statement in there will apply to your situation, but that's just it; you have to utilize best practices, make them your own and get used to saying them through repetition. The point I am trying to make here is you are selling your potential client on why they should let go of caring about the price point at this exact moment. They are trying to box you into a corner by which you must quote a rate and they alone will quickly determine based on factors you are unaware of if it's too much or worth listening more for. That's more power than you can give. At the same time, you are weaving immediately into asking another question, which forces your momentum train back onto the track.

Dealing with sales call obstacles, overcoming objections and making it to the close are all actions that require lots of practice, lots of poise and lots of precision. The "how much does it cost?" moment means your customer is interested, but you cannot abort the process of building your masterpiece.

There lies the second key point of this discussion: just because the client has shown some interest in listening to you does not mean you can stop what you're doing and head to a half-baked conclusion. You are involved in an intricate process; if you do not glean the answers to all the necessary questions, your recommendation will be shoddy and your chances of convincing the customer to change their current scheme to go with yours diminish greatly.

That is why the "how much does it cost?" moment is just another bump in the path; it is a good bump to a degree because it indicates you have done something to spark some interest. However, do not abort your process; stay the course, stay on target and finish your agenda so you can approach the apex of sales moments: the almighty close.

Closing the sale - like putting the finishing touches on a masterpiece work of art - is the apex of moments in the progression towards the sales transaction. However, like any commodity or good or service, many misconceptions exist about just what must transpire before that sale is "closed."

In essence, "closing a sale" is showing - rather than telling - a customer enough evidence to convince them that you have the cure for whatever needs and weaknesses exist in their current way of doing things, causing them to make a change from their current way of doing things. When their fear of changing is outweighed by their fear of standing pat because of your dialogue and they make the decision to purchase, the sale has been closed.

Referring to it as closing gives the connotation that a physical action on the seller's part is what iced the deal. While the burden of proof is certainly on the salesperson, who must operate like a prosecuting attorney assigned to quickly ascertain information through specific and targeted questions, the decision whether or not to buy is always the customer's.

The salespeople that forget that - the pushy ones, the unethical ones and the unsuccessful ones - tend to think they can force a customer to buy, but forceful closes only lead to buyer's remorse, product churn and dissatisfaction.

Closing a sale is a delicate and intricate process; like putting together a puzzle or baking a cake, all essential ingredients must exist, the proper nurturing must be done and any skipped steps lead to an unfinished, half-baked product.

The foundation for the sale is set when the salesperson states their business and quickly moves into finding out about the situation at hand. The reason asking questions is so critical to the overall process is because utilizing the customer's own words to weave the perfect picture together is the greatest way to achieve a successful sales masterpiece.

The questions serve to determine a customer's situation: the strengths and areas of opportunity for improvement that lie in their current strategy. You, as the salesperson, are conducting a needs analysis to determine (1) that your product or service is a fit, (2) how precisely you will match your service to their needs in their eyes and (3) what specifically to recommend to your potential client.

The presentation that follows must commence right away and is the point of no return - no stopping, no asking "does this sound good?", no drivel; from this point forward, you are presenting and concluding with a closing question. "Where would you like the invoice sent?" "Once you sign the paperwork, I go to work for you; would you like to use my pen?"

Your pitch must be a personalized recommendation based on the customer's whole picture, addressing the key items you learned in the fact-finding and ending with a question because it forces an answer.

Closing the sale also involves being able to diffuse and deflect (and often anticipate) customer objections. A customer objection means only that they need more information; they do not yet believe that your product or service is something that will yield a positive result, a profit or live up to its potential. It means your job is not yet finished.

Finally, the thing to remember about closing the sale (a.k.a. making their fear of standing pat outweigh their fear of change) is that it is NOT about spouting several random benefits of your service in the hopes they cave. You asked the questions in the beginning for a reason. You unearthed their needs and used them in your pitch for a reason. Often, you have to find five fresh ways to drive home that specific point - WHY they need to change, WHAT issues exist with their current strategy and HOW you and your product will fix a problem they may not even see.

In the end, closing sales is fun, it's sexy and it is exciting, but the best feeling of all is knowing that you made a difference for that customer, for your company and for yourself, all in one shot.

How often have you heard it? "You need to close more sales."

Unfortunately, unless you have a strong leader, that is where the conversation begins and ends. *You need to close more, but I am not going to shed any light on how it's done.*

To close more business, you have to ascertain why business is not being closed. Far too often, we hyper-focus on various parts of our pitch, we try harder during the close or get frustrated when we just cannot get over that customer objection. The truth is, no matter how good you are at the selling game, you will not close them all. But you close more if you can determine the hurdles and scale them.

Why are your customers not buying? What reasons are they giving you? Is there a particular part of the sales call or visit where it goes south? Or are you pretty much dispatched from the get-go?

These are vital questions when determining where to begin your process of increasing sales conversion. Truth is, no matter what line of work you are in from a sales vantage point, you will come across easier sales to close than others. Many sales gigs have that "low-hanging fruit" whereby the customer either initiated the purchase or it was a slam dunk. Let's call it what it is: that's not really sales.

If you are privy to such easy revenue, great; however it is what we do with the rest of our business that will determine our success.

The sales process starts with introductory statements and building the relationship, asking questions and uncovering, discovering and/or creating needs. You must show the customer why they need what you have. You must show the customer why what you have is better than what they are doing right now. You must show the customer the grass is greener on your side and that any cost on their part is justified because of the ensuing benefit.

So - where are you losing the customer? If they balk early, your focus needs to be on building the relationship and developing better reactions. If they balk after you have pitched, your focus needs to be on fine-tuning that pitch to address the customers' needs and developing better reactions. If they balk after your attempt to overcome their objection(s), your focus needs to be on weaving in their own words that you hopefully uncovered to ice the deal and make it a no-brainer... and on developing better reactions.

Spend a day or week just jotting down the customer objections you are getting: when do they shut you down? What do they say when they shut you down? What are you saying (or not saying) to address their shutdown?

Remember: if at any time a customer objects or hesitates, it must be dealt with. They may voice their concern early, but if you do not hear it or fail to address it and move forward, your likelihood at failure on that sale is high. Do not let it be the elephant in the room; ensure at all times that your customer is listening, understanding and on the same page with you. No better way than using their own words to brandish your pitch and ice the deal.

Sales conversion is not about trying harder to close. Increasing sales conversion is about realizing and acknowledging where and why in the sales process you are losing the deal or the customer's buy-in. Creating, practicing and executing on a more effective reaction and response to the objections you are getting will result in better conversion. You are already getting the "low-hanging fruit." You are already closing the sales that rely mostly on your knowledge and know-how. The ones tripping you up are the ones that require a quicker, zippier, more effective reaction and response.

Uncover that reaction and response, perfect your usage and delivery of it, and results and compensation will follow.

Often, when I have solicited my sales teams for training topics they are most interested in, they want the training to be on "overcoming objections." In addition, that has always been the most frequently asked question of me in my years of sales leadership.

However, while this indicates their heart is in the right place and they are yearning for more, this is NOT the most important question in sales.

Sales is determining the needs and weaknesses of a customer in a relatively short period of time and addressing those needs with your product or service. In order to "make the deal", "negotiate the sale" and come to terms you must show the customer you've got the cure for what ails them. They have to fear standing pat more than making a change. And, to ensure that happens, you have to make sure you set up a strong foundation for the sale through quality introduction, fact-finding and seamless presentation followed by asking for the sale.

All of that said, we spend our time trying to crack the customer code on all of these different objections. Why do we do this? I ask because - there is only one objection in the world.

Sure, there are variations on a theme. Sure, the customer will hide behind many different objections so they can slink back into their office and hope you exit. Sure, they will cough up deflection objections like having to talk to a spouse or partner or wait until next week or month or year or they are retiring or they are all stocked up on business; you've heard them all, right?

Objections are nearly all illusions. The Great and Powerful Oz of objections, hiding behind the curtain, is none other than LACK OF BELIEF. Period. Everything is a flavor of that one.

"Mr./Mrs. Customer, absolutely - I understand your gut instinct is to say you don't have the money / have to think about it / want to look over the information, but let's face it: if you believed this was going to work for you and bring a return on investment, you'd jump at it. For what specific reason do you believe this added feature / additional choice / extra revenue stream will hurt you?" Then STOP TALKING.

Customers have money. Customers make decisions without consulting their spouse. Customers – if the facts are the facts and you have shown them how you will fix their problems in their current plan of attack - don't need to think everything over to consider or pull the trigger on your proposal. If you settle for "just send me information" or "I'll think about it," leave a business card or walk out that door, you might as well put their face on a milk carton - it's likely the last you will ever see of them. You certainly are not getting a yes if you do not get any affirmation of your agenda.

So, instead of trying to dissect and discern all of these objections, remember it's just one. Lack of belief.

Acknowledge their objection, put it in its place, and move forward to your next agenda item - close again by asking the question that forces out the reason for their lack of belief.

Don't get me wrong - you can't close them all. However, your job is to get as far as you can in the sales process on every sales attempt and be able to look back and know the specific reason the customer did not believe. Your service may not be for everyone. Your customer may really truly not need it. But if you can answer why the customer doesn't need or believe every single time out of the gates, you did your job.

And you will never need to worry about the numbers because you'll look up and they will be there. Trust me.

# The Grand Entrance

Vincent Scott arrived at the Cellular Horizons location in Golden Valley, Minnesota, at 8:50 on Monday, February 7, 2011. Pulling into the lot, he straightened his tie and exited his black Honda Accord, 44-ounce Diet Coke and 24-ounce black coffee in tow. Old habits die hard.

Vincent strolled through the empty parking lot toward the store door. The "open" sign was not yet illuminated; however, he saw a figure inside. The person in the store, clearly recognizing Vincent as someone of importance, made haste to the door and opened it, making way for Vincent to enter.

"Good morning, sir," the character greeted him.

"Good morning," Vincent replied, entering the store.

"You're Vincent Scott," he stated.

"Guilty as charged," Vincent replied.

"I'm Jerry Smalls," the youngish male responded.

"Nice to meet you," Vincent responded, accepting the outstretched hand. "How do you know me?"

"I've seen your YouTube videos, sir."

Vincent laughed quietly. "I see."

The first person Vincent met in the business – Jerry Smalls – was a 29-year old wireless vagabond. Turns out, Jerry had made his rounds in the wireless arena of Minneapolis, having worked for several competitors, and had been with Brink since it set foot in this market 2 years prior. He was one of the first people hired when Wallace and Caminiti were ramping up their business.

"I really see myself as more of a trainer," Smalls said, as they got into the meat of some conversation. "I've been here since the beginning. I'm really excited to have you on board as someone who can recognize my talents."

It was not lost on Vincent that this scruffy-looking, oddly dressed and appearing character was 29 and was nothing more than a phone jockey in a cell phone store who likely did not bathe or brush his teeth often. A corporate trainer he was not.

Minutes later, Jordan Wallace entered, again wearing skinny jeans and a t-shirt and sport jacket.

"Good morning, Mr. Wallace, sir," Jerry Smalls groveled, greeting his superior. "How are you today, sir?"

Wallace strolled into the store casually, barely acknowledging the brown-noser. "Good, Jerry."

Thus began a bit of a dissertation on the operations of the store; Wallace did not give Jerry Smalls much attention whatsoever, in spite of Jerry's constant attempts to insert himself into the conversation or make himself sound remotely relevant. Wallace escorted Vincent into the back room of the store and eventually into the office as he showed him where paperwork was stored, how it was filed, the store cameras, and how the operation was audited and money was accounted for.

They soon departed the store and Wallace took Vincent around to several of the stores in his truck; initially, he had told Vincent where the locations were suburb-wise, but Vincent did not get the addresses and specifics until this day.

"You've got to be kidding me," Vincent muttered as they pulled up to the parking meters of the downtown Minneapolis location.

They parked at a meter right outside the Cellular Horizons downtown location. Not thirty feet away, towering above them like a castle, was the 45-story building that had once been home to Vincent Scott and his online advertising organization in his previous role before illegal ousting.

Belief and faith in a grand scheme to the universe is one thing that certainly keeps folks like Vincent Scott ticking throughout the murk of life. If everything happens for a reason, if everything is meant to be the way it occurs and if life is really one big movie, then this was certainly a sign to Vincent. His downtown store was right across the street from his former office and even in the same quarters as a restaurant he and his cohorts had once frequented.

Vincent took a long, hard glance at the gargantuan building; he and Wallace entered the store, and Vincent still had a hard time taking his eyes off of it. This had been the first time he had been here since he had walked out of it to the unemployment line over a year ago. Like running into an old lover on the streets, the memories came gushing back. It did not help that every few minutes, someone he had personally hired, coached and/or mentored into the business walked in or out of the building.

It was here that Vincent met downtown store manager Saul Portman. Saul was a former linebacker in college and – now 23 years old – a wireless store manager who had made rounds as a manager with a couple of other local outfits before landing with Brink when it was setting up shop in Minneapolis. He and Jerry Smalls were two of the three only employees who had been part of Minnesota's Brink Wireless operation since the start.

Saul talked a strong game, was conscientious about the business and well-respected by his team members. Whereas Jerry Smalls was clearly a joke and not well-regarded, Saul earned high marks even from Jordan Wallace which – Vincent quickly learned – was not all that easy to do.

Even the back room of the store, which had once been the bar area of the restaurant was still intact. It was not in use, but the bar, some tables and chairs and scores of cigarette butts and ashes to serve as evidence of its previous existence, adorned the joint. It was in this room where a going-away party for one of Vincent's old reps – Jane Daughtry – had been; she had been one of Vincent's favorites when he was first a manager, followed him to advertising, but left for Austin, Texas, to pursue a life's ambition.

Next up came a location south, in Bloomington. This store, along with the downtown location, was one of the most attractive. Store Manager Reggie Sherman was in attendance.

In his late 40's, Reggie was another journeyman of the wireless industry, having worked with three providers in kiosks and stores as a rep and manager over the years. Sherman was the third of three who had been with Wallace since he began his operation here. He was also currently running the Eden Prairie store, which was struggling mightily, in addition to the Bloomington location.

Once store visits ensued that did not include Wallace, which was shortly thereafter, these folks opened up candidly about Jeff Gemini, the former regional manager to carry the moniker before Vincent came on board. Few people Vincent would encounter were as vocal in their dissent than Reggie.

He met De-Metre Jones, the manager of the store in New Brighton, who was exceedingly raw managerially, but a true character and student of what he liked to call "the legal hustle" of sales. Jones had been one of the most vocal against Jeff Gemini; Saul Portman had literally been ready to walk, and De-Metre's top rep, Darryl Wilkinson, was also looking because of his disdain for their former leader.

Within the family of companies in Brink Management Company were three other owners, in addition to Jordan Wallace and his partners. The first Vincent met was that first weekend; he took daughter Elizabeth back home to Mankato to visit his parents, and stopped in to their mall kiosk where he came across Dustin "Bruce" Rollins for the first time.

The other owners in their mix: Bruce Rollins' best friend, "Logan" Aaron Tuncil and Chris Jeffries.

A drive out I-35W N towards Duluth and Fon Du Lac revealed most of the Jeffries stores: there was Hermantown, managed by looker Sasha Barnhart, Cloquet, managed by good-old-boy Cliff Watson, and, back closer to home, Plymouth, managed by self-proclaimed ideas man Jesse Fairbanks.

Tuncil owned the White Bear Township store, despite living in the heart of Minneapolis. He was not there often.

The final store visited: Greenfield. And, as irony, coincidence or destiny would have it, the store was literally located right across the street from the online advertising business group building that was formerly run by Vincent Scott. Two doors down from the store: Cullen's, the nightspot frequented by reps and managers alike where Vincent had spent many an evening throwing back drinks with his management team.

As Vincent made his way into these stores, mostly attempting to be anonymous and secret shop, he was typically already expected. In fact, as he came up on the employees of the Mankato kiosk, they were actually on YouTube watching his own sales leadership videos promoting his book.

But, in each store, the theme was common: he met people who acted excited to have him on board, who were very aware of his book, and who were pleased to hear his dissertation on people and process as the most important fundamentals in his coaching and leadership style. Numbers meant nothing but how well process was working; the right people following the right processes would lead them to greatness. Their initial skepticism was slowly won over. They just didn't know how long he would stick around, for he was obviously better than this position.

Immediately into his time with Brink Management Company and Cellular Horizons, Vincent's primary ally seemed to be Bruce Rollins.

Bruce proclaimed to be one of the ringleaders who convinced Jordan Wallace that Jeff Gemini had to go; the more Vincent heard about Gemini, the more he heard the words, "asshole," "condescending," "dictator" and "disrespectful." Rollins would state that Wallace was like his big brother, and every time he came to town, the two would spend time together and Wallace would crash at Rollins' house. Out of the gates, Rollins was selling Vincent on why his vote heavily mattered.

Bruce repeatedly offered to train Vincent on certain facets of the business: ordering, inventory, returns, and deposits. He was very outgoing, somewhat comical and was very high energy, often toting multiple energy drinks, always eating and regularly showing up fresh from the gym.

He also unabashedly shared the reason for his two names.

"See, my selling technique is like my women-chasing technique," Rollins would say, in complete seriousness, to anyone who would listen. Often, the recipients of said speech were his store employees. "Aaron Tuncil and I would start all of these Match.com profiles and go looking for girls. The name he used was Logan, like Wolverine, and I used Bruce, like Bruce Banner – the Hulk."

Rollins would practically deadpan this entire conversation, while Vincent was in awe that this was actually a Cellular Horizons multi-unit store owner. It was just a little more shine off the apple.

"So, it's all law of averages. I will send out 50 different messages to 50 different girls, right? 'Hey, how's it going?', or something like that. For every 50 messages, you'll get like 25 responses, 5 girls will agree to meet you, and 1 will fuck you.

"That's how you approach sales. I just hit up these lots with fliers or these businesses showing them a tablet, and play the law of averages. It's bound to pay off; playing the odds."

And he was deathly serious.

The Greenfield store was actually on the market, as Rollins was attempting to sell it to current in-store rep Gabe Blankenship so that he could use the money to move to California and start a medicinal marijuana business. The half-baked idea, ironically, had come from "big brother" Jordan Wallace himself.

Blankenship was getting the money from his wealthy father, but knew very little about the business and what it was worth. Rollins was attempting to unload the currently underperforming store for in excess of $65,000, while it made roughly $1,000 in net profit monthly – if that – in the best months of the year, if it was profitable at all. Under the current infrastructure with the lackluster staff, attempting to recoup the investment would be futile, but Rollins was selling like he was convincing an unsuspecting female victim that he was a somebody with his CEO business card and the Cellular Horizons logo on it.

The other in-store rep at Greenfield was T.J. Jones, the brother of De-Metre, but aside from their lineage they had literally no similarities whatsoever. Vincent's first encounter with T. J. had been a secret shop that revealed just how lazy and unimpressive T.J. was, but Bruce kept him on the payroll because, frankly, he cared very little about much else other than selling the business.

As he left each store, Vincent truly believed he was making a difference and was going to forge something magical as he left his indelible mark. He was part of a major company, but working with the freedom and excitement of being able to call his own shots. It looked like it could truly be the best of both worlds. That's what he kept telling himself.

The third owner in the Brink Management Company jurisdiction of companies was Chris Jeffries. Vincent knew little about him, but Chris and his wife Michelle owned the stores in relatively nearby Plymouth and in more distant Cloquet and Hermantown. An I-35W N road trip the first week took him to the latter two stores, and he visited Plymouth on his way back towards home.

The stores under the Chris Jeffries umbrella had a distinct feel; he and his wife were very close with the personnel, having them over to the house for dinner and gradually getting to know the ins and outs of their personal lives, for better or worse.

Jeffries's office was stationed in the back of the Cloquet store, yet his path did not cross with Vincent on his first few trips there. Being that the outing was a few hours away to hit the Hermantown and Cloquet stores and that – as Vincent found – these were the employees least interested in following Vincent's suggestions, best practices and mandates, these visits had a distinct feel as well.

Just prior to Vincent signing on the Brink dotted line, Chris had purchased Vincent's book. Stark differences existed in their personalities; he viewed Vincent as brash, arrogant and aggressive, while Chris valued the non-intrusive, customer service only approach. Aggressive sales were not the forte of him or his teams. It showed in their results as there was relative consistency in obtaining renewals but not a lot of new lines proportionately.

While Vincent would promote assertive ways to fact-find customers and earn their trust through infiltration of their walls of objections, Jeffries and his teams were more the infomercial type. There was no confident selling, follow-up or accountability. Jeffries was somewhat open to suggestion but not sure Vincent Scott would be the answer and was quick to debunk any suggestions he gave on sales or marketing claiming they had already tried and failed.

Hermantown prospered greatly because of its vicinity to Duluth and the military base. Further inspection by Vincent, however, realized massive struggling on their key performance indicators. They were leaving large quantities of money on the table on accessories and additional features. Much akin to Vincent's call center experience, he studied the statistics and analyzed the total quality, optimization and maximization of every facet of the job. He found every method possible to expound upon revenue and growth and expanded profits for all, focusing on areas they were missing out and creating processes to ensure these were no longer afterthoughts.

True selling indicators in retail – or practically any environment – are recognized with attention to additional acquisitions outside of the "low hanging fruit" or "gimmie" sales. Anyone can process an order or be a clerk; it takes someone intuitive and skilled to optimize each opportunity. That's what Vincent taught. Better than anyone else.

Hermantown, Vincent quickly discovered, was the top store in the entire region – by far – and it was because of a steady influx of traffic. Whereas many of the stores in densely populated Minneapolis would garner anywhere from 1-to-10 customers per day that would too often request phone troubleshooting or pay a bill, Hermantown would collect 30-to-40 customers daily from the military base just prior to their new assignments and in need of new lines of service.

With that math, they should have tripled and quadrupled the output of Vincent's other stores, but they did not. Their accessory-to-handset ratio, phone insurance conversion, total dollars per line of service, total television sales, Internet sales, etc., were all well below the levels of acceptability that Vincent was now putting a full court press on.

Having a Hermantown, who thought they had cracked the meaning of life, now hearing feedback on what they needed to improve rather than being left completely alone or blindly praised like Moriarty or Cellular Horizons did, was the first thing to wedge a bit of distance between the Chris Jeffries stores and Vincent. Hermantown was like the Promised Land, so how dare this kid who was working his first weeks in retail question them?

Vincent put measurements in place whereby the employees and managers would report summaries of their daily transactions. He quickly found that where his requests were often met with execution in the past, they were typically met with anything but in this environment.

Hermantown was managed by the very attractive Sasha Barnhart. In her fourth year working in this store and, to her credit, being there while the store grew, Sasha had seen the location liaise effectively with the military base. The relationship soared in part because the store closest to the base had gained a bad reputation for price gouging; to the victor went the spoils and Hermantown boomed. It didn't hurt that the men of the base thought Sasha was hot and word spread.

If there was one thing that Chris Jeffries's stores were certainly great at it was the clerking side of things; they were good at putting smiles on their faces, being nonintrusive and getting things right the first time. They did not expound upon opportunities, recognize the potential of each sale or actually uncover customer needs to sell to, but they produced enough money to keep Jeffries's bills paid and led the region in gross profit.

This was also very evident in Cloquet; an off-the-beaten path store whose employees felt Vincent did not understand their rural customer. Having grown up in a small town, Vincent was very aware of how to approach all types of customers, but Cloquet personnel – specifically store manager Cliff Watson – used the customer type as their ultimate excuse for lack of Minneapolis-style results.

With the saturation of stores in Minneapolis, many of the stores there would make anywhere from $15,000 to $30,000 in gross profit per month. After all overhead, payroll, etc., these stores were netting anywhere from $1,000 to $15,000 per month, depending on their demographic, quality of salesforce and marketing. And, with the primary stores in Brink being owned by Brink and its major investors, there was a little bit of money to go around.

The farther out from the major cities, however, the store points of distribution were more sparsely populated – giving an area like a Cloquet or Hermantown just as good, if not better chance of success.

This was what Vincent quickly discovered and had to expose: that each store was sitting on a potential goldmine of opportunity. The go-to-market strategies, the way to learn and satisfy the customers and the ways to advertise may differ amongst the teams, but the general system had to stay the same.

Vincent had learned that having the right people in place and following the right processes led to success no matter what. This situation would be no different. Getting people at Hermantown or Cloquet, who, inexplicably refused to take advantage of traffic at nearby universities in Duluth or Fon Du Lac or any of his marketing ideas, would be quite a challenge. He was trying to teach the comfortable dog a trick that would benefit it but that it had no interest in learning.

Doubling back from Hermantown and Cloquet brought Vincent to Plymouth. Jesse Fairbanks – who also managed the Golden Valley store – helmed the vastly underperforming Plymouth team. One of the first things that Jesse and Vincent certainly agreed upon was that – to maximize effectiveness of the stores – Jesse should manage just one store. His choice: Plymouth.

With the ability to type 100 words per minute, the fact he married himself completely and totally to his job and task at hand and the fact he never clocked out, Vincent sent a lot of work e-mails. Whether it was recognition, sharing a best practice he witnessed, news in the industry, sales scripts, or soliciting thoughts, feedback or objections that he could address, Vincent hit the team with a myriad of conversation starters on a daily basis. For many, this was quite the shock to the system and, with many of his employees between 19 and 23 years old with some or no college schooling and/or aspirations in life, his communications received mixed retention results. Vincent was used to people reacting and responding and hanging on his every word so as to suck up and gain his favor and eventual promotion; here, that was not the case. Only those who actually cared about the undertaking responded.

While Vincent did get a lot of good feedback from those who responded, which helped him get his early footing, Chris Jeffries was always one to respond with something Vincent did not quite expect: criticism.

One thing about Vincent, however, is that the praise, kudos and accolades did little to morph or shape his style or decisions; true constructive criticism with valuable tidbits was something he definitely valued. Chris Jeffries's e-mail retorts had some of this, but were often peppered with condescending lashings or potshots at Vincent and his persona. "The Vincent Show," Jeffries liked to call it.

Vincent's ability, however, to take the responses from Chris Jeffries in stride at least, in Jeffries's claims, earned his respect. However, Vincent heard a different story from people like Bruce Rollins or Jordan Wallace. Vincent would hold his own in these e-mail wars of words and supposedly gain Chris's respect, but then he would get a call from Bruce Rollins during a roundtable owners meeting where he claimed Jeffries ridiculed him at great length.

It also reached a point where Jeffries responded with pushback to just about everything Vincent suggested or advocated.

The stores Vincent directly managed as his own under Brink were showing traction. Chris Jeffries's did not; they lay dormant in nearly every statistical category. But Vincent could not force other owners, who were simply under management contract, to do his bidding. So he would have to learn to choose his battles, no matter how frustrating their decision not to optimize results would be. And he would milk the stores that actually listened and wanted to do better for all they were worth en route to the $200,000 per year paycheck Wallace dangled.

Very soon into his time there, Vincent realized more and more just how different this was from his old teams who were paid hefty salaries to do his will. A scheduled conference call with 10 or so participants would "begin" with at least half of them missing. He would be forced to text message some of them as a reminder, and would actually get responses like, "With a customer" or "I'm busy." No matter how much and often he stressed the importance of these mandatory meetings to their strategy and success, he would still never conduct a meeting without folks missing in action.

Saul Portman was more or less the go-to-guy and mentor for some of the other employees, specifically De-Metre, who had begun under his tutelage. Darryl Wilkinson, the top rep working for De-Metre in New Brighton, and Bryan Venison, his other team member, were also very much in this inner circle of trust. And this group socialized that there was no way Vincent Scott would stick around. He would figure out what he had gotten himself into and be gone within 2-to-3 weeks.

But the weeks piled on.

Vincent was less than enthused about many of the sales representatives in the store. It turns out that Jeff Gemini's strategy was to scramble to find someone whenever an existing team member left and just replace them with a warm body. The quality of employees was in serious need of an upgrade, and Scott spent a lot of the first few months conducting interview blitzes to proactively give his team a facelift. There was no bench roster or minor leagues; Vincent had to put on a full court press to develop a true team depth chart from scratch.

However, he found himself gravitating towards these core team members, showing Saul Portman, De-Metre Jones, and Reggie Sherman respect and getting it in return. They had their flaws, but considering how underpaid they were and how hard it would be to nab talent to do a job this complex for peanuts, he needed these guys to build his squad. They responded to the fact Vincent trusted them and let them run their stores, coupled with giving them valuable suggestions on how to improve results without berating, threatening or condescending to them.

Doug Wilson – the Regional Manager for Moriarty – and his sister-in-law Susie Wilson (who just happened to be the Account Manager from Cellular Horizons assigned much of the same territory) would check up on Vincent about once a week, typically attempting to meet him for lunch, and would ask him about his opinions on the business. Bruce Rollins called him practically daily and discussed the ins and outs of the company. Jordan Wallace – whenever Vincent started wondering what the hell he was getting himself into – would call and sell him on how magical the future would be.

This could certainly work. It had potential. Time would tell if it would all come together, but Vincent would always bet on himself. And he was seeing progress in the early going; he just had to keep growing this team. Feedback from Doug and Susie that had come from the region had been mostly positive, with the Chris Jeffries stores the lone holdouts.

Team members like Saul, De-Metre and Reggie really understood what he had set out to do. Without the foundation of those three in the beginning, Vincent would never have been able to find anything to latch onto here.

Vincent Scott accepted this Regional Manager position with Brink Management Company for a couple of reasons. One: he had been out of work for over one year. This was depressing, a severe blow to his ego and confidence and bank account.  Second: the fact it was with a major player like Cellular Horizons, who was huge in its industry, and it was a Regional Manager title, made it look like – on paper – that Vincent had bounced back better than ever.  The people who had seen him lay down on the sword for them saw him rise again.  The people who had despised him and anonymously attacked him saw him rebound from the hell they wished for him.

Nevertheless, the job was far from a dream come true.

Just a few weeks into his time with Brink Management Company, Vincent met the other prominent power players in the organization.

Lee Christian, who was the self-proclaimed Chief Operating Officer of Brink, though he was in essence no more or less than the Regional Manager for the Wisconsin market of 7 stores, flew into Minneapolis under the direction of Jordan Wallace and was to train Vincent and show him much of the operational parts of the business.

During his stay, Vincent was to glean from Christian the inventory database and all of its functionality, how to track inventory on hand in all stores in his jurisdiction, and pick up advice on how he was managing the "top region in the company."

They met at the Mankato Steak 'N Shake – a place where, seemingly a lifetime ago Vincent spent many nights talking and writing over coffee with the likes of lifelong buds Jack Johnson and Eddie Haskins and wooing the waitresses – and barely even visited the nearby mall kiosk.  What was teased by Wallace as an intense training was more or less a couple of hours of coffee and discussion and getting to know one another.

Lee showed Vincent some basics on the system, Vincent took some notes, but a few things were clear: Lee was interested in operations and was an IT wunderkind rather than an outgoing salesman, and the reason Wisconsin was successful was because they had 50% market share there, as opposed to Vincent's 18% in Minnesota.  To be fair, Lee was a great guy, his team loved and respected him and he was very loyal; both gentlemen saw where the other had attributes and skills they could learn from one another.

Together, they could certainly pack quite a punch.

Cellular Horizons was known for quality – quality which had improved dramatically in this region over the last ten years – but expensive price points.  That would be Vincent's big challenge in growing the business here.

Wisconsin was "#1" based on their ridiculously high market share, but had only 1 store exceeding $30,000 in gross profit monthly.  Lee ran one small market store that averaged around $6,000 monthly and his others ranged from $15,000-to-$25,000 per month. Vincent wondered how this was considered to be so amazing, but, then again, it all boiled down to the Benjamins. It was not a saturated market, they were getting a lot of door swings and people were buying. Like the Hermantown store, there was a lot of money being left on the table, but they were the current dollar champs and money talks.

The two hit it off; it was definitely good for them to speak with their peer in the business with a different vantage point. Lee was impressed with Vincent, as he had gotten pretty rave reviews from Jordan Wallace in the early going, and was curious to see what he could accomplish in this environment. Vincent found in Lee someone he could bounce ideas off of, vent to and – most importantly – learn from.

For, the reality that Vincent quickly realized is that no store was making anywhere near $30,000 in gross profit per month, save Hermantown – the requirement in that mystical $200,000 per year paycheck he was wooed with. In fact, the average of Vincent's stores the first month he was there was $11,000 per store. When only 5 of the 11 stores achieved $10,000, a new rule was announced by Wallace that was incredulously retroactive: that stores achieving under $10,000 per month would not result in a commission payout. Sure, it made financial sense for the profitability piece of the company, but Vincent was surprised at the ex post facto rule. It also chipped away at some of his earnings in that early going.

Be that as it may, Vincent was seeing some significant early progress.

February was more or less a period of immersion. March was when the big boom started happening.

Vincent, if he timed his day well, could make three good quality store visits per day in the city. This meant the core city stores would see him at least once per week. Bi-weekly, he would make the trek to Mankato with Elizabeth and break away for a bit from his parents' house to make a kiosk stop. Then, there was the I-35W N trip that he made once or twice each month. Considering those employees listened least, he visited them least often.

Most managers come in and immediately want to start nit-picking things, have knee jerk reactions to items they dislike or start barking orders to assume the management role. Vincent did no such thing.

He spent time learning his people. He would survey them on ideas they had in the way of company improvement and things they wanted to see. He got them involved on the conference calls, shared a lot of best practices and sent out scripts and ideas several times per day. He started to share "success stories" via e-mail, of sales rep best practices on closing sales, converting accessories or landing insurance. He utilized "over-communication" of quality information with a previously ignored market – and it was making huge impact with those who cared about the business. Those who didn't would be phased out.

Most importantly, he set the bars higher in each statistical category, made his team aware of each statistical category, got their buy-in on the expectations and started drilling them home every single day with strategies and processes and best practices. And it worked.

What was previously considered "the goal" was now what Vincent taught his team was the "minimum expectation." Driving it as the goal and accepting when someone fell short led to substandard results. Training these marks as the minimum expectation and etching out larger stretch goals that promoted growth led to surges in productivity – and everyone's paychecks.

It was at this time Vincent met the other major player to be in the Brink family: Aaron Hartley.

Jordan Wallace was very ambitious and had even more ambitious plans. Due to the success of his stores in Wisconsin, he was courted by Moriarty Wireless to open more and more doors. That was the function of a master agent: to acquire more and more doors under their own umbrella. Ideally, this could come from selling current dealers to take on more doors, which was less risk in their eyes than bringing on more outsiders for one or two at a time (specifically when they were as unprofessional as party boys "Bruce" Rollins and "Logan" Andy Tuncil).

Rather than stick his toes in the water, Wallace dove right in. He was opening 7 stores in the Dallas-Fort Worth area, all relatively close to one another, within a few months of one another.

Searching for a regional manager to helm this Texas endeavor, Wallace fielded a phone call from Doug Wilson, who put in his two cents for a recently fallen comrade.

Aaron Hartley had managed and overseen several central Minnesota stores for Moriarty Wireless; he had been the equivalent of Doug Wilson, who oversaw the Twin Cities. Hartley was 25 years old, had started with Moriarty Wireless as a rep at 19 and grown through the ranks, and this was the only world he knew.

Hartley made the same mistakes many young managers make – he was friends with his subordinates. When his best friend, Julian – one of his store managers – sexually harassed Hartley's administrative assistant, he was torn on what to do. They had been a tight-knit group, however, and while Aaron confronted his friend and it boiled over at first, Aaron and his assistant changed their stances and reported it weeks later. Aaron was terminated for waiting to report the incident.

Doug Wilson reached out to Jordan Wallace, knowing he was in need of a new regional manager for Texas, and they set up a Skype interview together to discuss logistics. It was a short process and Aaron was hired; being sold the same dream Wallace sold to Vincent Scott.

Another person angling for the regional manager position was Bruce Rollins. Jordan Wallace, not one to turn down a free chance to utilize someone to his advantage, agreed to let Bruce fly down to Texas, conduct hiring blitzes, do some training with the reps and managers and basically act as regional manager while he was searching. Bruce, of course, was under the impression he was in the running for the position, even telling everyone in Minneapolis he left behind that he was the "intern regional manager" (Vincent had to point out the incorrect spelling when he saw it change on his e-mail signature, as he clearly meant *interim*). In his chase of the position with Brink he basically abandoned his Greenfield and Mankato locations, leaving them to fend for themselves. He also pissed off countless new recruits and slept with a few of the girls he interviewed.

This had been why Bruce had been so attentive to Vincent in the early-going; he wanted to "train" Vincent on in-store operations, deposit drops and returns so he could and would do them for his stores in his stead. Bruce expected Vincent to act like these 2 of his 11 stores were his most important while he flew the coop and tried to get a job that was already promised to someone else. He figured that convincing Vincent why he was so important would coerce the new leader to shower his stores with more attention.

Aaron Hartley was originally from Minneapolis, and Jordan wanted him and Vincent to meet prior to Hartley's departure. They met at the Golden Valley store in early March, had lunch and compared notes.

Vincent, despite his charisma and experience, was very intimidated by many people in this industry. Until his learning curve was licked, he was not the smartest guy in the room; at least not on the product and the process.

Aaron talked a good game. He arrived, talked about some things he used at Moriarty Wireless, presented a job aid he had created there and then spilled details on his failed marriage and the divorce. He smoked incessantly and was overweight, but was astute about wireless and Vincent was sure from the results Hartley bragged over that he could be successful here.

So, the foundation was set; Brink Management Company owned 7 stores in Wisconsin, 5 of the 11 Minnesota stores, and would have a total of 7 stores in Texas. They held the management contract on 9 stores in Missouri and 4 in Minnesota. And, it was every indication from Jordan Wallace that this was just the beginning.

March saw some huge selling days for Vincent's new team.

It was a far cry from helming a department of 220 employees that produced $5 million per month in his past life in the advertising industry, but Vincent had to frequently remind himself: this was a new journey, a fresh path and a unique experience. There was no limit to where the experience could propel him and he was free of the enemies and mistakes of his past.

Jordan Wallace talked a big game; before too long, they were going to sell their management contract to Cellular Horizons stores all over the country. He would ask Vincent how he felt about traveling all over the United States to hire regional managers and get residual income from them. The questions were rhetorical; in every scenario, they would sacrifice and work hard for a while and then be millionaires, while Wallace and Caminiti kept partying like they already were. They pulled out corporate cards at every opportunity like they were Fortune 50 CEO's.

In February 2011, Vincent's region produced $119,000 in gross profit. This would be a benchmark for him; he came on mid-month, and it was vital that March be big.

It was.

A variety of things happened. Things started to click. Personnel were happy again. People like Saul Portman, who was on the way out, re-committed, seeing that Vincent was committed. The first few weeks of seeing just what a disaster this region was, how disorganized it was and how many gaps in the process existed did not scare him off.

This could really work.

The downtown Minneapolis store, which had just been opened in November, had its best month ever with $17,000+ in gross profit. Traditionally, this store saw the widest array of customer clientele; one minute, a Fortune 50 business executive could walk in for a device and the next, a bum could be seen defecating in his pants in the corner. Vincent helped a customer once who took her teeth out for him, and had only come in to have the cord on her old Walkman untangled – totally unrelated to their business. It was fascinating.

Many customers, with the stringent policies of Cellular Horizons, came up with needing to put down deposits; nowhere more so than downtown. But Saul was the best pound for pound salesman in this company. He had the respect of his mediocre team and he was constantly on the sales floor selling. While this was not the most effective way to manage the operations and lots of money went unaccounted for behind the scenes because of it, he was a phenomenal raw sales talent with potential to be a strong leader.

Hermantown also had their best month to date – a $43K effort – which truly made it easier for Vincent to lead this region to its best month in history: $190K in gross profit.

It was unheard of: a 59% month-over-month increase Vincent's first month on the scene during a traditionally slow month for the wireless industry. And it came about because his energy arrived, his organization and processes were starting to trickle in, he communicated, they were monitoring goals and tracking sales daily, and because this team's strong points – Saul, De-Metre, and Reggie – were implementing the high level talking points Vincent preached.

Suddenly, a lot of people took notice. Who was Vincent Scott?

Doug and Susie Wilson had, at first, chuckled and shown their bosses and contemporaries the Vincent Scott website and sales videos that were good for a laugh. The first video headlining the site featured Vincent turning into Superman, so it would take a lot to live that down or prove his mettle.

But a 59% month-over-month increase for this previously unheralded region, a best ever 35 new lines per door, a 15% increase in accessory take rate, a 100% increase in insurance take rate and an incalculable increase in the morale got the Cellular Horizons retail world chattering about Vincent Scott. Maybe the man could fly.

He was out there, though, they said. He was off the wall. He was "not corporate." Was he professional enough?

Susie and Doug Wilson were paid by Cellular Horizons and Moriarty Wireless, respectively, based on new line performance, and had bonuses and qualifiers based on customer service scores and mobile Internet sales. Therefore, these were really the only things they talked about when Vincent actually saw them.

Susie had 15 total stores in her jurisdiction; all but Mankato from Vincent Scott's fold rolled into her numbers. Doug had 16 in his, scattered throughout the Great Lakes region. Both had enjoyed mediocre success at best to this point. But with the resurgence of this region, their names were in lights – which they certainly liked and took credit for.

Weekly to biweekly, they would attempt to take Vincent to lunch to discuss the stores and personnel. It would always be a place of Susie's choice because of her picky taste buds, and she would typically complain about something, be it where they sat, the waiter or the time it took to be served.

Vincent wanted to trust them because they represented a possible gateway back into a more prominent role and company, and they talked a good game. Doug was extremely diplomatic. Coming from the corporate world as a business-to-business rep with Cellular Horizons prior to his Regional Manager gig with Moriarty, he knew the program, was very politically correct and watched his words carefully. Susie, on the other hand, clearly wore the pants in this relationship (even though they were in-laws) and spoke her mind quite freely.

The changes she would propose – like dropping dead weight employees right away or getting more display units or marketing, etc. – would cost time and money. With the skeleton crews that Wallace chose to employ in attempts to maximize profitability, this was often impossible.

Going a rep down in any store would leave the store manager and one – maybe two – employees, depending on how productive the store was. So losing just one employee would be 25-to-33% of the manpower gone in one shot. It was not feasible to just pull that trigger – even if, in a perfect world, it was the right thing to do. Vincent fully intended to phase out much of the staff, but this was a process that required finding the replacements and training them first. He was not going to leave his store leaders behind the 8-ball.

It became clear that people like Susie and Doug not only did not live in this world; they did not understand it. Frankly, Vincent was having a hard time understanding it but was getting better and better at it; somebody like T.J. Jones or Jerry Smalls needed to be terminated immediately. But, because there was no one waiting in the wings that was already trained, this was impossible to attempt.

He would have to (1) find replacement employees through interview blitzes, (2) hire on a few people in excess and go top-heavy in a store at a time to not make it stick out like a sore thumb on Wallace's payroll and (3) phase out the dead weight. It could take months to revamp the entire region to his liking.

The Susie and Doug conversations typically followed the same patterns; they were Monday morning armchair quarterbacks. They would typically call Vincent midday from the comforts of their own homes, with their children or their pets in the background, or from a brief store visit where they would meet each other prior to lunch, and tell him what they saw. The floor in Eden Prairie was filthy. T.J. Jones is a lazy idiot. They got a bad customer service review on New Brighton and Susie could not stand Bryan Venison. Cloquet was horrendous and they refused to market to the universities all around them.

Vincent always asked Susie and Doug the same question when they recounted these things to him: "What did they say when you covered this with them?"

Their response was always the same: "Oh, I didn't get a chance to do that; I just wanted to let you know so you could cover it."

So – what was the function of Susie and Doug, aside from taking credit and getting paid for Vincent's team's successes?

Initially, Vincent thought Doug had 40 stores or so, which was why he was always traveling and never in his stores. It was not until later he discovered otherwise.

It was rather amusing; Susie would call Vincent, unbeknownst to him right after a lunch with Doug. Ten minutes after they got off the phone, Doug would call about the exact same thing. It happened so frequently, Vincent referred to them behind the scenes as the two-headed Wilson monster.

Vincent would also be lauded by Susie's boss Steve Flowers and his boss Kurt Stillwater in the rare instances he would run into them. It was clear that Vincent was the new success story on the block.

What was also apparent – especially to Vincent – was that this place was a mess, with no processes in place for anything, too many bad employees and no accountability. The job was so beneath Vincent and was not a good environment, conducive to his skills. But it was his job and Jordan Wallace superbly kept selling him on a bright future after sacrifices and hard work.

Wallace's primary "leadership" style was pitting his regional managers against each other. He would beat Lee Christian up over the huge gains Vincent made in every area and ask Lee why Vincent trounced him in every key performance indicator. He would beat Vincent up on why Wisconsin's stores made more gross profit (despite the fact they got 2-to-5 times the traffic per store) and had better year-over-year improvements in gross profit. It was not until much later, when Lee and Vincent began to vent to one another, that they realized this is what Wallace was doing to attempt to bolster results.

It did, however, work. When Jordan Wallace gave Vincent his first "report card" and graded his early marketing efforts an "A" but gave him a "B" in sales and a "B" in operations, Vincent was aghast. A "B" in sales?!?!? He wrote the book on sales. Literally.

What more could Vincent be doing? What other person on the planet could have taken over this mess and produced the turnaround-in-progress Vincent was achieving?

But he trudged along and continued trying to fill in the gaps every day in every way he knew how.

Vincent was led to believe the sale of the Greenfield store would happen relatively early into his time here. He also assumed – very wrongly – that a Cellular Horizons owner or a potential Cellular Horizons owner, approved by Moriarty Wireless, would be a somewhat well-to-do or intelligent individual. However, the more encounters he had with super hyper Bruce Rollins and flaky Gabe Blankenship, the less he believed this to be so.

The rumor was Bruce Rollins was extremely fond of steroids and cocaine. Regularly, he came into his store to raid deposits, eating huge sandwiches, double-fisting energy drinks and bragging about how many times he had had a bowel movement that day, all while sporting his gym clothes and talking about the girls he was screwing behind his girlfriend's (and child's mother's) back.

Gabe Blankenship was just a blank slate; there was not a lot of activity going on in his head.

He and Bruce fought like a married couple, and Bruce was his own worst enemy in prolonging this deal, which was a steal for him to begin with.

With Bruce flying the coop to Texas, trying to become a regional manager for Jordan Wallace, he basically left the entire store in Vincent's and Gabe's hands. Only Gabe and T.J. worked in the store to begin with and, considering neither of them were even passable sales employees, it was clear to Vincent he needed to get an actual store manager in there as soon as possible. So, he started interviewing.

It was different for Vincent to be on this side of the human resources coin. He was, for all practical purposes, Brink Management Company in Minnesota. He recruited, hired, trained, coached, built processes, implemented procedures, delivered the high-level message, managed employees and kept his pulse on the morale. He also had freedom to do things the way he saw fit. He may not be making the same money he had in recent years, but it was nice to be able to do things his way…and, because he was not the type of person to abuse that power, to see the fruits of his labor in all areas.

For a store manager requisition, Vincent would get hundreds of applicants. He found the most efficient method in this case was not even looking at résumés, but sending an invitation to every single applicant inviting them to an open interview forum. As he was the recruiter, HR team and hiring manager all wrapped in one, this made his job easier. The applicants would – maybe – appear, Vincent could screen them in a brief conversation and if he liked them would continue the interview.

Vincent had long not been a fan of the résumé. It really, in the grand scheme of things, meant nothing. Even if the items on it were actually true, it could not speak to how these candidates would fare in situations that they would face daily should they be selected. He wanted to see personality, character and real-life responses to realistic scenarios.

His favorite after following this process for the Greenfield opening was Terry Bunche, a former business owner in his mid-40's who was the top rep of 200 at call center for a wireless competitor.

Terry said all the right things; he was actually selling wireless currently, had run his own construction business and wanted this job because it was an opportunity to be unchained from the desk and to make a difference as the head of a store. He was not turned off by the anemic starting salary and came across as legitimately interested in what he could bring to the table.

Vincent assumed that Gabe Blankenship would want to be front and center in the proceedings of selecting a store manager for the store he would be purchasing. Vincent served as the first face the candidates saw, he screened them and he gave his three finalists to Gabe – figuring he could do an interview.

Unbeknownst to Vincent, Gabe was completely inept; while he put on the façade of machismo and bravado, he was very clumsy with words and unimpressive in nearly every way. It was a big reason the sales results at Greenfield were so poor. He did little more than confuse those he met with, and completely scared away Terry Bunche.

It had been a couple of weeks since he had last talked with Terry, and Vincent was a bit surprised he never heard back from him. This is when he started piecing together Gabe's incompetence.

Gabe was starting to get immense pressure from all around: from Bruce to close the sale of the store, from Jordan Wallace to come to terms on a management contract for the store, and from Doug Wilson, to get a store manager, because those results ultimately rolled up to him. Vincent was caught in the middle; he knew what needed to be done, had done everything he could, and was growing antsy on all sides.

Finally, a conference call spearheaded by Doug and including the others involved forced Gabe's hand; he ceded carte blanche to Vincent to hire a manager…but was it too late? Bruce Rollins, as per usual, condescended to Gabe and they got into a tiff on the call. Gabe revealed he was apprehensive about signing a two-year deal with Wallace. The hinges were coming off of this deal.

Vincent called Terry, hoping against hopes that he was still interested. He left a message and hoped for a callback.

Terry called Vincent later that day.

"Yeah – Terry – how have you been?" Vincent asked.

"I'm good. I was a little surprised to get a message from you, but wanted to call you back to let you know about my conversation with Gabe."

*Oh, no, here goes,* Vincent thought.

"Do tell," Vincent responded, coolly.

"It was actually pretty short," Terry continued. "We went into his office and it was mostly just me talking. He really didn't ask me any questions. He was showing me a sales tracker. That's it. He talked about the results of the store. He didn't even sound like any growth was possible. He said he was glad there were just two sellers in the store so they could both make some money."

"Wow, okay," Vincent said, feigning shock, but not really. "Now it makes sense why I haven't heard back from you. Gabe will strictly be an owner, and that's *if* this deal even goes through. The other thing is I have been in this position for 2 months and I just assumed Gabe would represent his interests well. Clearly, he didn't, and for that I apologize. You would report to me, it would be us working together. Frankly, there's a ton of potential here – the location is solid, we just need to rebuild and I need somebody with the business sense and tenacity to do it. I'm interested in your talents for this store, and would like to offer you the job."

There was a pause.

"Okay," Terry responded. "Yeah, I admit, I walked out of there and was done with this."

"I can imagine," Vincent stated. "Which is what I pieced together after not hearing from you and spending more time with Gabe. I'm asking you to give this a shot. This is a potentially prime location; with the right leader, we can make it happen. I know you're the guy."

"If that's the case – if I'm working for you and everything we talked about is true, I'm in."

"That's what I want to hear."

"When do you need me?"

"Well, I know this sounds ridiculous, but our current owner is in town for another day, and he really wants to spend some time with you and give you some training," Vincent answered, closing his eyes at the absurdity of this whole situation. "Can you come in later today, and spend some time with him tomorrow?"

There was another pause. Terry, on the other end, was also wondering what he was getting himself into.

"Sure, what time?"

And, there it was. Unlike the corporate bureaucracy of a huge company where it took weeks and months to even implement small decisions, this was a fly-by-the-seat-of-your-pants non-stop thrill ride. Possibilities were limitless but support and structure were nil. Fortunately, guys like Terry Bunche and Vincent Scott were thrill seekers who worked well with zero structure and gobs of potential.

Terry started at the end of March, got a crash course on the store from Bruce Rollins, put in a lot of time, started putting his mark on the team, and began seeing what Brink Management Company was all about: loads of potential, but no plan. Vincent, Saul, Terry and the few others that were "getting it" were just making it up as they went along… and somehow it was working.

# "The Surviving Game" by Vincent Scott
## The Essential Elements of Successful Sales Leadership

The sales manager: occasionally (and hopefully) a more highly evolved salesperson who exists to lead, guide, assist, remove obstacles and eliminate excuses for, set the example, coach, train, serve and protect the salespeople reporting to him or her.

Sales managers are all around us; those in the selling game have likely encountered multiple. Like salespeople themselves, they have a wide range of qualifications, personality traits and work ethics, but the role of this figurehead is one that ties them all together.

This crucial leader is in place because of the people he or she leads, and this is a fact that can never be forgotten. Often, these coaches were once players of the game - likely above average or exceptional at that - but this is a new role, with new responsibilities and unique challenges. Whereas the salesperson is responsible for and accountable for one set of numbers, results and efficiencies (their own), the team leader must manage processes to achieve optimum results for their entire team.

Yes, that's right - the sales manager's primary role is management of process and people in perfect harmony.

In the realm of managing people, the boss needs to learn and understand them - their needs, strengths, areas of opportunity that need improvement, their potential and their pitfalls. It is important to stress to the team they manage that they exist to support them, answer questions or know where to find the answers (and know when to give them and when to require the work fall upon the seller), and that they take responsibility for doing their part in the salesperson's career path.

For, in any selling environment, sales manager and salesperson have a contract: upon issuance and acceptance of job offer, both parties agree to give their all, fulfill obligations in training, effort and results. Neither party can forget these promises.

The manager's role in managing process - like any other facet of management - can have many different styles and approaches, but it boils down to one thing: the mechanics of successful leadership. Time management, ensuring that the training and coaching needs of his/her employees are being met, spending the right amount of time on each project and investing the proper attention and energy in the appropriate places - these are all incumbent upon the sales manager.

We will never see everything the sales manager grapples with, which is why an unclear picture of their worth sometimes exists. But an effective leader is so pivotal to any organization; their motivation, their wisdom and their ability to create and foster an environment that is conducive for results can and will make or break teams, offices, departments and companies.

Sales managers are an extremely valuable resource. They, too, must be trained, coached and shepherded along the path to exceptional leadership.

Just as a quality investment of time in a sales representative can positively impact every futuristic call they make, quality training and molding of a sales manager will trickle down to the hundreds of actions they undertake in a day, the hundreds of situations they face and the hundreds of employees who prosper under their tutelage.

The role of the sales manager - like any other rung on the ladder of the salesperson hierarchy - is imperative to make the sales wheel go around, be it for any part of the holy sales trilogy: the customer, the company and employees.

There is a prominent cross-stitched sign that reads, "Anyone can be a Father; it takes someone special to be a Daddy." Now that I relish my relationship with my daughter more than any experience my life has enriched me with, those words ring true. It is not challenging to father a child, but the investment and reward of being a Daddy is the best there is.

In that vein, anybody can wear the moniker of manager. Companies make mistakes, people are often picked based on nepotism or the old boys' club nonsense, but it takes someone incredible to be an actual leader.

My years of sales and corporate experience have shown me a lot about the operations of the world - good and bad - so I have seen my fair share of horrific management. In fact, of the several people to be my boss over the years, only a couple of them really ever did anything to help me and I have learned more of what not to do than what to do from them.

To learn leadership without any guidance is not an easy feat, yet many of us find ourselves in this predicament. Real innovation and quality, respectful leadership are often endangered species – but they don't have to be.

A lot of the same relationships and variables are similar no matter what stage of the food chain you are on - customer, rep, manager or manager's manager. The trick is to always take care of the people, constantly remember that without their presence there is no need for yours, and to consider yourself part of the team rather than on an undeserved pedestal. Your job exists to make theirs easier and more profitable.

My management success was due to allegiance to my team but holding them accountable. One of the most frequent mistakes I have seen managers working for me make is their tendency to want to befriend their team members. At first, this can lead to a surge, but when the "friends" see what they can get away with, they try to get away with more. When those outside the circle of buddies see what those "friends" are getting away with, their resentment grows. There is an unhealthy balance on the team and eventually this can lead to unrest and upheaval.

Team synergy is important; momentum, managing processes (and not necessarily people) and figuring out how to impact the most futuristic actions possible that your team undertakes is the key to mastering management. Care about every issue. Learn when to show them how to do something and when they need to figure it out of their own devices. Either know the answer to every question or know where to find it. And never leave their questions unanswered. Like a child modeling themselves after a parent, they notice everything and forget nothing.

In addition, view every time you pull your team members out of the trenches as an investment. Far too many managers have trepidation about pulling reps off the phones or out of the field because they think it jeopardizes revenue. However, if you are giving them quality coaching that will benefit every futuristic action that team member does, how is it not a worthwhile investment of time by both parties?

Follow-up is also vital. In fact, lack of follow-up is the biggest contributor to ineffective training. The manager must lay out the course of action from the current standing to the goal. The parties must agree. The leader must follow up to ensure the steps are being implemented. When their words are not being heeded, repercussions must be there. The true leader never disciplines anyone who does not see it coming.

Finally, remember it is the leader's job to remove obstacles. Again, the manager does not exist unless their subordinates do. They are the ones who directly impact the manager's paycheck, they equal their results and their presence is what justifies the manager being in that position. Eliminate obstacles, remove objections and make sure the reps have no excuses not to perform.

Do not, however, lend credence to nonsensical excuses; personal issues and excessive complaints have no place here. As a supportive figure to the team, you empathize when team members struggle with an outside force yet cannot allow this to be a chronic inhibitor of performance. Your job can be your sanctuary from the outside world; if employees allow their dismal personal life to destroy their business life, their sanctuary is lost and things only get worse.

Get everyone on the same playing field, coach the ones who want to be coached, cultivate the talent that exists and cut bait on the ones who do not have the skill or will and desire to obtain it. Fear of disciplining or terminating where necessary is a management weakness; you are cutting them loose so they can go on to a career they are destined for. You both come out winners in that equation, as evidence indicates this is certainly not the fit for them.

Never forget: the goal of a leader is to lead, to serve and protect. You will constantly be challenged and tested, fires will regularly pop up all over the place, but you can never let them see you bleed, never let yourself be taken off the path and you must prioritize: the team and the results always come first.

A manager is a dime a dozen. A leader is a rare breed, destined for success and able to make magic happen as their team members follow them like the Pied Piper.

Which are you?

In order to effectively lead in the arena of sales, one must possess the abilities to sell, inspire and endure the ebb and flow of the selling game terrain better than most. While there are not enough truly great sales leaders in the world today, no reason exists why you cannot be one.

Like any endeavor in business, there are two governing principles: people and process. If you have the right personnel in place following the right procedure, you will be successful. The numbers will be there. It's like the House always winning and playing the odds; when we stop relying on tried and true methods, this is when we fail.

Many managers find inexplicable (for them) failure because of this very reason: they try to follow a process with the wrong people, or they fail to provide the right process to the right ones. They get too caught up in chasing numbers, telling their team they need more of a metric without showing them how to achieve it or why it's important, and they fizzle out for that very reason.

The vital first part of your process as sales leader is building the relationships. No team will respect someone who shows up on the scene and starts barking orders; and why should they? This manager has not established trust, gained respect and earned the right to lead.

The manager title is one thing, but the two-way communication that a leader evokes to foster a winning team is essential. Building the relationships can involve the leader rolling up his or her sleeves and being in the trenches, learning from the front-line employees what actually transpires and is needed for improvement, and seeing through their own eyes what is working and what is not. There is no better way to diagnose the business, and you cannot introduce necessary changes to the process without being able to make that diagnosis.

Once that diagnosis is made, focus not on selling more. Focus on what prevents sales in each metric you are held accountable to and eliminate those obstacles. You gain trust and results by eliminating obstacles to selling because there is nothing left to do but sell.

Furthermore, you must often sell your team on why process tweaks are beneficial; they fear change just like a customer does. This is the "sales food chain" – your relationship with your team is akin to the rep relationship with a customer in that you must ask questions, learn their existing process, gain trust, expose gaps they may not have even known about and convince them to change based on need. When you make their fear of standing pat outweigh their fear of change, your salesperson can make the decision to do so. Either way, you will call upon them to get outside their comfort zone. Your ability to keep them away from their comfortable ways of failing or mediocrity will determine your success.

This is done by a variety of methods; recognition is chief among them. You must also document the progress: where we've been, where we are, where we're going and what steps we are taking to get there. And you must hold accountable; did they take the steps to get there? If not, why not?

Like anything else – following a recipe or directions – steps must be taken to elevate our team members to their potential. They will rise, they will fall based on their choices and abilities. But it is you who must lay out a clear road map for them to follow and a "why" behind their process; is it for promotion? Is it more money? Is it accolades? Or is it just holding on to a job and benefits?

Whatever their motivation, you must know your people (see "build the relationships") so you know how to put together their personal plan of attack to obtain or keep what they want in lieu of losing what they fear losing out on. Know that and you can drive them by reminding them of their goals and their trajectory based on their actions. Know that and you can praise them as they rise and you can build a crucial succession plan for your business.

Once you have the right people following the right process, your job is one of checks and balances. You will have fires that pop up but never let anything take you away from the top priority of proper staffing and proper protocol; the fires will lessen as you reach optimum levels in both. There will be people you must set free to find their true calling in life once you establish this is not it. There will be changes in industry and landscape that you must devise new process for. There will always be challenges that call upon the final essentials – patience and consistency. But reminding yourself of the big picture, that nothing happens overnight and that you are working toward something great will always keep you focused and on track. Consistency in your process will garner consistent results.

Strive for perfection. Strive for personal goals that are bigger than the commitments you must meet for your company, and term your company "goals" as minimum expectations. Do that, and even barely falling short of your stretch goals (larger goals that provide the ideal growth you are striving for) means you are very much ahead of the curve.

Adhere to these essentials of sales leadership and you will become an essential cog in your company's wheel.

\*     \*     \*     \*     \*

## Bumps in the Road

Life does not really come with any kind of finite instructions. Certainly, there is some semblance of recommended road map. There are always people more than willing to give you their two cents. Nevertheless, the decisions are yours and the harsh reality is that things seldom go according to plan.

Vincent Scott, while not exactly sure what place it was, was in a completely different one than he had ever encountered with only his intuition and experience to guide him.

For starters, he had crafted a book that had illustrated his selling and leadership techniques and tactics, found a publisher amidst 953 rejections and achieved the dream of becoming a published author. However, his publisher turned out to be a deadbeat, tried withholding royalties and did nothing to market his book or live up to the promised end of the bargain in their contract. The reality of the distribution was not as it had been guaranteed, the man was rude and dishonest and the whole ordeal was disappointing. That wasn't in the roadmap.

Vincent had been illegally removed from his previous position and was realizing more and more that not only was justice not swift, it was painfully slow and he could never move on emotionally until this saga was complete.

Vincent had first filed with the government agencies responsible for vetting his case prior to trial in January 2010, a prerequisite to getting any wrongful termination suit filed. At that time, he filled out paperwork and waited two hours in a waiting room just to see an overly grumpy employee who attempted to convince him that his case did not fit the standards and guidelines. Considering the Civil Rights Act of 1964 specifically prevented sexual discrimination, harassment, hostile work environment, racism and the retaliation that took place from reporting it, this was clearly not true. However, after thirty minutes of selling, Vincent got her to at least put through the complaint.

Over one year later, not much traction had been accumulated on the case. It was just David versus Goliath. The file was assigned to a case-worker: Jon Jefferson. Jon met with Vincent and tried to convince him that his case was not covered. Jon ignored the hundreds of pages of proof and evidence and documentation Vincent provided and failed to call, contact or return the calls of 99% of the witnesses who came forward.

In short, Vincent's case was not getting its just due. He knew these things could and would take time, but this was absolutely outrageous. And if they didn't pick up his case, which was clearly in their jurisdiction, he was going to have to come out of pocket for a lawyer and all subsequent fees, which would total in the tens of thousands. That wasn't in the roadmap.

His former department was laying off another 50% of their workforce by the conclusion of 2011, which was fitting, but was little consolation to the weary Vincent Scott.

And much of his situation was certainly better, even if a lot of it was not. He had freedom. His ideas mattered. Heck, he *was* the show. And he knew it – more and more as time passed. It's just that the lack of direction, support and structure all throughout Brink, Moriarty and Cellular Horizons was not in the roadmap.

Vincent was making his own marketing decisions as he learned the ins and outs of what wasn't working and contemplated how to better reach out to potential customers. He had taken generic Cellular Horizons fliers that touted a phone or two in a land where only 18% of customers were with his carrier, and was developing new pieces that would attract shoppers currently with competitors with an offer to buy out all or part of their contracts. He was developing this market and making it his own.

With the marketing techniques he had learned in being the chief marketer of his book, he started social media pages for his stores and started getting thousands of followers and connections for them. He was turning this into a science and a process, and working towards putting it on autopilot – the ultimate dream of any leader: a perfect process with the best people possible (albeit here on a shoestring budget with a lot of house he needed to clean) that required only checks and balances from leadership.

And, all the while, he was not afraid to roll up his sleeves and get in the trenches. He would go out in the heat and put hundreds of fliers on cars as many of his lazy employees watched. He would make his own cold calls to business owners to "form a mutually beneficial partnership" in hopes they may co-market and turn into purchasing customers; it was the tried and true philosophy of offering to do something for them first, gaining trust and seeing how they could help one another.

Some of his onlookers joined in. The ones that mattered respected him more and more.

Vincent's outlook had changed. It was not that time had healed the wound, it was that enough wounds had scarred over that he had forced himself to forget many of the things that caused his pain to begin with. In fact, Vincent had repressed so many memories that he was strictly living in the moment and for the future – axes to grind and all.

Too much closeness – to anything but Elizabeth – was too much for Vincent. His innermost thoughts and self was not something he was comfortable sharing. Those he had committed to most had destroyed him, broken him and left him for dead. Sure – he had chosen to let them in and take, but he could decide to bolt the doors going forward so as to never be ravaged again.

He had driven off Casey Carnes with his inability to commit, and was now in the process of doing the same with Emily Nance – on-and-off with both of them for months in separate stints.

Vincent liked being able to be himself with another human being to a degree, but pull back when he felt like it, be alone when he felt like it. He maintained a rigorous workout routine, kept up writing in his journal regularly, put together his detailed sales reports and put in way too many hours on the job to keep him away from anything he was not ready or not willing to do in the way of companionship.

Anything to take his mind off the past or the unfair penance.

He had plenty in the present to focus on, anyway. Work never let up. These employees, being without leadership for so long, were lapping up his teachings like little lost puppies. Their phone calls to Vincent were frequent and incessant. He was in a seven-day-a-week business and he was tugged on all seven days. While he lamented this mentally, and it did little to help his growing anxiety, he could always use work as an excuse to get out of anything, anytime, that anyone else – including Emily – wanted him to participate in.

The chief difference, however, in this Vincent and the one from years ago was that he shared his success stories and tips and *still* beat everyone. This Vincent was no longer as self-promotional; he was gracious and even though he was doing more work than anyone, he gave all the credit to his team.

While, privately, in the recesses of his mind he knew he was worlds better than this job, he took great pride and lengths to dominate, but to also make everyone aware of what he and his team were doing to dominate.

It was all not without its unique, pungent challenges, however.

Darryl Wilkinson, touted by Saul and De-Metre as the next obvious management choice, flip-flopped when offered the Golden Valley management spot vacated when Vincent granted Jesse Fairbanks' wish of relinquishing it – and put in his two weeks' notice.

Jesse Fairbanks, upon being moved out of Brink's actual ownership and to the Chris Jeffries store chain, used Jeffries as some sort of shield from Vincent's expectations in the way of reports, observation forms and conference call attendance. He had an excuse for literally everything and the move caused quite the chasm between them. Vincent would typically kill him with kindness through gritted teeth when they spoke or he visited, but he could not force Fairbanks to do anything to make them both more money and both were well aware of it.

The staff in the relatively faraway White Bear Township store was atrocious enough that even when their mostly absentee, burnt out manager, Jackie, left to pursue a career in insurance, it was actually a loss. They had made a habit of firing and re-hiring the same terrible employee multiple times because he would always come back, even though he lied to customers and was a terrible liability from multiple angles.

The situation was so dire, and it was so difficult finding replacement people, that Vincent had to resort to moving worthless T.J. Jones out there, dangling a management carrot if he could train the two new recruits he was lucky enough to find on Craigslist, of all places. T.J. was the only person willing to move there and Vincent was learning to use whatever resources he could to forge this fractured ship forward no matter what the armchair quarterbacks said.

Terry Bunche called and was already in need of being talked off the ledge; after logging some 80 hour weeks, revamping the Greenfield store out of his own pocket and building a passable team, he was being ordered by Bruce Rollins to process illegal, fraudulent equipment returns to get reimbursement from Moriarty Wireless with fake, made-up "problems" cited as the reason so Rollins could stay financially afloat. He'd process these claims on phones or equipment that were not selling to give him enough of a credit to get phones that would sell.

These were challenges that working in the framework and methods of a big company never could have ever prepared Vincent for. This was baptism by fire; having to rely on bad employees, having to be creative to recruit, having to fly by the seat of his pants and having to tolerate managers that did little to nothing of what he asked them to do because if he fired one, only he suffered. Marketing on a nickel, relying on personnel who were severely underpaid and getting nothing constructive from the people paid to help; Vincent could see why his predecessors were so unsuccessful… and why he was the only person who could somehow will this into a win.

At the end of the day, he did all he could do and then some to pull this rabbit out of his proverbial hat. He would then retreat into the calming healing of cuddling with his daughter when he had her and with a fifth of vodka when he didn't.

Admittedly, he was once fully entranced with the Kool-Aid of corporate America. Vincent had been his respective departments' biggest advocate, buying into the smoke and mirrors and tirelessly selling employees on products that did not work and a company that treated them like nothing more than statistics. He thought he would retire from there and eagerly lapped up all of the bullshit they fed him – that he was going to run the company someday – and, when they unceremoniously and illegally dumped him, his belief in forever was vanquished.

Now, 32 years old, jaded, distrustful, tired – Vincent was a completely different person. He questioned his limits. His anxiety attacks from the height of his battles with his old boss and with Abby that he thought were behind him were back. His drive seemed to have lost a step, even though it was more than anyone else's.

Was this what he had fought so hard for? Was this what he had sacrificed his career for, standing up to dictators and illegal practices? Last he checked, the corrupt bastards he fought were still there, running his ship into the ground (and quickly at that), and Vincent's name was a curse word, his career derailed, his finances severely impacted and his future cloudy.

In spite of all that, there was this fellow Jordan Wallace. Sure, he answered to investors, but he was his own boss, and he had that cavalier attitude and swagger that Vincent was actually jealous of. Was this his training to be an entrepreneur, a business owner and would it bridge him to the next facet of his life? Or was he wasting his time?

Could this be done?

There was no answer to that question at this time; all Vincent knew was that if Brink Management Company could be a win and a success for anybody, Vincent was the best person to make it that way.

As for his axes to grind, they would live to be resolved another day. Right now, Vincent only had his crosses to bear.

All he heard from Jordan Wallace was about Wisconsin success (that he never saw proof of on any report) and the need for year-over-year growth (which he never saw lack of from any report). All he heard from Doug and Susie Wilson was that his stores were best in show, so he was very much in the dark on what precisely he was striving for.

Hermantown, despite the fact they did literally nothing Vincent requested, carried these numbers and masked the inadequacies of several stores. In March, when they spouted off $45K in gross profit, that was fine and good, but with a slower start in April, the numbers were gruesome a couple of weeks in. After posting $190K in gross profit in March as a first step to greatness, the region was already taking a major hit, on pace for $148K in April with just a couple of weeks left to play.

Vincent was slated to fly to Indianapolis for a retailer convention conducted by Moriarty Wireless. Upon landing, he met up with Lee Christian, who had just flown in, and, over lunch and a few drinks, they discussed the organization.

Both gentlemen very passionate about success, this meeting actually helped them bridge any gaps forming between them from the influence of Wallace's leadership style.

Lee was a simple man; he had a heavy IT background, had started as a sales rep, was promoted and then promoted again as Wisconsin's store count grew. His ambition was to one day run his own stores and make enough profit so he and his girlfriend could live happily ever after. It was warm enough. You couldn't help but like the guy.

Lee was actually just as taken aback by Wallace's attempts to antagonize them with each others' results as Vincent was, and it was interesting to learn – for both of them – that he had the same approach with the other.

Jordan Wallace's flight landed, and Lee and Vincent picked him up in their rental car. Flights, Jordan Wallace's biweekly ski trips with his wife, wine and scotch tasting trips with Lyle Caminiti, nice hotel rooms, and the night that ensued all indicated that this was the life. Jordan Wallace was clearly living the dream we all think we dream of having, though how he could afford it was a wonder.

Heading into the lavish dinner Moriarty Wireless hosted was a sight to see. It was young money on full display.

Surrounded daily by people like 23-year old Saul Portman, 22-year old De-Metre Jones and others their age that had adult problems, families and were scraping by for a living definitely made Vincent feel his age and gain perspective. They were him, from 10 years ago, without his experience or privilege, making the kind of money he made as a meat clerk and assistant manager at Cooke's Grocery Store in Mankato.

Moriarty Wireless was founded by current CEO Stuart Moriarty's father, Sheldon, 20 years prior, as a small outfit for cellular phone retail. This was in the early brick phone days, where products that suit Gordon Gekko or Zack Morris were commonplace, and it began on the premise of outfitting other small retailers with consistency and quality.

Sheldon bequeathed the business to his two sons – Stuart and Samuel – and they served as CEO and COO, respectively.

They were in their early 30's, as were those who served on their executive board. The most prominent was their Chief Strategy Officer, Seth Schmidt, who sat at the head of the dinner table on this night. He was the senior officer representing Moriarty Wireless.

Vincent and Lee followed Wallace, who seated himself near Doug Wilson, and the night of excessive drink and food began. And it was not just any food; it was oysters and crab as appetizers, lobster, steak and caviar, and it was vodka, scotch and bourbon aplenty for all to indulge in. It was any previous celebratory meal Vincent had encountered on steroids.

It was enough to make Vincent rethink any doubts he had about this place – which meant it did its job. If this kind of money was flowing, surely he was onto something; he just had to tap into it by being the best damn resource in their business. This he could do. This was familiar territory for him; par for the course.

As if the dinner was not enough, it was precursor to an evening of barhopping and a strip club, all expenses paid by either the Moriarty or Brink Management Company tabs. Everywhere they went, corporate cards were flashed, be it by Schmidt or Wallace.

The more Wallace drank, the more obnoxious he got; strutting around downtown Indianapolis with his sunglasses on at night wearing his hat sideways and hitting on every woman that moved. He even nearly got into a fight with a bar bouncer because they were charging a cover to get in and Wallace tried unsuccessfully to leverage his large group getting in for free. Always selling.

*This is my boss*, Vincent mused, becoming less impressed with him by the moment. But he caught himself, and realized that once upon a time, he too had exhibited behavior along the same lines.

Watching the money flowing like water all around him was intoxicating, and maybe 10 years ago this would have completely captivated or entertained him far more, but he was not the Vincent Scott of old.

One of the other owners was an extremely attractive brunette named Kristen, who sauntered over to Vincent – quietly sipping his drink in the corner near Doug Wilson – and started hanging all over him. Her breath, reeking of booze, and her overaggressive approach, which would have worked on the old Vincent, sent him to an early turn-in. He could have easily taken her back to his room; the fact he did not left Wallace, Lee and Doug in bewilderment, but his priorities had completely shifted. He was a Dad; not a drunken douche bag.

Vincent had once "suffered" from what he called Peter Pan Syndrome – a refusal to grow up. But, as he played in this band of misfit toys called Brink

Management Company, he realized he was the foremost adult in the group. What a sobering realization.

Jordan Wallace was Peter Pan. He had all the money and toys – a Dodge Viper on the company dime, these frequent non-business trips – and a beautiful, devoted wife, while he lived by no rules in Neverland. He cheated on his wife like it was a sport, seeing how far he could push it. He was the center of attention and liked being the golden boy of Cellular Horizons and Moriarty. He had left Cellular Horizons and started his own business because being a CEO could get him away from being managed and could get him what he felt was the power he craved.

Jordan Wallace was Dustin "Bruce" Rollins; just on a completely different, puffed up scale, with actual charm and sophistication. Jordan Wallace was what Vincent Scott might have become, had it not been for Elizabeth blessing his life. In fact, that unbridled pursuit of pleasure in all of its forms every day is what many do and would indulge in if given the chance.

This was why Rollins looked at Jordan Wallace as his brother and idol: he was everything he hoped to be.

And Vincent realized this as he watched Jordan Wallace; he knew Jordan was drunk on the power and money; given the same blessings his talents had managed to bestow on him, Vincent had made several missteps of his own in the past before an awakening and reshuffling of priorities.

Vincent sat in the dealer meeting conducted the next day, where several different vendors gave dog-and-pony shows, where Stuart Moriarty spoke and gave the gospel according to Moriarty Wireless.

He was so irreverent, so politically incorrect, and the audience loved him. Any corporate human resources employee would have had a field day on his vulgar mouth, sexual innuendo and crude jokes on stage in front of hundreds of his employees, but they were seemingly none the wiser. This was incredible to see.

Part of Vincent certainly gravitated towards this. Money was in no short supply. There was a loose structure, but it was not as stringent and forced. If Vincent could make a splash here, and his trajectory thus far indicated he could, perhaps this was a viable place for him to hang his hat.

It was typical of Vincent's time here thus far; when he became downtrodden at the odds against him, something would occur or someone would come along and he'd start to think he could really make this an endeavor to remember.

That night, Moriarty hosted a bowling event downtown, and Vincent had the opportunity to meet Stuart, laud consummate nice guy Doug Wilson to him, and meet several others in the organization.

He turned in early, took a bus to the airport in the morning, and flew back to Minneapolis, rejuvenated and now knowing his place in this world: rising star with limitless potential.

The coming week, Vincent was also slated to meet with Paul Gemini – the other chief investor in Brink Management Company and his predecessor's father. Gemini flew in with Wallace from Wisconsin and Vincent tagged along on a few store visits until meeting up with Doug Wilson for lunch.

"You know, when I first heard about you, my initial thought was 'how pompous does this kid have to be to write a sales book at age 30,'" Paul Gemini said upon meeting Vincent. "I said 'that's the kind of kid I want working for me.' I love it."

Vincent smiled and returned the handshake.

The more Vincent observed this business, the more he also realized that the money very much dictated Jordan Wallace's actions.

Jordan Wallace had some raw management ability, albeit mostly with some shady or suggestive sales practices that somewhat misled the customer from the true message. While it was not downright wrong but perhaps somewhat creative in a deceitful way, it was far from masterful, effective technique. He was well educated and very intelligent; his reasons for breaking ties with Corporate America were quite valid.

That said, Jordan Wallace had not earned his stripes. He had happened into money and privilege in this arena. He had not earned it the hard way yet. He had not scratched and clawed his way to the top, or, much less anywhere – he wanted and was used to short cuts.

On the other hand, Vincent wanted so badly to "earn it"; to finally obtain what he had fought so hard for. He felt he had always done all the right things and made the proper moves in the face of whatever circumstances he encountered: he worked hard, he saved money in excess and lived like he was much less fortunate so he could save for the future and protect against the down side. Things were going swimmingly until he met Abby Winters, and then his financial life took a massive hit. His illegal termination was another significant blow.

Wallace made it look easy and he flaunted his fortune. Vincent would have liked to have lived a day in his happy-go-lucky world. But was it real? Sure, Vincent could have flaunted what he had, but he chose not to; always stocking up for a hopeful future of promise and peace.

Vincent had earned the stripes, but he had also paid the price for his courage and stamina. Others had used him until he ceased to be valuable to them and became a liability to their world of secrets and lies, only to discard him and leave him worse off.

Vincent was sure to infuse his rekindled passion into his actions and conference calls. He had seen now what they were a part of – the grander scheme. Moriarty Wireless had grown from nothing and continued to gain momentum. They were major players – one of the biggest family of companies of its kind in the Midwest – and there was no stopping them. They were onto something, but clearly needed drivers like Vincent Scott. Vincent saw his role and what he could do in a business that let him run free.

Doug Wilson seemed pretty cool in a passive, nonintrusive, buddy type of way, and if he had found this much success and $100,000 per year paydays with Moriarty, what could Vincent Scott do?

It was important for Vincent to communicate what they were a part of to his mostly 20-something team. With the right coaching, organizational skills and polish, there was no reason why they could not have been just as good – if not better – than many managers he had managed before in a huge corporate setting that made 2-to-10 times as much money as they did.

And it was effective. His core team – the Brink-owned stores – understood what he preached. Terry Bunche quickly latched on with Vincent and, despite the fact his paperwork was shoddy and he was inconsistent about execution of Vincent's orders, he was a good sounding board for the oft-frustrated Scott and he could produce raw results. Saul, De-Metre, Reggie and Terry were – slowly, but surely – showing progress on all of their focus items, like key performance metrics, scheduling events, executing some cold calling initiatives and marketing. The foundation was being set.

Unbeknownst to Vincent and contrary to the Wallace diatribes (out of his strategy to further drive his managers), the region was besting year over year numbers on a large scale.

But all of the good and the progress continued to be lost amongst constant setbacks.

Vincent had allowed De-Metre Jones to watch over Golden Valley in addition to New Brighton because of their proximity to one another, the fact it plugged a hole and because De-Metre desperately needed the financial help.

However, New Brighton's numbers sagged while Golden Valley was stagnant. The reps complained he was never where he said he would be and that they were not getting coaching.

Theft started occurring; phones would go missing either in the cloak of night or even in broad daylight in a few stores here and there, which took up plenty of Vincent's and his managers' time.

Day-long interview blitzes would turn up 5 people, meaning the time Vincent spent putting them together and the day in question were mostly wasted and he would have to take the gamble again if he still wanted an improved staffing situation. Managers would not keep up with their daily and weekly paperwork, meaning inaccurate auditing of equipment, inventory and sales. They would not log in consistently to Vincent's conference calls. Vincent would ask for things and make basic requests and get no response.

Brink Management Company was providing Vincent the most dramatic professional highs and lows he ever thought possible. He legitimately wondered how long he could do this, how much he could put up with. His paycheck would be off by $2,500 or his employees would be paid improperly on a biweekly basis, morale would take an intense drop, and he had to somehow keep bringing himself back every single day, without fail. Moriarty could not have thrown enough lavish dinners to keep Vincent ensconced in this current muck forever.

Sales results were ridiculously inconsistent. They did rebound in April and, while they bettered their mid-month $148K pace and finished at $171K, it was still well down from the $190K March. This was certainly not going to be easy. At all.

But any and every time he started to seriously consider leaving Brink Management Company at all costs, old Jordan Wallace would pull a rabbit of futuristic promises out of his hat.

Vincent just could not shake this feeling that he was meant for so much more – in all areas. He was never satisfied. And Vincent – being his own toughest critic – constantly wondered if he was where he was supposed to be and doing what he should be doing.

May was traditionally a strong month in the wireless retail business thanks to the conclusion of the school year and the kids heading back home, according to the Doug-and-Susie-Wilson two-headed monster, and it started out strong. After the initial week, Vincent was on pace for a $200,000 gross profit month for his region.

The frustration, however, was that it seemed no one could see the business through his eyes no matter how hard he tried to impart his vision into everyone he encountered.

Jordan Wallace wanted to talk constantly about doing more and more even before reaching their initial goals, and profitability, and growth year-over-year, which was all fine and good. But the traffic simply was not there, and any time a good (or even decent) marketing idea was floated his way, he would tell Vincent to write up a proposal that would die on his desk. When it came to signing the check, Wallace would kill the initiative through inaction.

There was no doubt in Vincent's mind that he was a Godsend to these people; they said as much regularly. But even with Vincent's amazing process (that many ignored, to their detriment) that was increasing every statistical category by 30%-to-200%, it was a challenge to "grow the business" in Wallace's definition because there was little-to-no traffic.

Stores like Plymouth were a good example. Not that Jesse Fairbanks' boring personality could set the world on fire, but Vincent would stay there for a day and see five customers enter the store. To their credit, they did some cold calling initiatives that drummed up new business, but they were fighting against their own worst enemies – bad location and no traffic.

Vincent would exhaust himself conjuring up strength from somewhere he did not know it existed. His day would begin at 6 AM, and, if he did not have Elizabeth that night, it would sometimes end at 3 AM the following day, only to begin again a few hours later. He got so excited and drove himself and his region and was so passionate about doing whatever it took – against all odds – to get the growth he was charged with getting.

And he had to accept where it worked when it worked. It was gradual in most areas. But, in overall revenue, his region could not best March 2011.

He would plug gaping holes in the ship with his own body, only to have to leave to tend to another one. The ship could hemorrhage and Vincent was wearing himself out trying to minimize damage so they could drift a few yards farther.

He would overexert himself only to have to slink back into the recesses of his empty apartment ignoring the nonstop phone calls from his team to recuperate.

And where did it all go? What was the purpose to this?

A corporate hellhole had a structure, paid him handsomely and gave him health benefits, but smacked his hand and beat the living daylights out of him when he got out of their narrow guidelines with his spirited innovations or refused to break the law as instructed. They took months to approve any of the necessary policy changes, verbiage, observation forms, marketing ideas, etc. that he proposed there, but could accomplish here in mere hours.

On the flip side, people listened and had to obey him because they were so terrified of losing their jobs and the $100,000 per year paychecks they did not deserve. In fact, it was that very subservience to the system that kept them there after the truth was exposed. Those people would not have been capable of the effort and drive Vincent was exhibiting here at Brink – for less money than those traitors made now.

Where was the justice?

Vincent was consumed with these thoughts, these axes, and this hatred. He could not let it go.

If he had just shut up and said nothing about all of the crimes, he would likely have another promotion under his belt by now. If he had just conformed, and been a cookie cutter assembly line drone or proud, card-carrying boys club member, he would be making even more money than he had made before.

Here, he had to deal daily – if not hourly – with incompetent owners like Dustin "Bruce" Rollins, the cocaine-addled, steroid supersized idiot running his Mankato and Greenfield locations into the ground through his sheer stupidity, shortsightedness and horrifying people skills, whose employees he had to talk off the ledge on a regular basis. Rollins would withhold money from his employees' paychecks, claiming it was for insurance but he never enrolled them for insurance. He would call female employees at 3 AM after a night of drinking and drugs trying to meet up with them for sex. And there was nothing Vincent could do about it, outside of listen, for he assuredly got every phone call reporting it.

Here, Vincent could meet decent-to-good candidates that could make a difference in his business, but he could never afford them. His only hope was to sell them on a potential future…like Wallace had sold him. Vincent did not even have the heart to tell the business degree candidate requesting a minimum of $50,000 per year as a rep or manager that Brink paid $1,000 per month and offered no health benefits. Heck, he himself had just paid $170 for a doctor visit and $344 to get his hands on one prescription's worth of the antidepressants keeping him afloat.

Would this job take him somewhere? Who knew, but at least it had gotten him a little money, gotten him off the couch, out of his severe depression and back into the selling game. It was something.

He believed in signs and destiny; the irony of his placement across the street from two of his old hotbeds was not lost on anyone, least of all himself.

He just wanted perfection. He was giving so much – when would it pay off?

He found himself picking everyone and everything apart. Cellular Horizons and Brink and Moriarty. Abby. Emily.

But this was a case in point: was anyone ever going to be good enough to live up to these standards Vincent had set?

Of course Abby wanted Vincent back when she found out about Emily. But he could never get over the past.

A mid-month collapse in results caused by a huge traffic drop-off, major chargebacks in stores that were off to big starts like downtown Minneapolis, morale being clipped by incorrect paychecks and a slew of other things out of the control of Vincent Scott plummeted his May to an abysmal $167K finish.

Used to using his Midas touch to immediately turn things to gold, this was something Vincent had never experienced: trying literally everything and having it not work as expected because of occurrences completely out of his span of control. Just like his court case. Just like his book publication. Just like his shoddy relationships. The things he had given his all to had nothing but disappointment to give back – except for Elizabeth.

His statistical metrics kept surging to new records, but the things Jordan Wallace and his investors cared about – profitability and more revenue growth – were not happening in correlation with his tireless efforts.

And the insanity did not stop. Bruce Rollins – now back from a whirlwind tour in Dallas where he bragged he had sex with five of the candidates he interviewed, despite his girlfriend and their daughter back home – was growing more and more into a nuisance trying to cover his own tracks. He imploded his own raw deal he was trying to push on Gabe Blankenship and was running seriously low on funds.

Terry Bunche, however, was hanging in there. With his misfit team – lead rep Jerry Smalls, on loan from Brink and not being paid by Bruce – he catapulted Greenfield to a $15K gross profit month – by far their best ever. However, when Bruce used the cash surplus to settle some old debts and celebrate with his favorite nose candy, it put the hurt on him when they sputtered out of the June gate.

Any time Vincent plugged a leak in this ship, he had to immediately turn his attention to another enormous leak – there was no rest. Ever. Bruce Rollins was threatening to lay off his manager at Mankato, even though that manager and only one other employee were covering all seven work days! He was threatening to lay off Terry's top rep, Alicia, because he had initially agreed to let her come on at an elevated base salary of $1,200 per month to secure her services and he now regretted it.

He was in over his head.

Now he was desperate and blaming Vincent for not doing enough and living up to his end of the management contract (so he could try to get out of paying it to Jordan Wallace), Terry for not doing enough and spending too much time off the sales floor (managing the operations of the store, for Bruce). It was pathetic, and it severely ruffled the feathers of the only people still in his corner.

It was a Sunday, and Vincent – at Emily's – was still conducting business, calling Susie and Doug Wilson and requesting a meeting first thing Monday morning. Dustin "Bruce" Rollins had to go. He was a menace to their society.

Vincent had been brutally harassed and bullied in business before. Now, he had the position to fight back and destroy this clown. And he played that card. He met with the two-headed Wilson monster over coffee the following morning and planted the seed for the removal of Bruce Rollins. And the wheels jumped into motion quickly.

Moriarty cut off his inventory ordering capability, citing his overwhelming debt in the $100,000 range that he would never be able to come back from. This, however, was the least of the issues with Rollins; he was running off his employees, terrorizing them in hopes they would just quit and not file for unemployment insurance and he was trying to cast blame for his downfall on everyone but himself.

Rollins made good on his threat to lay off Max Yastrzemski – the manager at Mankato's kiosk – and – despite all of the disparaging words he uttered about Terry Bunche, put Terry in charge of the additional location and allowed him to bring on a part-timer.

Spending a day at the Mankato kiosk together, Terry came to Vincent excited with a marketing idea to attract attention via drawings and lead generation. The two of them brainstormed for two hours that day over subpar Chinese food and a notebook and hashed out a revolutionary idea.

The end result was this: they would purchase a toll-free number, landing pages and a marketing database to house their leads. All of their marketing – fliers, social media, ads in any form – would feature this theme prominently and they would run different promotions for the various product offerings they had. There could and would be campaigns for different regions, for wireless, Internet, television – you name it. Bundled pricing, touted savings – anything to capture consumer attention, including Vincent's contract buyout offer.

113

The beauty was that it was nonintrusive. And with their market share under 20% in their territory, it did not discriminate. With general messages like "Find out how to save up to $500 per year" and a wide net with a toll-free number or website a consumer could visit on their own time, it would conceivably appeal not only to the 20%, but the 80%, too.

Vincent was ecstatic. They crunched numbers. He contacted Lenny, the marketing and flier connection who had faithfully served Brink Management Company since inception, and he calculated they could cost effectively obtain 50,000 fliers per month for all of their stores in the region. With 11 stores getting just shy of 5,000 fliers apiece, if each store only got 500 inquiries per month, or even 100, and they were able to convert 20-to-50 into sales at $150-$200 a pop, that was anywhere from 20%-to-70% lift on what these stores were producing currently. It was enough to make the reps and managers more money, Vincent a huge name for himself and an extra ski or wine-tasting trip for the powers that be.

Things moved quickly. Thanks to the all-but-guaranteed profitability, it was an easy sell to Jordan Wallace, and Terry and Vincent moved forward in purchasing the domain. The possibilities promised to them by the marketing group Terry located online seemed endless – capabilities to utilize drip marketing campaigns, upload and reach out to their existing customer database and do nearly everything shy of providing world peace.

The idea Terry spawned and Vincent developed was not only something that would revolutionize Minnesota, but it could work wonders for Wisconsin, Missouri and Texas. Then – Wallace promised and dangled – he could package it to thousands of stores across the country.

"Something else I want to talk to you about," Wallace began. "But kind of keep this under your hat. I've been talking to some other dealers, making connections and whatnot. What it looks like is that, over the next year or so, we will be expanding by 100 more stores. Moriarty is helping me get in touch with these guys to sell our management contract. I'd see putting somebody like you out there to the different regions to get them started, do some hiring blitzes, put a regional manager in place and then they would report to you. Can you see yourself doing that?"

Vincent of course would say yes.

"Can you imagine?" Wallace continued. "We would get a cut of every store in our jurisdiction. Let's say you had 100 stores reporting in to you, doing the average of $15,000 in gross profits. They would have a regional manager, but let's say I pay you even 2% kickback for getting them going and keeping them rolling.

Heck, that's $30,000 per month take-home for you. $360,000 per year. We'd be millionaires in no time."

Here came those wild numbers again. They rolled right out of his head and off his tongue without missing a beat. And it was never a modest sum – he always talked in the millions of dollars.

But they always achieved their intent: Vincent Scott bought back in to this mission: impossible, gave it another 70+ hour work week at a top capacity higher than anyone else could achieve, despite all obstacles and against all odds – always with just a little less left in the tank than he had in reserves before.

All while he kept receiving horrible, disappointing results every night in his e-mail from his store personnel, if they even completed the forms correctly or sent them at all. All while he continued conducting conference calls with shoddy attendance. All while he would get hammered on little minutiae by Dustin "Bruce" Rollins like why didn't he review the past few days' deposits for him when he managed to stop in and talk a few of his employees out of quitting. All while an incompetent rep made sexual harassment charges against De-Metre and Vincent had to put on an investigation when she was trying to cause a stink because he rebuffed her flirtations. All while he applied to 57 jobs at other companies and received nothing but rejection notices. All while he was being billed thousands of dollars in attorney fees for getting majority custody of Elizabeth while Abby was trying to get back in his good graces. All while he would sit in traffic to and from these thankless store locations, trying to hash out a revolutionary marketing plan that these employees would probably drop the ball on and he would wonder what on earth he was truly supposed to be doing.

Thank goodness for his little princess. She was the only thing keeping him somewhat sane.

All of that – and it was not enough to break him.

This was like the Wild West. It was constant, unorthodox and unsanctioned insanity with no real law and few keeping the peace.

What really threw Vincent for a loop was that he was being faced with ten times what he was faced before in his career…for less money, less recognition and less… Well, just less.

How much more was he going to have to take? When would this job actually start fulfilling any of the Jordan Wallace promises?

*Lead generation*, he had to keep reminding himself. Not if, but *when* this takes off, he will make so much money that this stupid stuff will not matter and everyone who helped kick him to the curb could kiss his ass.

He would wake up in the morning, excited in spite of it all, and have himself knocked down twice by lunch. How many times could he keep picking himself up off the canvas?

As if there wasn't enough distraction going on already, Susie Wilson put a full court press on Vincent to get his team to enter the Cellular Horizons Superstar competition. It was a great reflection on her if someone from her market competed and placed.

The entry method was simply a video, talking about and pitching the benefits of mobile Internet service by Cellular Horizons. Vincent promised he would attempt to get his team involved. Unfortunately, no one had any desire to take the time to enter the contest and film a video.

Vincent initially teased that perhaps he would film a video, but, with his animated team at New Brighton, they hatched the idea to film something more elaborate.

It was in late May that Darryl Wilkinson, who turned down Vincent's initial attempt to promote him and left the business, returned as a rep to New Brighton. They were again starting to move up on the sales charts and times were high; they also were known for their personality and unique interactions with customers that prompted them to bring food and desserts in for their crew. Darryl was being groomed to take over the Golden Valley store full time come June.

So, it was set: Vincent spent a day in New Brighton filming. The back of Darryl's head was to serve as President Barack Obama. Doing his voice was dead ringer Bryan Venison. Store manager De-Metre Jones had a cameo as a Jamaican ambassador to the United States, as he played it with accent and his considerable dreadlocks came in handy. "Obama" called the Jamaican ambassador as prelude to his golf trip to Jamaica, looking for a mobile Internet solution. They three-way called the store, looking for answers. Vincent Scott is on the receiving end of the call.

Vincent – at the conclusion of the video – ran towards the camera from across the store, removed glasses he was borrowing from Venison and pulled open his shirt to reveal the Superman emblem – off to hand-deliver the product directly to the White House. Throughout the presentation, he had woven in references to Superman and Cellular Horizons taglines. It was beautifully done, and enhanced at the end with John Williams music. And he won the local competition handily.

Susie called Vincent to congratulate him and inform him of the surprising news that he was headed to Chicago to compete on a national level.

He had entered simply as a joke, and now he was headed to Chicago to put on a sales presentation in front of Directors and Vice Presidents with Cellular Horizons corporate, competing against kids 10 years younger than him who literally did this job all day every day, knew the specs and could talk tech.

What had he gotten himself into?

Part of Vincent wanted to pawn this task off on someone who could potentially better represent the market with their existing knowledge of the products and services. However, Vincent knew this was a perfect opportunity to play the political game and gain some clout with the brass of Cellular Horizons. He could not refuse.

Little breaks in the action were always good. As luck and scheduling would have it, amidst all of the craziness with New Brighton and Bruce Rollins and Abby, he was headed to Chicago for the Superstar competition. The day he was slated to return, he was asked by Michelle and Chris Jeffries to give a Chamber of Commerce luncheon speech on their behalf in Cloquet; it would require the earliest flight back possible and a 2-hour drive upon touchdown, but he agreed. Lastly, he was also asked by Doug Wilson to be on a featured panel of experts for Moriarty dealers at a roundtable meeting in Des Moines, Iowa, the day after returning from Superstar, requiring leaving directly after the Cloquet luncheon – a 6-hour drive on little sleep. He accepted.

The lows were tempered with the highs. But surely, this could not keep up, could it?

All of these ridiculous lows in his business, but this week would be great for his career between Superstar recognition and a panel of experts appearing in front of all of the Moriarty brass. Plus, he could finally bury the hatchet with Chris Jeffries. It was victory all around.

## "The Surviving Game" by Vincent Scott
## The Marketing Game

Marketing. Promotion. They are literally all around us – everywhere we look. There is no escape. For those compiling the countless ads that flood your television screen, Smartphones and mailboxes, there are concepts drawn upon that mirror those utilized in successful sales.

These concepts can be quite complex when it comes to the analytics behind who is viewing your material, your target demographic and what's working versus what's not. Breaking down marketing to the lowest common denominator goes a long way in determination of the best way to master this facet of business and success.

Great content is material that is relevant to your audience - whether they know it or not. Like marketing and sales, we must deliver a high-quality product, service or information in a convenient package that is pleasing to the senses and satisfies some desire: for knowledge, motivation and betterment of some situation. Great content is created when we take the needs of our viewers into consideration and are able to utilize our experience and infuse our passion into whatever mediums we choose to use: written word, video, social media, articles, advertisements and other branding in a way that accomplishes the aforementioned.

No brand or company or person can succeed without getting their name out there in a positive fashion, to be seen and remembered by the masses. Our adage in advertising was that without utilization of some medium, be it print, Internet, billboard, television, etc., you did not exist. You're the best-kept secret, and why would you keep yourself a secret from those whom you want to buy from you? Furthermore, having one of these mediums without proactively driving traffic there – via search engines, social media and the like – was like having a billboard under water. Your message must resonate, or you are not remembered.

Ensuring that your brand is in front of the right people through the right methods is the marketing game.

First: nothing is out of bounds, unless it is politically incorrect and will offend. The more unique the better. It is the memorable ads that stick with people long after they have aired; the Super Bowl ads people are talking about around the water cooler the following day (or on Twitter and Facebook just seconds later) made an initial impact because of originality.

Think about something that is synonymous with you and your brand; what do you stand for? What is something in the public consciousness that you can relate to that you want others to associate with you? Like plot topics for movies, many of the ideas and common themes are taken, but if you are able to pluck something from obscurity or create a new association that resonates with your audience, you win.

Second: Who is your target audience? As a small business owner, a website developer or a lemonade stand owner, you have a target demographic, and that is who you are speaking to.

Think about marketing like diverting or stealing traffic from your competition. Who are your competitors – big and small? How can you differentiate yourself from them? How can you make consumers who are looking at them look at you instead, or in addition to?

Metaphorically, if people are traveling from Point A to Point B every day to reach your competition, you want to plant your billboard in-between. Where are people looking right now to find your competition? Trade magazines? Internet listings? Search engines? Radio? Television?

Your target audience is the people who can or could utilize your product or service; someone for whom you want to show that a need exists. Right now – like sales – they are either using something in your place or they are unaware that a need exists. Your goal is to find the best way to virtually "meet" as many of these people as you can, as cost effectively as you can with as powerful a message as you can.

The thought process on marketing is daunting for those who are uninitiated; everything proposed to you either sounds good, or you just don't yet know what the right cocktail is. The fact is, most companies have employed a plethora of different marketing strategies over the years with varying levels of success.

There is no silver bullet, which makes this even more of a gray area. Like a job search, you do not want to discriminate against any possible user of your wares yet you do want to amplify your efforts to those who will be the most likely and lucrative.

Provided you are aware of (1) how many people you can be in front of with this marketing avenue, (2) what the monetary investment is on your part and (3) how easy and likely it will be that you will make substantial enough return on your investment, you know what you need to know to make the decision. It's also so important to (4) have a way to track the results so you can show what worked and what didn't and know if this will be something you pursue in the future, if you tweak it or scrap it.

What is your average customer worth? Tabulate how many customers it would take to yield a significant enough profit and deduce from your exposure levels how likely that will be to achieve.

Third: Medium is important. What is your best medium or mix of mediums? Key to remember here is that you never want to leave out a potential piece of your target audience while playing up your message to your constituency. Find mediums that will allow you to market your services to as many people as you can with as many uses as possible; this increases your reach, influence and likelihood at return.

I learned this in my years building and leading an advertising sales team peddling a cornucopia of marketing tools - you never know where you will land the big fish. You also cannot rely on big fish alone; you have to eat, so finding the parts of the stream where you can attract tonight's dinner is important, too. It might be helpful to attract customers to items you can sell in bulk and while they are getting to know you, building the case for your bigger ticket items in the process.

Then, of course, add to the mix that you also want to attract the most people for the least amount of investment possible. This will heavily affect which mediums are feasible and potentially effective for you. If you are a dentist in San Diego, California, you won't want a nationwide ad, a statewide ad or an ad in the *New York Times*. You will examine where you want to pull clients from, mediums that exist which can be geographically targeted to people looking for the industry you represent. This can be done in a myriad of ways – specifically in these days of Internet prominence, television, print and radio.

There are countless mediums and options available to you. If you are a business, it's likely you have been solicited by a multitude of them already. Making heads or tails out of which ones are conceivably a fit for your business can be a daunting task. Nevertheless, it comes down to potential exposure, size of investment, potential for return on investment and the tracking mechanisms in place.

Simplification of this process and what it implies is the best approach. Cold, hard facts, historical data and tracking and tweaking the process will lead to you finding the right blend for your brand.

Each marketing technique likely has some merit and will work given the right circumstances, but someone with a niche product and narrower audience will need to enlist methods that will put them in front of just those people. The Internet has been a marketer's dream for that very reason.

The Internet enables the brand to be advertised on sites specifically designed to tout the product, on social media, banner ads on a variety of other sites, and through the secret sauce of search engines. The common theme is writing ad copy for your product is like writing a slogan with a call to action or penning sales verbiage; you have to quickly capture your audience's attention, expose a need or weakness they may not even know they have, and invite them to act now.

Online tutorials are readily available for those who want to learn how to capitalize on the opportunity of search engine marketing and search engine optimization. There is also a plethora of professionals out there on these topics – many of whom are employed in just such situations. The Internet is ever-changing and the means available to you to develop and promote your brand change just as often; staying on top of the changes, what the search engines are currently favoring and what consumers are after will greatly impact your success.

Leave nothing to chance and give yourself the best chance at success by employing a variety of ways to tout your best foot; your quality message.

Social media is huge in this day and age. It is more and more common to advertise through special pages on Facebook, Twitter, Pinterest and other sites that are part of consumers' daily lives. Admittedly, I knew little about advertising through these means until my first book was published. After some research on how to market via these means in a very cost-effective manner, I opened pages on Facebook, Twitter, YouTube, WordPress, and others to add content about what I wanted to promote – *The Selling Game*. I learned that search engines liked the content I could post on free sites like YouTube, blogs on WordPress and the like, and Facebook and Twitter make it simple to put out any message you desire and connect with a large number of people.

Like anything in marketing, I proceeded through the aforementioned steps. My target audience was people who would enjoy reading a book about career, interviewing, selling and management. My chief competitors were people who had written similar works in the annals of history. With that in mind, I set out connecting with people on Facebook, Twitter, LinkedIn and YouTube who had taken an interest in those people, whether they "liked" or "followed" or commented.

Statistically, depending on my ability to send a personalized message as a greeting, anywhere from 10%-to-40% accepted my request for connection. From there, each website typically has a method to simplify or automate your connections, your automated messages and your follow-up with your connections. As I do not wish to necessarily endorse one over another, I encourage you to do a web search for programs that will follow new followers on Twitter, YouTube and the like.

LinkedIn requires a personal touch, which was visited fully when we talked about searching for employment. The same concepts apply here; we cast a wide net, branch out to those with whom we can form a mutually beneficial relationship and find nonintrusive but informative ways to build that relationship.

Each of these can also intertwine. Your Facebook page can be regularly promoted on Twitter. You can automate posts so you do not even have to be at your computer when a post is going out about you or your business. The possibilities are endless as to who you can connect to, how you connect with them and what you will do from there to engage them and build a relationship.

Nothing happens overnight; this is another process that takes time to build a foundation, compile quality content and strategically add target audience based on geography, interests or other factors. It's fortunate that the Internet will allow us to define those parameters however we wish.

Like anything, you make a goal and you step in the right direction daily.

And you can never be afraid to learn by doing. I've talked to many business owners over the years who are flabbergasted and overwhelmed with marketing; they have tried so many things and are frustrated with the lack of results. Sure – any solicitor is going to make their product sound good. But without guaranteed results, it's all a crapshoot.

You minimize your risk by knowing you are putting out quality content to the right people with a good probability at return on investment. You may have little success in certain mediums, with certain messages or with your first attempt. But you keep putting something out there, you track it, you tweak it and you continue. Making money without marketing yourself is impossible.

Finally, find something to relate to in your audience. Make yourself relatable. Give them what they want, be it humor, be it information, be it savings, offers, a bargain, an enticing entry into your world. You have something that you feel they should and would want - right? That is why you embarked on this endeavor. So find the best way to introduce yourself to them in a nonintrusive way in which you challenge them to think again about what they do now in the arena you present a better solution.

You have an answer to their needs. They just don't know it yet. But if you choose the right target demographic, your ultimate goal is to steal traffic from those who do similar things to what you do - right? In my world, these are people who are interested in leadership, success and greatness.

So - what's your goal? Mine is to form mutually beneficial partnerships, meet new people with whom I can share ideas, learn from and grow from.

What's the end result? The most rewarding things for me in my career have been meeting people from around the world with whom to have intelligent conversations about success, leadership and common goals. For you, it may be to revolutionize the food business, the retail business or the work-at-home, network marketing business. But no matter what your calling, ignoring your target audience and their needs and their wants and where they are hiding out will result in falling.

Also rely on the statistics when formulating your process; customers typically make the decision to purchase after seeing a brand an average of five times. You may resonate the first time but want to consistently convey your theme over time as you build your audience and brand.

Furthermore, research shows consumers forget 25% of a marketing message a week later and nearly all of it after a month. A consistent stream of quality marketing that they receive on *their* terms is the best way to show them why to change so that when they're ready – they will.

Like sales, we do not force their hand in making a change. We show them why our choice is better so that when they fear missing out, they will choose us.

Where is your target audience looking right now for what they are getting? Plant yourself there. Do it often, consistently, with a repeated message. Sometimes, it is not about saying fifty different things to win over your audience; it's about saying the same thing fifty different ways until it prompts them to make a buying decision. Ultimately, you want to be scoped out and given a shot. You will get that shot with a unique, respectful and consistent approach to the people with the highest propensity to buy you and your services.

The "fifth contact" that prompts your consumer to make a purchasing decision could be via Internet message, social media post, phone call, e-mail, and search engine result. Unless you are where your audience is looking, they can't choose you.

Marketing and promotion are vital, but they are also fun. Do it right and be yourself, and the rest will fall into place.

\* \* \* \* \*

## Superstar

Vincent Scott always adhered to the plan of arriving at the airport with 2 hours to spare. It left him plenty of wiggle room and often time to read and grab a quick bite prior to takeoff. His ritual was to bring a James Bond novel for every flight he took, and this flight was no different.

On this day, he quickly recognized Ben Kennett – a store manager for a Moriarty corporate store – and Kurt Stillwater – Director of Retail Operations, who was Susie Wilson's boss's boss – in the airport and made conversation with them before the flight. Kurt – of course – sat first class, but Vincent and Ben sat next to one another in coach.

Ben was 26 years old, hailing from Minneapolis and fancied himself a musician as he was an avid guitar enthusiast. He was good friends with Aaron Hartley, as Hartley had been Kennett's boss at one time, and Ben had been crowned the other regional winner of the Superstar video competition. Ben's winning entry merged pitching the company's Internet service with his favorite Bob Dylan lick. The two had met previously briefly at a Cellular Horizons training function.

Ben Kennett was pretty green, but was an ambitious manager wanting to move up and learn everything he could. They talked a lot on the flight and had lunch prior to the competition in the Peninsula in Chicago where they were being put up during their stay.

Ben marveled at Vincent's wealth of leadership knowledge, picking his brain on how to manage the problem employee, how to market effectively in the area and how he was recruiting and training. Vincent loved talking to young sales managers getting started in their leadership career; he knew just what to tell them to ensure solid footing in those early years. Vincent had no shortage of stories about good moves, risks that paid off and mistakes he learned from to educate young Ben.

Just prior to the competition, all of the competitors convened in a downstairs hallway just outside the ballroom hosting the event. There were Kirk and Randy, who were in their early 20's and went back and forth at these events between winning; they were debating whose turn it was to win this time.

There was Marcy – a beautiful 21-year old, bubbly store manager. There was Paul, a 19-year old store rep who knew the specifications on every product front and back. There was Connor, a 24-year old assistant manager who had been doing this for years. There was Ben – 26 and a store manager who had been in this business his whole career.

And there was Vincent Scott – 32-year old regional manager and book author who had never even been trained on the computer systems and knew just what he had overheard about the products. He tried to keep up on everything online as articles flooded his e-mail inbox from the searches he set up, but his dance card was pretty full. He had been in retail a grand total of a few months.

Which of these things was not like the other? Vincent could not have felt more out of place.

Once each participant found out their scenario, they would retreat to some corner of the hotel hallway outside the door of the competition, pace, and recite lines of what they planned on saying. In other words, they were hardcore and obsessed with winning this thing.

Vincent did not even take a moment of preparation. In his experience, he did his best thinking and reacting off the cuff and knew that over-thinking this and preparation would be his downfall. He went in fresh, unfettered and relied on his sales instincts.

What his experiences and age had given him was the ability to be pretty tough-skinned to what would rattle most individuals. The job interviews, the public speaking – these things did not faze him anymore. This was a man with tens of thousands of views for his sales videos across the world. He spouted off just enough techno-babble to impress, threw in some comedy to get the role player and the judges laughing and on his side, repeated the role player's name multiple times, made a real connection and closed the sale. He just wanted to compete.

There's an adage in sales that if you get your customer laughing, they're yours. Vincent knew how to put on a show and he did just that on this day in the Peninsula Chicago.

The Cellular Horizons brass took the contestants to a baseball game that night and Vincent would automatically get a little prize money for showing up. Then he would fly home and dazzle some Moriarty owners and delegates at a roundtable discussion over best practices. Overall, it should be a rewarding, if tiring, experience.

Then – the unthinkable happened.

With everyone waiting with baited breath for Kirk or Randy to be declared the winner, or even Ben or Marcy, Vincent Scott was announced as the Superstar. He still had it despite being away from this game for so long and against a young crop of kids who thought they were better and wanted it more.

It had not been about the most technical knowledge, the repetition or the spouting of facts; it was about being personable, being confident and being genuine.

It was an affirmation for Vincent; during all those minutes, hours, days, weeks and months between depression on his couch and his computer to apply for jobs, he wondered what he had left to give. He began to doubt his abilities. He was unsure if he could conjure up his sales persona and be the best once more.

Now, however, he was the best salesperson in all the Cellular Horizons land, with a trophy to prove it. He was a force to be reckoned with, no matter how long he had been out of commission and how damaged he had become. And this experience, this notoriety – now with Cellular Horizons bigwigs from across the country – was another step toward the complete and utter retribution of Vincent Scott.

Ride shotgun with Wallace for now, be a huge part of this lead generation and 100+ store ramp-up and then latch on to Cellular Horizons corporate and really wreak some havoc. It made him smile ear to ear. The future was definitely bright again for Vincent Scott.

Cellular Horizons wined and dined Vincent and the other competitors that night and, of course, he was the star of the show. He was so in his element in this situation; he so graciously accepted the kudos, so seamlessly segued into intelligent banter about the industry or sports or whatever the situation dictated – even when he didn't really know what they were talking about. That was his genius – and he so easily left his indelible mark on these people. This time, Vincent would do it all again – the team-building, the relationship-building, the partnering with peers and liaising with leaders – but do it right.

In true Vincent Scott fashion, he, Ben and Kirk met three girls at the hotel bar who happened to be in town for a fashion magazine catalogue shoot. They whisked the three boys away for the night of carousing. Vincent felt 10 years younger again.

He did not feel so young 2 hours after his head hit the pillow for shuteye when the alarm signaled it was time he and Ben had to hightail it to the airport.

No matter. He arrived back in Minneapolis, bid Ben adieu and drove to Cloquet with a hearty helping of caffeine in his system. The nearby military base meant armed forces and their families were in attendance at the Chamber meeting; Vincent added some thanks to them in his speech and he blew the room away.

The keys to the ultimate speech: start with a joke to ensure you capture attention and spice things up. Check. Vincent cited that he thought Chris Jeffries and Michelle only asked him to do this speech to see if he could actually make a speech in less than five minutes. The room laughed.

He peppered the speech with resounding respect for the Jeffries family, their store personnel and the unparalleled customer service. He probably believed about one-third of all the things he said, but this was Vincent Scott – the salesman extraordinaire – we were talking about here. Again, he was in his element. He spoke powerfully with commanding presence and didn't think. He just spoke.

For, this is what he loved to do. To feel needed and wanted were the two most basic elements of this warrior. Jeff Gemini could not and did not do these things. Jordan Wallace could not deliver like he did. Vincent Scott was the real deal. Even Chris Jeffries was starting to believe.

With Vincent having to get on the road pretty quickly, Chris gave him a ride back to his car at the Cloquet store. They talked extensively, and the more Vincent got to know Chris, the more he liked him.

Chris and Michelle were from Las Vegas. He had had a difficult life, but had always stayed true to his morals and principles and worked hard. And the two realized just how much they had in common in the way of work ethic and priorities.

Funny that, in the beginning, each thought the other was a pompous ass. Even if they were right, they were starting to value the others' part more and more in their business relationship.

On the flip side, Vincent was starting to see how the people who were supposed to be supporting and helping him and his team were not as great as he initially believed.

Back on the road from there, Vincent stopped into Minneapolis and met up with Saul Portman, his companion for the Moriarty conference.

The extensive drive gave these two – who had already developed a mutual respect – to get to know one another even better and truly understand the other's motivations. Saul recounted stories of run-ins with abrasive coaches that sidelined his football career and how he got into the wireless business. He talked about his history with Brink, how they and specifically he had been strung along by Jordan Wallace for years now and how he had been very ready to bail just prior to the termination of Jeff Gemini.

Vincent told Saul about his business past; it was not something he discussed too often, specifically in its truest form and exactly how it went down. Saul was flabbergasted, as anyone who heard the story was.

But the two saw the similarities in their very different pasts: both had worked hard, prioritized family and had been batted down previously by people who were supposed to be leading them.

Along the way, Vincent also fielded several phone calls. The downfall of Dustin "Bruce" Rollins was very much upon them.

Terry Bunche was in a panic, as were his employees; with inventory cut off, they were now not receiving paychecks from Bruce and they had no idea what was going to happen next or if they would have a job the following day. The climactic conclusion for Rollins was clearly coming to a head.

Bruce was once again scrambling to do fraudulent returns to try to get Moriarty to let him order phones. They were onto him, specifically because Vincent had already reported his scam to Moriarty via his calls and meeting with Doug (and Susie) Wilson, so he was trying to obtain Terry's system password so he could file the illegal returns under another name.

That was the eventful ride to Des Moines. Saul and Vincent checked into the respective hotel rooms and went for a drink before calling it a relatively early evening.

The Moriarty event was well attended. With stores spread all throughout the Midwest, and owners, managers and reps welcome to go to this roundtable and best practices sharing event, there was a solid turnout. Vincent and Saul represented Brink, as no one else came from Wisconsin, Missouri or Texas; Jesse Fairbanks and Cliff Watson – both portly fellows – were happy to attend on behalf of the Chris Jeffries stores and take in the free meals.

These events were good for the morale. Moriarty hosted a dinner the night prior that Vincent and Saul had missed, a breakfast on this morning and an all-day program with a seminar and lunch before it broke mid-afternoon.

Karl Reinhold, an author and guest speaker that Moriarty used frequently (in Indianapolis, for instance) was also a featured component of this program. He gave his spiel; there were some team-building exercises and a workbook everyone got to follow along with. A few vendors were there that hocked phone equipment, accessories and marketing packages. Then, the featured panel of experts. Finally, the finale: an awards banquet for first quarter successes.

Reinhold's message was on leadership; as he was speaking predominantly to owners and store managers, it was well received and relevant. Vincent's mind, however, always wandered during these things. He had seen such programs before; people with an outsider's view about the business came in and spouted generalities that were – to him, anyway – common sense. The room was in awe because he was articulate and intelligent, but Vincent knew he could have had more of an impact.

*Patience*, Vincent told himself.

The panel of experts experience was fun for Vincent, however, and a real treat for those in attendance. Doug Wilson and his boss, Kent Smyth, were more or less the conductors of this event, taking turns doing introductions and leading the ceremonies along. They led off the panel of experts by introducing the panel from left-to-right on stage, purposely putting Vincent on the far right.

He was introduced last and, after mention of his book and regional successes, his winning Superstar video was played for all to see and applaud. His status as Cellular Horizons company Superstar was also made known to the crowd.

Vincent did not disappoint as the time came for him to contribute.

The topics of the conference, with leadership as the focal theme, centered around a Q&A from the audience. Questions were posed by different audience members as conversation starters, and members of the panel of experts with experience in that aspect of the business would offer their insights.

The panel as a whole was a dud. There were six people comprising the assemblage, including Karl Reinhold, who had a few noteworthy things to add here and there, albeit good general observations. Vincent bit his tongue to allow everyone else to speak prior to his contributions; he found himself realizing that the old Vincent would not have shown such restraint.

Then, he put on a clinic.

He put on such a show that Saul Portman, already impressed with Vincent and happy to have him as his boss, was more in awe of this man who had come to Brink Management Company just a few months ago. Jesse Fairbanks and Cliff Watson – already planning an early exit to eat one last big meal on the road on Chris Jeffries' tab – actually stuck around and were shocked at just how much this character they mostly ignored knew what he was talking about. The audience was blown away; afterwards, many made way to introduce themselves, swap business cards and meet author and sales leader Vincent Scott.

It was his forte; Vincent talked about what his region was doing and what it had done for results, complimented his team and teamwork above all else and was as unselfish as could be. This was a new Vincent; he knew what to say to get these people to listen and understand. They were buying in even more than before because he was gracious, selfless and teaching them unique methods to do business that were working beyond belief.

Previous incarnations of Vincent made it about *him* and what *he* did; this version talked about how *the team* was growing their region exponentially better than any other in the country and what they were doing from the front lines selling to marketing to recognition. He had a captivated audience.

And, in reality, he was putting on the show for Kent Smyth. This, coupled with his Superstar win, was going to really propel his status within the Cellular Horizons and Moriarty families. From there, there was no telling what Vincent's next step up the ladder would be. He was winning the crowds. He was being politically smart. There was nothing he couldn't do.

There was not a topic in the discussion that did not elicit a lengthy but spellbinding response from Vincent. He was the star attraction. From talking about their lead generation to come, to observation forms he created, how they hire, how they coach, how they communicate and the unparalleled results they were achieving, he and his team were on full display. There could not have been a better advocate or delegate on Brink Management Company's behalf.

Of course, this was prior to an awards banquet where Brink won first place in every category – new acquisitions, year-over-year-growth, renewals, you name it.

These amazing highs; they kept Vincent ticking and motivated. Of course, they were always prelude to returning to the disasters at home. On the ride home, Vincent got a pretty telling phone call alluding to what awaited him.

Unable to pay his employees, Bruce Rollins was on a brink of his own. Jordan Wallace revealed that he would be shut down inevitably and that Wallace was going to pick up Mankato on his payroll to keep them from quitting after everything Vincent had done for them.

In recent weeks, Vincent had convinced Bruce to use some of the savings of having Terry watch Greenfield and Mankato toward hiring two part-timers at Mankato. The lead generation was ripe for a solitary location like Mankato. Vincent didn't want to see his hometown's lone representative knocked out of the game.

Wallace framed that as a favor to Vincent which – from Vincent's experience with such management tactics being used on him – meant that he'd better make them successful.

The following morning, upon his return to Minneapolis, Vincent met up with Terry Bunche at the Bloomington store – away from the hubbub and chaos of Greenfield. However, as Terry arrived, he came bearing news: Dustin "Bruce" Rollins, aware that his time was up, had locked the door to his Greenfield store, changed the locks, stripped every piece of inventory from the walls and shelves and left the building dark.

Vincent made a call to Bruce, who surprisingly picked up.

"Yeah, what's up?" Bruce asked.

"You tell me," Vincent responded. "We're just wondering what's going on."

"You know what's going on, man. I'm just protecting my interests. Nobody else is," came the response.

"Where are you?"

"What does it matter?"

That meant he was headed to Mankato – his other location – to do the same.

Vincent made phone calls to Steve Flowers, Doug Wilson and Kent Smyth within the business and to the Mankato mall security and police department in an attempt to head him off at the pass.

It was to no avail, however as, while mall security briefly subdued him, his name was on the lease and he made off with everything of value. Considering his massive debt in excess of $100,000 on equipment alone, he really had no right to take what he had on hand. Vincent – knowing Mankato had just had its lease on life extended – was none too thrilled.

Rollins also left several people very much holding the bag. He failed to pay any of his employees, so he owed many of them a few thousand dollars apiece. Jordan Wallace agreed to pay the Mankato team since Vincent had just signed two brand new reps and the last thing anyone needed was for them to just walk, but the Greenfield team was completely shafted.

Not only that, but Vincent and Wallace lost the management contract by abandonment on the Greenfield location; it was purely money and effort lost on Vincent's part. After everything he had done, contributed and endured for these two stores, they were now completely adrift and Vincent was taking a pay cut. Wallace added Mankato to his Brink-owned stores yet they would have to outfit the location from scratch after Rollins' recent heist.

But this marketing plan forged ahead. Terry Bunche effectively sold Vincent that he had everything under control on their make-or-break lead generation platform; he had located the marketing group who was housing their database and was coordinating with them everything Vincent requested.

Vincent met again with Lenny, Brink's marketing designer, and strategized the July release of the 50,000 postcards which would kick off this campaign. There were some setbacks to the overall schematic of Brink as usual, but it was full steam ahead with the countermeasures.

During this time, Vincent became increasingly close with Terry Bunche and Saul Portman. He talked frequently as well with De-Metre, Reggie and Darryl (by now his Golden Valley manager), however he had formed a stronger bond of mutual respect with the aforementioned two.

While Vincent certainly had learned his lesson about befriending his employees after 99% of them abandoned him post-termination, this was a different type of bond. They found themselves talking one another off the ledge nearly daily with the frequent drastic ups and downs their business environment brought.

Terry had hit the nail on the head with this job: they had encountered a brick wall with their results increases and were stagnant until something new – like lead generation – could plow them through the next level. They had gotten this far simply on Vincent's back, and his energy and charisma, but they were not going any farther without the mandatory structure. Vincent could not have agreed more.

The generation of leads – if done properly – could not miss.

Brink Management Company was already touted as "the best dealer in show." They took home every award at the Moriarty convention, they had the top numbers in Minneapolis and there was nowhere to go but up.

Vincent believed he had the best people in place possible for the pay and circumstances in most instances. There were a few stopgap people like Jerry Smalls still hanging around, but, after robbing from two stores, people like T.J. Jones had flunked out. Vincent's rampant interview blitzes had plugged in the rest.

If the brand new marketing campaign, centered around 50,000 monthly postcards, social media and anything else they could think of like local fliers, events and coupons, all routing customers to the toll free number or web addresses and capturing their data, worked – great. They would all be rich.

If it failed – what was next?

Vincent never should have won Superstar, but it proved his mettle here and now, to himself and his employees. He sat on the precipice of rolling out something that would revolutionize this business and possibly the industry. The sky was now the limit.

\*       \*       \*       \*       \*

# "The Surviving Game" by Vincent Scott
## Surviving Business Politics

Politics. It's all around us. Our daily lives are governed by it, we are told what we can and cannot do because of it and you will never, ever escape it no matter what you do. So you'd best learn how to play the political game and get politics on your side.

From the moment you attempt to make your grand entrance into your next working endeavor until the day you retire, you will have varying levels of involvement in business politics. Whether you work for a big name corporation, a small company, get loans and licenses and work for yourself or you do anything outside of living under a rock, you are going to be some part of a political system.

Knowing that politics exist – as we discussed in looking for a job and networking – changes the game and how you go about looking for a job. Unfortunately, it is not what you know, but who you know so you have to get to know the people that will care about what you know. Networking with the right people will aid you in playing the political game getting through the first door: employment.

Politics makes sense in a lot of ways; of course it saves time and energy for a hiring manager to bring on someone he or she knows can perform the role or someone a contact of theirs has vouched for. It is not wrong – and certainly can be good for the person who has networked – but for those of us who are overqualified for the role getting passed over that is little consolation. It's not necessarily the best candidate that gets the role, but it is the one who played the game most effectively.

In a lot of ways, the politics we witness firsthand in employment and business mirrors that governing our countries; misconceptions and lack of knowledge lead to unnecessary suffering. Having the knowledge of getting in front of the proper connectors to enhance your job search makes all the difference in the world.

Just like managing politics assists you entering a company, your duration there depends on playing the game. You will not agree with every decision and every policy handed down by those above you. Fair or unfair, decisions will often be made without consulting you or anyone with first-hand knowledge of the factors affected. You may work for those whose priorities are not in line with yours or where you feel your leaders' priorities should be. When these things happen, whether your goal is gainful employment with benefits or climbing the corporate ladder you have to remember who signs your paychecks.

When we enter into agreement to carry out a business relationship, no matter what it is, we are agreeing to the terms of said agreement. In the same token, so is your employer or anyone with whom you enter into agreement with. That said, just as employees often forget these vows, employers can also waver from that first contract. Reigning them in – however – looks quite different from how an employer will reign back in a rogue employee.

In short, a company decides to provide us paychecks and benefits. They have the right – provided nothing is done illegally in the decision – to renege on that process of paying us. They also have a lot of power on their side; superiors will hold their recommendations in high regard and trust that due diligence was done. If an employer wants to cease paying you, it is highly likely they will find a way.

Your role at any stage of the game is to be an ambassador for the company to the members of the sales food chain who come after you. By this, I refer to your next leg in that food chain: for associates, you must endorse the company to the customers. For management roles, you must champion the business to the associates, and so on up the ladder. Most challenging is when those aforementioned decisions and policies are etched in stone that we disagree with; we have to either outwardly trumpet the company's praises or simply bite our tongues.

The chances of landing a role in the working world that does not require you to occasionally bite your tongue is not likely. You could be an actor grappling with politics around roles and rewards; you could be a teacher bound by rules and regulations and a small business owner forced to comply with city ordinances and landlord laws of the land.

Know the needs and wants of those you are in business with. Specifically when they have a vested interest in your behavior, it is highly likely they will make you very aware of what they wish it to be. A great way to stay in their good graces is to consult them on "difficult decisions" (even if you really don't value their opinion or plan to follow it), accept rulings (whether they cared to hear you out on your opinions or not) and move forward, and learn how to pick your battles.

You will often have to decide which are the battles most worth fighting for in order to make it into a position to best help and support others.

This is specifically tricky when you are governed by especially bad management.

You will know poor management when you see it; they will not value you or your opinions on how to run the business, they govern through fear and intimidation, and they use politics as a weapon. Just as politics played can assist you, going against the political grain can very quickly be your undoing.

Often, people of all statures in business will have political allies. The strength of these alliances is all determined by what is at stake. Power players will unite to have more power and more strength in decision-making or more clout when decisions are made that concern them. Alliances can make for interesting bedfellows and align interesting, contrasting individuals. Nevertheless, political relationships serve quite a purpose in all levels of business across all industries.

Embracing the place of politics in business is to your advantage because without doing so, you can have quite a bumpy ride. You can have a very decorated, glowing résumé and never gain entrance to the corporations you seek out. You can be a great employee with innovative ideas and the love of your employees and strike out mercilessly trying to show senior management why they are running their company into the ground. You could be an owner and let the red tape and ordinances and lease agreements trip you up so your brilliant idea fizzles out.

We play games of chance where we know the odds and make calculated risk. Sometimes we play games like Candy Land where the outcome has literally nothing to do with anything but luck. Your career will fall somewhere in-between. Set yourself up for the best chance at success and know where politics falls in the surviving game: it's front and center, it's unavoidable and – if played properly – it can give you quite a leg up on your journey.

## Fever Pitch Frustration

Monday, June 27, 2011: Vincent had an all-manager meeting scheduled in Golden Valley at 1 PM to unveil and launch lead generation: the most exciting day to date in this Brink Management Company endeavor, if not the company's history.

After weeks of communicating back and forth with Terry Bunche – who was floating around without a store to manage and no one really knew what he was doing – the websites were live, the database was ready and waiting and the fliers had landed.

The concept was simple. It touted the capability to save up to $500 per year on home phone, Internet, television and/or wireless – a catch-all for any consumer. *Who the heck wouldn't be interested in such a catchy offer?* To find out more, one would be routed to the toll-free number or Internet landing page of their choice. Once there, their information would be captured, and the team would follow up. It could not miss. It was shooting fish in a barrel.

Vincent strolled into the store and the clock ticked toward game time. This was his bread and butter: selling a new program or innovation to a team with detailed delivery, exceptional execution and outlining the results expected. He had put together an organized synopsis of the meeting with high level bullet points that he would expound upon with passionate dialogue. The mission of the meeting was to educate his team on this plan, how it works, why it works, what to do with it and excite them on what was in it for them.

This was the single most important meeting in Brink Management Company history and probably that many of these employees would ever see, and Vincent had been drumming up the excitement around it for weeks.

Jesse Fairbanks, however, took a vacation, and chose not to dial in to the conference call line. Cliff Watson took a vacation day and did not dial in to the conference call line. Reggie Sherman was at a customer's home, installing a home phone unit. (*What???*) Oscar, the newly minted store manager at White Bear Township (also hailing from Craigslist), said he was coming but never showed nor called into the conference call line. A call to New Brighton revealed that De-Metre was helping customers and that was why he was not in attendance.

Vincent sat there, in awe and bewilderment. *What is this? Where the hell am I?*

Recent results had continued to drastically underwhelm. These goofs could not even be excited about a kickstart to their business like nothing they had ever seen. They didn't understand it; they didn't get it. It's why some people would be permanent under-achievers in life and would just bounce around as sales reps for the rest of their days.

And Vincent couldn't understand them; he couldn't fathom a world where someone wouldn't gravitate toward a leader who believed in them and broke his back for them. This was specifically pertinent because Vincent wanted such a leader so badly for himself.

He could not wrap his head around people so stuck in their one-dimensional, small world that they hadn't planned well enough head to get to the meeting. They were committing cardinal sins of management: stuck in day-to-day minutiae that sales reps could perform for them while huge initiatives that could make everyone lots of money were being presented to near-empty rooms.

Vincent could not do this anymore…

They were on pace to barely achieve $160K in gross profit for June. Mankato was a disaster; a store pulling in a few thousand bucks per month was taking up too much of Vincent's time. He had to find a new manager, talk his whole staff off the ledge while Bruce Rollins bolted and did not pay any of them, all while personally carting inventory and deposit money back and forth from Minneapolis to Mankato just so they could open.

This was not at all in the roadmap. Vincent was giving these people everything he had; putting on shows for the parent companies, winning awards and giving Brink Management Company the best press possible. On the flip side, he was dealing with fallout like he had never seen before with no help, leading a team that was mostly clueless because he could not attract top talent on the peanuts they were getting paid, and pinning all his hopes on lead generation marketing through an unknown marketing company and the occasional help of sometimes reliable Terry Bunche. A wing and a prayer.

What was the answer?

Vincent had put up with his last employer for 9 tumultuous years. He was 4 months into this experiment and he was fried. Now, these lame reps and managers would drop the ball on lead generation; their store leaders couldn't even bother to show up to a damn meeting. Conservative estimates showed they could grow the region by $10,000 in gross profit per store per month if it was done right. Yet, he could not even get store managers to follow a basic instruction and attend a meeting or call into a conference call – even after showing the considerable gains in commission they would make and their reps would make.

A few did, but collectively they didn't care… and Vincent could do very little with apathy outside of what he had already done.

Nevertheless, Vincent just kept blindly trudging forward. He always just trudged forward incessantly. He conducted the meeting in style, pocketed his emotions per usual, filmed a video explaining the lead generation platform in depth that he made viewing of mandatory, and the whole groundbreaking experiment was underway.

Highs and lows are normal in any forum, but Vincent had never seen anything like this. Jordan Wallace would call him up and tell him to meet up with Dustin "Bruce" Rollins and give him two separate drops of $3,500 apiece of walking money for the items he ripped off out of his stores, causing major chaos. Apparently, he and Wallace had made some deal on the trailer he had packed up when gutting his store and abandoning ship and Vincent got to be the golden errand boy – not once, but twice. Who knows what backroom deal they had going on.

Rollins was also best friends with Aaron Tuncil, the White Bear Township owner, who decided to vacate his management contract by way of simply not paying.

In essence, Vincent lost 2 of his 11 stores in one fell swoop, with Mankato given a death blow Vincent would have to resuscitate them from. When he had signed on 4 months prior, Jordan Wallace promised they would be adding locations. Now he was losing 18% of his territory and bonus potential on top of an already relatively lackluster base.

While he sputtered to a $163K finish in June – accounting for his loss of both Mankato (who remained closed for the rest of the month) and Greenfield, the numbers were misleading: he still continued positive trajectory of every single key metric and statistic.

Unfortunately, he got paid on raw revenue. So, for him, with lead generation upon them, it was now or never.

Vincent would work so hard, exhausting himself, and was forced to take a step back. Some days, he just could not do any more. Terry laughed at Vincent's "bull in a china shop" approach, but it was the only way he knew how – complete, total, wrecking-ball domination of everything in his sights at all times.

Bring on the leads! May they be the salvation this project so desperately needed.

## "The Surviving Game" by Vincent Scott
### Training: The Biggest Miss in The Selling Game – But it Doesn't Have to Be!

We can be great at sales, strong at leadership and have the best of intentions. Yet if we fail to properly train and – more importantly – follow up to ensure the material sinks in and is consistently executed upon into the future, we fail as individuals, as teams and businesses.

We have seen it dozens of times: a new initiative is unleashed, we undertake continuation training on a component of our business or we embark on initial training in an organization… and the ball is dropped. This can take multiple forms: unorganized curriculum, hapless material, lack of engagement from trainer or the presentation and failure to track successes, follow up and ensure *long-term* success.

Let's begin with initial training, as it is typically chronologically first in the cycle.

Always remember that training – at any stage in the game – is an investment in your people. It is necessary we take the needed time, provide the proper resources and ensure success for it – every step of the way.

When you train your workforce for the first time, they are in many ways a blank canvas. You can never assume your team knows anything about the business you want them to master, the customer base they will be satisfying and the tools needed with which to accomplish that goal. Training needs to be comprehensive and informative, but it must also be engaging, enlightening and hopefully entertaining.

There are stark contrasts in the spectrum; some training classes are arduous and strictly academic, with reading through text and mechanically going through the motions of the material. Other training sessions include games, skits and humor. Neither is completely right or wrong; finding a mix of the two is ideal to grab the attention of your audience, keep it and fill their minds with knowledge that you want them to retain.

There are also multiple schools of thought on the duration of training; do not skimp this initial investment into your team. Research and workforce surveys reveal that lack of training is often one of the largest complaints across occupations. We are certainly in a rush to get our teams out into battle, but failing to arm them with the arsenal necessary to join the front lines will not bode well. All the time you spent recruiting, selecting and hiring will be wasted if you improperly invest in your talent's future.

What are the most important ingredients to your future team's success? What must they know? Like raising children, we can never give them everything they will encounter; their best learning comes in the field. Nevertheless, it is our duty to prepare them for the experiences they will face.

Make the itinerary first. Map out your syllabus with an approach conducive to adding pieces to the arsenal in an order that makes sense and increases the likelihood of retention. Like anything, build a strong foundation.

Your team needs to know about the company they have enlisted in. They need to understand the innovation of the products and services, the target audience and why people need what you provide. They need to know the benefits of the products and services. They need to know what they will face – scenarios, examples of types of situations they will encounter, and mixing in field work with a partner already in the field can greatly enhance their learning. They need guidance on compiling a go-to-market strategy and they will continue to need development and evolution of process along the way.

We often see training curriculums that are either too long or too short; avoid those pitfalls by mapping out a learning plan which sticks to exactly what is needed. Arm your team with the essentials of knowledge about the business, the products and services, the customer base and their responsibilities. Make it fun. Give some down time to digest the information; provide breaks in the action so they can take a step away and not be overwhelmed.

Selecting the trainer is another core ingredient in this mix; finding someone conducive to deliver this message who has credibility in the field is vital to the success – especially in initial training. Companies will often bring in someone they deem to be an effective trainer because they have trained in other environments, however this can have poor results if they themselves are not properly adapted and assimilated into the new material.

Training the trainer is just as important if not more so than training the team; this is the face and general who will be prepping new recruits for battle in the weeks, months and years to come. Make that choice wisely and prepare them fully for that responsibility.

No matter what business you are in, continuation training will prove to be necessary at many times along the path. We are constantly developing; new products are introduced to the marketplace and our consumers' needs change. Our people are also often on different places in the learning curve and we need them adept at fielding queries and proactively promoting everything in our product line. Continuation training enhances existing knowledge with your workforce, is an investment into future results with that knowledge and also helps build long-term growth and success.

Continuation training can take many forms. It can be a one-day crash course pulse check seeing where your team's knowledge is and apprising them of what's new in the hot topic. It can be a week-long event that drastically shapes their knowledge on your hot topic. Or it can be a daily or weekly meeting or conference call, regular correspondence and communication with your workforce and following up to make sure you are getting the desired results.

I am a firm believer in over-communication (of good information, of course); it goes hand-in-hand with the fact you never take for granted what your team knows, remembers or how they would approach a new situation. It is the job of a leader or trainer to prepare the team, anticipate obstacles and bestow the knowledge necessary to barrel through or jump over those hurdles. When we painstakingly communicate these things regularly, find new ways of talking about the same vital things and we inspect the results to ensure it is working, we manage to plug gaps in the knowledge and savvy of our teams.

Ladies and gentlemen: the biggest miss in effective training is tracking the results and following up to ensure the process is consistent and the knowledge is retained.

To what level are we holding our trainings and trainers accountable? On the flip side, are we putting too much on their shoulders and putting them to task for things way outside their jurisdiction?

No matter how well we prepare our teams or cover the material, things will change. Important nuggets of information will get lost in the shuffle of the daily minutiae. More new things will come to the table to further compound our mission.

Also, the needs of our workers will change; perhaps we tweak our training to make sure it is up-to-date in its quest to adequately satisfy the people it serves. Perhaps we examine the employee retention of a training class to make sure we have prepared people appropriately. We survey our trainees and teams to utilize their first-hand knowledge and experience as we reform our training curriculum. We use exit interviews to get further feedback on where training and continuation training can fit more and more into the job.

In short, we examine the needs of our people and audience and equip them with everything they need to follow the process; when it changes, we once again bring them back to the table, re-equip and regroup.

What results are our people having after leaving these training courses? How are we tracking this?

Look at the results of the performers for the first quarter after leaving training. Look at the sample group's results in the weeks following a training day or week and examine those results versus those in preceding days in the same metrics. The digital age has made it all the easier to keep account of every possible result and component of the job and our employees' performances. Use this information to hold yourself accountable to provide the best training – and follow-up – possible.

Evaluation and holding trainers and yourself accountable to deliver the best possible training will up the accountability and results. Actually planning the curriculum and doing so around the pressing needs of your organization and teams will keep the material relevant to the task at hand. Making sure the course is illuminating and entertaining at the same time will keep the atmosphere light yet focused on absorption. Re-convening with the team regularly to revisit the topics and study real-time results will make sure the effects of training last for a long, long time.

Gaining the buy-in and contribution of your team and the people who have been trained will also make certain this vital component of your business is impactful in every way.

# Comebacks

No matter how apathetic you try to be or how many painful memories you repress, and regardless of how much you try to prepare yourself for the worst in any situation, life will never fail at unpleasantly surprising you.

Vincent's phone rang on the morning of Sunday, July 17, 2011. Any time he saw a Mankato phone number that his Caller ID did not recognize at some random time in the day, his heart would freeze.

It took him back to May 14, 2006, when his mother called from a strange number to tell him that his father had suffered a heart attack.

"Hello?"

"Vincent…" his mother responded on the other line, with clear strain in her voice.

"Oh, God," Vincent managed, knowing immediately it regarded his Dad and he instantly feared the absolute worst – bracing himself in preparation for it.

Vincent was alone in his apartment, reading on his couch and he bolted up, swiveled around and planted his feet on the ground.

"First off, your Dad is okay," she responded. "He had a stroke."

Vincent blinked hard. Tears came immediately, no matter how impenetrable he thought he was. He allowed himself to love so little because for what he loved, his fear of losing was so great. But his love for family was absolute; their support for him during his most trying times was the *only* love that had not wavered.

"He is in the hospital now and they are running tests to make sure everything is okay with his heart," Kay continued. While Vince was her rock and companion, she was holding up rather well.

"What happened?" Vincent asked, his eyes opening slightly and masking the anguish in his voice.

"I talked to him this morning, and he was a little unresponsive," Kay responded. "I thought he was just tired. I went out to do my morning walk, and I just felt something was wrong. So I came back to the house and checked on him again and he seemed okay. A few minutes later, I was out on the deck and heard something fall. When I went inside, your Dad was standing in the kitchen and had dropped the milk jug and was unable to move.

"I knew immediately he had had a stroke," she continued. "There was no way I could get him in the car by myself, though. I ran up the street and got Earl.

Thank goodness he was there. He came down, helped me get your Dad in the car, and I took him to the hospital as fast as I could."

"Wow," Vincent responded, processing this information. He had arisen from the couch, made it to his room and was already starting to prepare for the drive to Mankato.

"Are you okay?" she asked.

"Am *I* okay; are *you* okay?"

"I am right now," Kay answered. "In a little bit of shock. They measure the stroke on a scale from 1-to-22. They said on that scale this was a 5."

"That's a relief."

"I do have to tell you, though, that your Dad can't talk. The right side of his body has been affected considerably, and he has a droop to his face," Kay said.

"Will he recover?"

"They don't know."

"OK," Vincent responded slowly. "Well – I'm on my way."

Vincent fought back tears and tried his best not to think as he quickly showered, packed a bag for the foreseeable future and took off. This trip was all too familiar.

The real bright spot to Vincent's challenges of the last several years were that they made him quite emotionally strong. Nothing, however, could ever prepare him to see the man he called his hero, who was always a pillar of strength and good and right in this cold, cruel world, ravaged by a stroke to the point he could not feed himself, speak or go any amount of time without considerable outpouring of emotion. Physically, the man was his Dad, but Vincent Scott, Jr. felt helpless and unable to communicate his predicament.

The day was a blur; so many visitors, lots of tears and very little food or sleep.

A constant during times like this was the Haskins family; Vincent's Godparents, Paula and Duke, and his best friend since birth, Eddie. Even Eddie's sister Gina reached out to Vincent and Kay to offer her services as speech therapist as Vince got his bearings and immersed himself in the road to a comeback.

Vince was alive; for that, Vincent and his mother were most thankful. It was, however, in the moments when Vincent could not control the tidal wave of his thoughts and emotions any longer, harrowing to be so unsure if his Dad would ever be the same again.

To watch him struggle so mightily with communicating even the most basic of requests or statements, to see him grow so frustrated over it or his physical therapy, and to witness him overly emotional as a result of the trauma to his body was so difficult for Vincent Scott the son. These days were the worst of his life to date, and he was not even the one going through the physical ordeal.

This period certainly put into perspective Vincent's year-long forced sabbatical. While those days were distressing and full of seemingly unending sorrow, this was infinitely worse. Vincent knew he had at least some control over his career and would hopefully eventually get where he deserved to be; the frustration was the waiting and the agony in between. However, when it came to the lack of control over the well-being of those he loved, he was in petrified turmoil.

He had just seen them the weekend prior; Vince and Kay had come to Minneapolis to visit that prior Sunday. They played board games, had lunch. There was never any possible noticeable precursor to such an event. The only solace was that they always cherished one another as a family, no matter what past struggles they had endured together and individually.

Eddie got Vincent out of the room for a while and they had a semblance of a meal in the hospital lounge. Eddie even called Jack Johnson, now a Lieutenant Junior Grade with the Navy who was on land and in Washington state, with the news, and Jack reached out to Vincent that evening. Vincent spent an hour on the phone with Emily, who was a hospital nurse supervisor and knew the ins and outs of strokes and what to expect.

During the days to follow, Vincent was running on fumes with little sleep. He urged his mother to go back to the house to sleep or shower or change, yet he did not leave the hospital at any time. He could do nothing but wonder if his Dad would ever be the same again, or if he had seen the last of the man who raised him, as he had come to know him.

Vincent learned how to be a Dad from this man; he still had more he wanted to learn. More he wanted to say. More he wanted to talk about. More moments in his life to come that he wanted his Dad to see.

Lots of people lost their Dads much earlier or had absentee fathers; Vincent couldn't handle another loss at this point – not one that would be the most significant of his life to date amidst a handful of other debilitating blows.

On the first morning after the day of the stroke, Vince, Jr. sounded better and seemed better, but, by mid-afternoon he was sluggish, frustrated and emotional. It was difficult to decipher anything he was trying to say, and he was overcome with emotions from the aftermath of the stroke. It was horrible.

And, as horrible as it was for Vincent, as he retreated to corners of the hospital waiting room to be alone and fight back tears, it had to have been a million times worse for his father.

The phone rang off the hook; so much so that Vincent finally unplugged it. People were coming in all day; so much so that Vincent and Kay agreed that they would limit the number of visitors.

Vincent sat in the chapel, talked to God, and prayed for nothing short of his Dad to be taken care of.

The thought dawned on him, however: during his forced sabbatical, Vincent had started reading "comeback" books like *The Death and Return of Superman* about the Man of Steel's comeback from death, *The Natural* detailing fictional ballplayer Roy Hobbs' return from a nearly career-ending gunshot experience, *The Color of Money* about Fast Eddie Felson's quest to return to best Minnesota Fats and the like. However, it now seemed his own Dad would teach him a firsthand comeback story for the ages. If anyone could do it, he could and would.

Accompanying his Dad in the physical therapy sessions, Vincent watched in awe just how stroke-affected all of the other victims were. Many were overweight, few had any true determination and most seemed confined to the fact that this occurrence would limit or inhibit their future actions for as long as they inhabited the earth. However, he watched his father fight through and never falter.

The therapists would ask him to do a lap or two; he would do five. They would ask him to recognize people and things, answer questions about his past and present and perform various tasks and, even if he could not immediately execute, the fire and desire of recovery never left his eyes and demeanor.

On the third day, Vincent could not help but laugh when his Dad managed to find the words to ask to go home. And the doctor let him.

The road ahead would be lengthy and difficult, but mid-day on the third day, Vince left the hospital and was determined to take the path to wellness.

So many things were going in his favor. After checking into the hospital in 2006 at 202 pounds, he was now a svelte 175. Kay, though she took some flak for it, kept him on a strict regimen and he relatively quickly returned to his golf, basketball and volleyball. His chief concern now was that he would not be able to play basketball again; a game he played at 66 surrounded by men in their 20's, 30's and 40's where he could still teach them a thing or two and rained 3-pointer after 3-pointer over their outstretched arms.

That evening, with Vince stable and resting in his home, Kay with everything under control and work and Elizabeth back in Minneapolis, Kay and Vincent agreed it was time for Vincent to head back.

Vincent, however, had an even stronger and more profound regard for his parents and their relationship. Watching Kay tend to Vince's every need, the unbelievable bond they had and how seriously they took their 38-year old vows to one another was inspiring and moving. Vincent could not imagine having a relationship like that; which was the very reason he had not to this point. How could anyone compete with this pedestal he aspired to?

Kay quickly enrolled Vince in the physical therapy sessions and outpatient speech therapy programs prescribed, and Vincent Scott returned to Minneapolis to lead a small band of misfits to victory.

Abby, having heard from Elizabeth's babysitter that Vincent's Dad had been hospitalized after his stroke, reached out to Vincent via phone call and subsequent voice message, sounding sincerely concerned and offering to help with grocery shopping and the like.

Work quickly greeted Vincent's return with ample activity; Chris Jeffries was being courted by Doug Wilson and Moriarty Wireless to purchase and acquire the reigns to the Greenfield location, in addition to his Hermantown, Cloquet and Plymouth duds. It had moved far enough along that Susie and Doug scheduled – what else? – a lunch to discuss. Any excuse to eat free on their companies' corporate cards was a good one.

It was also shortly thereafter when Susie and Doug would start making Hermantown and Cloquet road trips down I-35W N with Vincent in tow once per month. Since Vincent was making them regularly, they figured this would enable them to hang out together, eat together on the road and knock out these two stores in one shot.

They would meet in the morning at Susie's choice of meeting place, drive to Hermantown, leave when Susie prodded them to do so, go to Cloquet, eat lunch at Susie's choice of restaurant, visit the Cloquet store where the seasons never changed, and leave so Susie could get back home by 3 PM every day. Susie would use these opportunities to gang up on Vincent and on Chris Jeffries so she could push her agenda on personnel, follow-up policy and anything else to stop the descent of numbers in her region.

While every store in Vincent's region was rallying and making drastic improvements (Bloomington, while perennially a powerhouse for Minneapolis, New Brighton and Eden Prairie had all just come off their best months ever),

Hermantown was steadily descending in overall numbers. While they were still the #1 store in the region, dropping from $45K in gross profit in March to $37K, $35K, $32K, and, most recently $30K, and new activation productivity from 105 to just 68 in July (Bloomington was 2$^{nd}$ with 50), the Hermantown descent meant every other store had to make up all of that difference with considerably less traffic. It just was not feasible.

And, with the Jeffries' stores not wanting to put forth the effort to perform on Vincent's innovative, revolutionary ideas (now through no fault of Chris's), they were likely going to remain stagnant and in freefall. There was little Vincent could do; he at last realized that visiting them once per month and wasting little time on them was the right answer. "Move the middle" who wants to move up.

To the credit of Chris Jeffries, he and Vincent were getting along well now and Chris was more and more of an advocate for Vincent and his teachings. Nevertheless, his managers who had ignored Vincent's innovations to this point did not want to actually put any additional exertion into their business now.

Vincent had found a system that was working in the stores that chose to work it, and it was paying some dividends. Sure, he had to fight for every yard and his team was a lot of riff raff – but they were making some gains.

Hopefully, lead generation would make up the difference. He had vowed to achieve $200K in gross profit in April, but had yet to eclipse that total. In fact, they were going downward – not upward – and losing stores was certainly not helping.

Vincent spent much of the time over the next few weeks back and forth between managing lead generation and taking care of Elizabeth in Minneapolis, and heading back to Mankato frequently to be with his family.

Vince, Jr. continued his progress; while he was making huge strides in his therapy sessions, he became discouraged at the lethargy that came much more quickly and that he had difficulty remembering what he once could.

On the work front, Vincent, Terry and Saul were planning their next big move; they needed to push a realignment that would give this project legs and hope for a bright future.

It was the end of July, and Jordan Wallace returned to Minneapolis for a midyear review with Cellular Horizons brass. Regional Director Kurt Stillwater, his subordinate Steve Flowers and Doug and Susie Wilson would all be in attendance and the plan was to cover the progress of Brink Management Company thus far in 2011.

Prior to the meeting, Wallace met Vincent at the downtown location where he and Terry Bunche were finalizing the lead generation platform and rolling it out. Wallace had not previously met Terry in person, though Vincent had been sure to talk Terry up frequently in the wake of the new marketing mechanism.

Jordan Wallace – knowing he had a meeting this day – did not stroll in wearing his typical t-shirt and jeans with sport coat array; he actually sported a turquoise dress shirt with a tie that was a slightly darker shade of blue.

"Terry, this is Jordan Wallace. Jordan – Terry Bunche," Vincent said, motioning one to the other and vice versa.

"Hi, it's nice to meet you," Terry reacted.

"Likewise," the always cool Wallace responded. "So Vincent tells me this leads idea you guys cooked up is going to really take off."

"Yeah, it's exactly what we need to do," Terry responded.

"Let's see what you've got," Jordan said.

They stepped into the back room. Saul Portman was off that day, so he was not privy to this meeting of the minds.

Terry showcased the database, how it recorded and recalled leads, the methods by which they could reach out to potential customers and the current state of the website landing pages and 800 number they had been given as part of the bundle. Vincent let him steer while he added cameo comments from time to time to expound upon points.

"This is good stuff," Wallace responded.

"And this is just the beginning of what this can do," Vincent continued. "Anything we want to run through this thing; any type of campaign, any promotion – we just set the system up to handle it and store a different promotion code. It will tell us what promotion they are calling about so we know what we're talking about when we engage them. It also tracks what promotions are working and which ones aren't so we know which ones to drop and which to keep doing."

"Really?" Wallace said thoughtfully. His wheels were in motion. "I think we could integrate this in directly with the other projects I'm looking to start."

"Sure – probably. What other projects?" Vincent asked, a little startled.

"Have you ever heard of Berkshire Hathaway?"

Vincent and Terry quickly exchanged glances. "Of course – yeah," came the collective reply.

"You know, I really have no long-term interest in cell phones. Let's call it what it is – it's a saturated business with little profit margin."

*Where the hell was this coming from?*

"I really just like starting businesses. I have no interest in running them for the long haul; I just want to launch them and get residuals off of them until the end of time," Wallace continued. "I want us to be a holding company, like Berkshire Hathaway. We've got a mobile hot dog stand that Lee and Lyle and I are starting, called Wally's Weenies. I've got an idea for a restaurant marketing company. I also checked out some property last week in North Carolina and am looking to start a saloon-type restaurant chain. Then there's a website designed just as a one-stop-shop for everything wireless, that we could use to sell to Cellular Horizons stores all over the country. Why stop with what we have?"

Wallace stopped for a minute to gauge the reactions of his audience.

"Sure, absolutely," Vincent said slowly. "It could do all of those things. So are we getting out of this business?"

"Possibly. I mean, I'll probably always have some stake in wireless. It's where I started," Wallace said matter-of-factly. "But I get bored easily. And can't you imagine, guys, you traveling around the country selling this lead generation to people!? What if I just sent you guys to meetings around the U.S. to talk to owners and sell this product! That's a true management company. Then we'd get a cut off of everything they sell."

Wallace – per usual – was getting caught up and excited in his own train of thought.

Of course, these ideas would sound great if the previous ideas – like pitching their management company to the 100 stores that were joining them (instead of losing stores in their jurisdiction) were coming to fruition. Sadly, they were not and there was no sign they would.

"I've got investors for all of this shit," he continued. "And they fucking love me. They just love throwing money at me. I just sit there and sell what I like to call the 'blue skies.' That's how I got Vincent. I never would have gotten him otherwise."

There was a brief pause. Vincent wondered where this was going.

"Of course, there is a *chance* things can pan out the way you pitch them," Wallace continued. He was on a roll. "But it's pitching the 'blue skies': the perfect scenario. You know, like that if we got all of these stores cranking out $30,000 gross profit per month. It *could* happen, but it isn't happening anytime soon. Hell, we're not even close."

The words that had just escaped Jordan Wallace's mouth were not at all lost on the audience; specifically Vincent Scott. This man had just said he duped Vincent with hopes of nearly $200,000-per-year paydays in order to secure his vastly overqualified talents. Terry Bunche, meeting his "leader" now for the first time, was also less than impressed with what he heard.

Vincent's issue with this was predominantly the fact that while he certainly knew how to sell a bill of goods to someone, it was not his style; he would never have coerced a life-changing decision from someone or led them on for his own gain. He always managed to sell reality – specifically to his followers. It's why they followed him through thick and thin.

"Sure, OK..." Vincent began, digesting this new information but attempting to stay on track with their agenda. "But that said, we *are* in this business. We all signed on for *this business*. We are selling a good product, it's something we believe in and all have a stake in."

"Yeah, I will definitely keep that in mind," Wallace said, almost flippantly. He was clearly not even focused on this business anymore. "There's so many things on the table. I mean, as things are right now, we are looking at making some pay sacrifices – all of us. We've got to delve more into net profit; there is a lot of money going out of this business and we are just flat out not profitable."

This was due to the ski trips and winery visits and overseas voyages by Wallace and his wife and Lyle Caminiti and his girlfriend on a biweekly basis. The fact no one on the front lines was even privy to a profit and loss statement did not help, either – Vincent and his leaders had no idea what the real expenses were so they had no way of managing against them. Sure – many of them would get a monthly nasty-gram from Lyle over a hefty heating expense because it was nearly impossible to keep their stores warm in the dead of a Minnesota winter. But the company as a whole was bleeding through unchecked, rampant wastefulness and lavishness at the top.

"Pay cut?" Vincent asked. He processed this information quickly. "Honestly, Dan, I can't really do this for any less money than I'm making now. I came on because of the – what did you call it? Blue skies? I'm already making far less than I expected and sacrificing and still waiting on the store openings and the globetrotting to sell our management contract."

"Hey, we all make sacrifices for six months and – between these other businesses I want you to take a part in, the marketing you guys are putting together and the management company we are going to have across this entire industry, we'll all be fucking millionaires."

*Was he serious?*

Pay cuts for regional managers? So not only was Vincent on pace to hope for $70,000 this year coming off multiple six-figure paydays and being sold on making $200,000 here, but now he may make even less? The last time he made only $70,000 was as an entry-level sales rep back in 2002. Now, being in this position that a plunge backwards, he realized the penalty for standing up to the corporate corruption: only he suffered.

It could have been worse, of course – and he was fully aware of that. But he should not have faced this punishment at all.

Every day, as Vincent would pull into the parking lots of these stores and see the revered Cellular Horizons title above the door, walk into a store where he called the shots and enjoyed the mutual respect with his employees, he felt like he was doing something: learning to build his business.

But after being smacked multiple times per day like a crowbar with the fallacies and gaffes this company and its hapless support was rife with, Vincent could not see any hue of blue in these skies.

"Working here, doing what we do is like getting your Masters' degree in running a business," Wallace often said. And, for every Wallace-ism that was utterly ridiculous, like the ludicrous financial figures he threw around with ease and carelessness, he actually said some things that made sense and Vincent agreed with.

"Your entire job is about support. Whatever these guys need. Do everything you can to just meet their needs and see that they are taken care of," Wallace told Vincent when he came on board.

But as Vincent started to see how much of an absentee boss Wallace was, how often he checked out and how he never, ever followed through on anything he started (any idea, any plan, any process) it was obvious this would not be the mentor he craved. He was too much of an acting-rich playboy for that. Sure, there were some good fundamentals and Wallace had been a good sales manager years ago. But now he was so drunk on the freedom and other people's money that his business was falling apart. Quickly.

Ironically, Jordan Wallace needed the same rude awakening Vincent had gotten.

The conversation at hand did not look up; Wallace left to go wherever the next party was while Vincent and Terry ended up engaged in a lengthy parking lot conversation about their futures and the future (or lack thereof) of this business.

"He told me everything I needed to hear in there," Terry said. "I'm not here for him or for anything else. I'm here for you. I know what you can do, and I believe in you. That's how all of these guys feel. And hearing him say those things – he doesn't even want to be here!"

"You're right," Vincent lamented. "So we are going to push these things as far as we can…and take over this company, one way or another. Come hell or high water, someone will have to listen to us then."

If Jordan Wallace did not have the interest or the infrastructure to give them the direction and guidance and support necessary, they were going to take it to the next level themselves. Surely these things would not go unnoticed by the Cellular Horizons and Moriarty brass and the investors in Brink Management Company. Their desire and ability to will themselves to the next level would ensure a victory here. It had to. They would make enough noise that someone would pay attention to them.

Wallace agreed to let them start their marketing program in Minneapolis and hinted that – if and likely when successful – it would be something they could duplicate in the other markets. So that is precisely what they would do.

They had gotten the victory at hand, despite it being an ugly one. They'd take it, and press on.

The concept of dropping pay for regional managers sent Vincent into a pretty immediate mental and professional tailspin, but his resolve was clear: once he showed Jordan Wallace how much money he could make him and save him and how he could basically run the company himself, surely there would be a case made for his greatly increased compensation. Put in the time, build your case for promotion or a raise and then make your request from a position of strength.

Vincent would continue working to support and promote his team, but this time he was going to make the case through numbers and innovation and unparalleled leadership that Brink, Moriarty and Cellular Horizons should be fighting to sign his whopping paycheck. A leap of faith, sure – but Vincent was again willing to bet on himself.

The following day was the politicking event Wallace was in town for; the Cellular Horizons, Moriarty and Brink leaders sat around a table and everyone congratulated each other and patted themselves on the back and touted 150% year-over-year improvements in total new acquisitions. Vincent was complimented heavily by everyone in attendance and the vibe was utterly feel-good.

Peppered throughout were individual action plan talking points for each store, but the theme of the meeting was how proud everyone was of themselves for the huge turnaround in this market since the baton was passed from Jeff Gemini to Vincent Scott. The market had their best results in history.

Much of the next several weeks included transition; Chris Jeffries and his wife Michelle re-opened the Greenfield Cellular Horizons store under their umbrella and Saul Portman was tapped for a dual-management role to assist and get it on its feet. It was a goodwill gesture from Vincent; loaning out his store manager to Jeffries to help him get a non-Brink owned store off the ground.

Vincent and his principal players spent much of the time doing interviews to plug holes and upgrade staffing. Vincent found himself doing most of the work on the lead generation platform; Terry Bunche, who was not currently assigned to a store was typically difficult to reach and doing God knows what. He sporadically kept Vincent up to speed on his progress, but Vincent was not seeing the movement he wanted as quickly as he wanted it.

With everything that had happened and now that Vincent was seeing Terry might not be as reliable as he initially hoped, Vincent planted the seed with Chris Jeffries that they start fresh with a new, hand-picked store manager. Terry had no interest in immediately returning to that grind because he was drifting around in his Director of Marketing role; it also gave Vincent and Chris the opportunity to select someone who would give Greenfield his or her full attention.

Progress was also being made in other areas; New Brighton, under the leadership of De-Metre Jones, celebrated its best month ever and first over $20,000 in gross profit.

It was the same old from Jordan Wallace; in between a trip to Napa Valley with his wife, he talked about a $4 million offer being on the table to buy his business as he was supposedly being coaxed out of the Cellular Horizons business – allegedly by Paul Gemini.

Conversations between Lee Christian, Aaron Hartley and Vincent started becoming quite frequent, as the three filled each other in on the content and inconsistencies of their own conversations with phantom owner Jordan Wallace.

From this point forward – August 2011 and beyond – much time was spent by these three major players in the organization wondering what was going to happen to the company, when it would happen, and what the fallout and result for their own careers would be.

Lee confirmed that Wallace was filling his head with visions of sugar plums and being franchise-starters as well; a holding company like Berkshire Hathaway.

Vincent had to keep moving onward; he could not allow himself to be sidetracked by the distractions. He made quality visits to his stores, developed individualized marketing plans with the teams there, tried to get them energized, put on sales clinics and drove results. He was doing everything he could think to do and it was continuing to make a difference – especially in his management team, who saw him leading excellently by example with his passion and enthusiasm. Vincent knew his process and he kept following it, undeterred by whatever uncertainties existed in the business under a leader who didn't even want to be in the industry. It would work itself out.

The reminders came daily that he had his work cut out for him.

In the old days, he had made rousing speeches and ridiculous paydays. He had generated countless millions of dollars single-handedly through his innovation, motivation and execution. He was a rising star, the crusader, the Pied Piper and Robin Hood wrapped into one. His top reps were well-polished, high-adrenaline, high-octane, respectable and respectful future leaders of the corporation.

Here, they were snot-nosed brats who lived with their parents and had no intention of ending up in this racket. Lisa, his top rep here, threw a fit when Vincent recognized a new female rep for a solid sale, sending a text to Vincent that the new rep got praise because she kissed his ass. And what was worse? Vincent suspended her, but he could not fire her…because it would only hurt him and store manager Reggie Sherman and the $1,000 a month base salary was not going to attract a rep that was better than she was.

He gave speeches to near-empty conference call bridges. If a great speech falls in a forest and no one was around to hear it, did it really exist?

He was moving the needle by thousands of dollars here and there, surrounded by too many people that did not even belong there.

Here was a one-man band making a fraction of the paychecks of yore, trying to pretend to the outside world that he was in a better position…when he most certainly was not.

Vincent Scott felt extremely mortal.

He was taking on more responsibilities in this business, and making less money – as he was only paid a cut of the profitability of the stores and had lost stores since the project began. He was developing a marketing plan from Terry Bunche's initial brainchild, and would see no huge gains from it because these lazy teams were not doing the necessary legwork.

And yet the roadblocks did not end there. The commitments the marketing company made about their lead generation platform went unfulfilled. They had promised the ability to send messages to their existing customer database, yet weeks and weeks of inability to, truncated messages and failed attempts ensued. Finally, the company confessed their inability to deliver and – by then – the game was already full-force in motion.

Vincent was excited about the quality of the products his team pitched and sold daily. However, he was worlds better than this job, this money, this predicament. He had not deserved this banishment. And he had spent a year applying to jobs just to get here.

His personal life was not looking much better. He had been off-and-on with Emily Nance for months and, when forced by circumstance (Elizabeth starting preschool) to be around Abby for any lengths of time, she made clear again she wanted Vincent back. With another break for her and Chris in full swing, her target was back on Vincent.

It would start somewhat subtly: inviting Vincent to dinner the night of the open house at school. They would quickly and easily fall back into the somewhat flirtatious banter – the things that had caused their initial attraction to one another were still present, they joked and both attempted to say or do things which would be alluring to the other for absolutely inexplicable reasons.

And it was all quite the conundrum; he wanted to be with Elizabeth every second of every day, and being with Abby would give him that chance. She claimed she had matured and changed.

Being with Emily meant some semblance of a family unit; her son idolized Vincent and the kids enjoyed playing with each other. But he was nowhere near able to commit to anything and he just did not feel the cosmic feeling he wanted…a feeling he had felt only a few times before.

He wanted a conversationalist with ambition and work ethic. An equal. A beauty. Someone who was independent but wanted to be treated like a queen and made Vincent feel secure and whose actions made him feel special. And she had to be deemed worthy to be around Elizabeth. The women he spent his free time with might fit into one or two of those categories, but none posted a clean sweep.

It begged the question: could anyone?

His relationship history, coupled with the massacre that left him unemployed, left Vincent extremely unwilling to trust or open up to anyone. First love Janie had dumped him by phone so she could quickly move on to a new crush while away at school, lied about it and then tried to get him back. Vincent was briefly engaged at 21 because he reached an impasse in his college partying and thought he needed to settle down – until he came to his senses.

Then Julie Lansing came along. She and Vincent were kids, but they moved from Mankato together and were Vincent's longest relationship to date. Julie eventually missed home and Vincent fell in love with his career and they drifted apart; when Vincent learned she was secretly plotting to move home, they came to a cataclysmic conclusion when Vincent kicked her out.

When Julie did not soon follow her pattern of reaching back out to him to reconcile – in fact, she did quite the opposite – Vincent decided he absolutely had to have her back because he couldn't have her. The inability to obtain what he wanted no matter what he did had done a number on him and he went without committing to another woman until Abby got pregnant 4 years later.

Relationships left far too much out of Vincent's control – something he did a poor job of handling in his personal life.

When *The Selling Game* was released, Vincent had a book signing at Cullen's Bar in Greenfield. True to her word, Julie made an appearance. She had grown up quite nicely – stunningly beautiful, physically fit and her smile had the same effect on Vincent as it had years ago when they first met at Cooke's Grocery Store in Mankato in 2000.

The encounter went well; Vincent introduced Julie to the others in attendance who were mostly old friends and co-workers, and then ignored them as much as possible so he could be around her. Uncharacteristically nervous Vincent decided to ask if she wanted to get together sometime for coffee or dinner and she quickly accepted with a smile.

However, two subsequent dinners revealed no chemistry. It did, however, give them closure as lovers, allowed them to part as friends and Julie went on to meet her future husband in the months to come.

Great for her. Nothing but another closed door for Vincent.

Things fizzled with Casey when she wanted a commitment. Things fizzled with Emily because she wanted commitment. And – here came Abby again – whom Vincent had sworn off multiple times but still found himself wondering *what if* about. Until they were ruled out and down for the count, they were still potentially in play – no matter what common sense or the odds told them.

Abby and Vincent were like a rubber band; with enough time apart, they were relaxed and able to fall into the old act. After spending some time together, they would grow more strained and stressed before snapping completely and requiring distance yet again. They didn't work together but they hated when the other was with someone else, did not enjoy fighting and bickering and wanted peace.

Abby's primary beef with Vincent was that he would not let go of the past. Vincent's contention was that history kept repeating itself and he wanted Abby to live up to her potential of being the person she could be. She was Elizabeth's mother and time with her meant more time with Elizabeth. They also had an undeniable chemistry, even if they could not figure out how to keep it from becoming a catastrophic volcanic eruption.

With Vincent throwing himself into his work and Abby not wanting to be alone after another tiff with Chris Hurst, these two walking calamities re-entered each other's lives. They both knew they did not want animosity to exist between one another; they just had yet to find a delicate balance between one extreme end of the spectrum and the other.

The same problems existed – Vincent felt unappreciated despite everything he did for Abby and Elizabeth to support them emotionally and financially. He had dropped everything when his world came to a halt with the news of Abby's pregnancy and had gone above and beyond since Day 1 to deliver everything he could – far more than any other man would have done in the situation. Sure, he had made mistakes, but he always did what he felt he had to do. He felt disrespected frequently – like his needs didn't matter. Abby felt unloved and that Vincent did not trust her, and she had a point – Vincent would not allow her back into his heart under any circumstance. His head wouldn't allow such a breach of common sense.

And it kept coming back to this fact: while Vincent longed for a family and wanted a true love happy ending, Elizabeth Scott was all he allowed himself to need. She was true, unconditional love to him. She was teaching him patience and how to love someone on another playing field and the epitome of how bringing someone else joy warmed his heart.

If a cosmic relationship would come along – great. If he and Abby could figure this thing out once and for all – great. But, if not, he was going to have to survive solely off his love for Elizabeth Scott, his career and his writing.

The working part continued down an odd trajectory; Jordan Wallace continued to roll out one harebrained scheme after another in an attempt to save money so he could keep spending it in the manner with which he had become accustomed. All the while, the morale and the paychecks and the potential of the business suffered.

First, it was an idea called Outreach 200. This idea morphed considerably from its initial conceptual stage, but the gist was this: every employee in every store within Brink's business would reach out to 200 people within their circle – through social media, phone calls, texts, etc. – and invite them all to an event that would be hosted at the store where Wallace would authorize $50 of appetizers and sales were expected to occur. (Another example of shoestring budget; $50 of appetizers for a handful of store employees and 200 guests would not go very far.)

As with most Jordan Wallace schemes, in theory, parts of the idea were not terrible; it would utilize the networks of those employed in the stores, would potentially close some additional business between all of their product offerings and could make some money.

However, as most employees explained, they had already reached out to these people dozens of times, made it clear they offered Cellular Horizons products and services, and the chances of them just showing up to an event with a miniscule finger foods budget to have cell phones hocked to them when they were all already in contracts did not really appeal to the masses.

Wallace reached out to Vincent and introduced another plan to him that Aaron Hartley had already fully endorsed in Dallas: the full utilization of 1099 contractors to supplant sales representatives in the stores.

Bringing 1099 independent contractors on board to push wireless was actually utilized by some other dealers. However, those dealers had infrastructure, they fully trained their people for 8 weeks and they had fluid payroll process. Betty Bendis – the payroll administrator, secretary, HR and Legal and Labor department all wrapped into one here at Brink – produced at least a 30% error rate on payroll every two weeks, which did little to boost company faith and morale. These factors combined, and this idea did not impress Vincent from the start.

The reason Aaron Hartley fully accepted the plan for his Texas region was because the decline of his market was so rapid he could barely afford to pay the people he had on staff. After the initial success in Wisconsin for Brink Wireless and Brink Management Company, Moriarty sent Doug Wilson in to close Jordan Wallace's tremendous ego on venturing into Texas – where, in reality, no dealer with fewer than 100 stores had ever been successful. Wallace was easily coaxed, opened 7 stores all in one shot, and they were horrendous as a unit. Only a couple of stores showed some traction; one store was quite profitable, but many of the rest ran much debt and just kept going in the red.

At this point, the budget did not allow for payroll for staff, and Hartley was forced to reduce all expenditures dramatically. 1099 enabled him to bring on individuals without overhead, pay them on performance and "hire" as many people as he wanted. Furthermore, Hartley wanted to change over every current employee to 1099.

This backfired immediately in the way of employee morale and belief in Brink's sustainability, despite Hartley's attempts to spin it as a win. There was a break-even point, where if a sales representative generated a personal total of $5,000 in gross profit in a given month, they made more on the 1099 program, but a scant few in this market were even reaching that number. And new 1099's being hired, getting minimal training (and ineffective training from ineffective managers, at that) were certainly not going to cut the mustard.

Vincent vehemently refused to turn his entire existing team into 1099 contractors. It was not going to happen. At the end of the day, Vincent's role was to serve and protect his people – and this was not in their best interests.

But it did not end there; Wallace and Hartley were forming Outreach 200 around the 1099 project, and the 1099 contractors could not graduate training until they held an Outreach 200. Wallace and Hartley made some changes to what the original incarnation of Outreach 200 was intended to be and the new version was just handing over 200 leads to store leadership upon arrival in the store, calling them and closing them, and – based on their success of their own leads – their success or lack thereof in training was determined. They would be given subsequent necessary training if – and only if – they could generate revenue from their own leads.

In essence, everyone with a pulse was "brought on" as a potential 1099 contractor, their leads were taken and they fizzled quickly out of the business. Anyone desperate enough to take such a position likely did not have much of a network to work with to begin with, and this looked like it would be a dagger to the heart of any potential success Brink as a whole could have – especially if it was forced down their throats.

Vincent continued to lead Minnesota to consistent across-the-board successes; Wisconsin continued to post more revenue because they had three times the penetration of the market, but Vincent showed year-over-year gains in every store every month and big secondary metric productivity. The distinction of market with the largest year over year growth was Minnesota, far and away.

Forcing his employees to forgo their base salary was certainly not the answer in taking his business to the next level; lead generation marketing, big marketing events getting the team out into the community and cold calling to new potential business and consumer customers was.

Sensing a need to come to consensus on several items morphing in the company, Wallace flew Aaron Hartley, Lee Christian and Vincent to Wisconsin for a week. The intention was to have all-day sessions at the corporate office (the back room of the first store in Madison, Wisconsin) to agree upon how to move forward on 1099 recruitment, training, marketing and commission.

It doubled as a wine-and-dine event, where Jordan and Lyle would end each day by taking the assemblage to a fancy restaurant, to Jordan's home for an exquisite meal or they would hit up Lyle's before a night on the town. The highlight: Vincent played shuffleboard for the first time and won $1,000 off Lyle.

He foolishly turned right around and lost it.

During the meetings, all of them sat down and got to share thoughts on their own job descriptions and responsibilities as they restructured the entire company. Vincent, Lee and Aaron all lobbied considerably for pay raises as they found a variety of money-saving exercises that would reduce expenses by $750,000 per year. The result: the three of them got honorary title enhancements with basically less pay as they were going to all share a part in managing all open markets… but Wallace kept them so boozed and well fed throughout the trip that they barely realized their pay cuts and misfortune until they sobered up on the plane ride home.

Vincent had certainly witnessed the man behind the curtain.

Returning to their respective homes, each of them (now carrying a generic, bogus, meaningless "Regional Vice President" title) had one charge: hire as many 1099's as possible, institute Outreach 200 widespread and cut costs. In fact, they and store managers would be given a small bonus if they were able to convert their entire staff to 1099.

Despite all of the cost-cutting, they came away "sharing" the revenue for the entire company on the same compensation plan, meaning Vincent – who was making the most money currently – took a pay cut. Lee Christian took a pay cut and, while Hartley made a little more on paper, Jordan Wallace was no longer going to pay on the company-provided $3,000-per month apartment that Wallace put Hartley up in when he coaxed him to Dallas from his home of Minneapolis. This meant Aaron and his girlfriend would have to move out or pony up.

The new "Regional VP's" saved him $750,000 per year on paper with their cuts and re-allocations, but walked away making less money. And it was clear that Jordan Wallace had no idea what they did or dealt with in a given day, week or month. His input was miniscule during the process of mapping out how they would go forward managing the company; it was disheartening for Vincent, Lee and Aaron to see that and to walk away feeling unappreciated, less compensated and still uncertain of where they were going.

Another part of the new program were company-wide daily rally calls for all managers each morning, training calls for select groups across the company one afternoon per week, and occasional all-employee calls – all led by Vincent Scott.

From Vincent's standpoint, he was buying in again thanks to his larger presence and stake in the company and his knowledge that if anyone could make a significant impact across the enterprise and increase company revenue (and commissions for the new Regional VP's), Vincent could. Sure, he would be making the same as his two peers but he once again reminded himself that this visible position would get him where he wanted to be in the Cellular Horizons and Moriarty hierarchy.

But the very first of these all-team calls was truly indicative of the typical spirit of these things.

Vincent logged in to spearhead the call and his roll call set the call off on the wrong foot: of over 100 employees in the business, there were roughly 20 folks who dialed in.

Lee Christian, who touted himself as the Chief Operating Officer of the company, was MIA – apparently on a call regarding Wally's Weenies. *Where the hell am I?* thought Vincent.

Aaron Hartley, who touted himself as the Vice President of Sales, and a sales guru, had little to say outside of, "I agree with Vincent 100%." It became a frequent joke of the Brink employees that this was the extent of Hartley's contribution – agreeing with Vincent Scott.

Yet Vincent still remained undeterred – he plowed through these calls, gave motivational speeches that fell on likely deaf ears and remained the only beacon of hope for Brink Management Company while he was losing hope for himself here waiting for the life raft. It was clear to him and anyone else who cared about this business that Vincent was going to have to carry this thing on his back from here on out if there was any chance at success or even survival. And even those things were in serious doubt.

The phantom Jordan Wallace was actually on this call, but said little and was not a participant in many of these calls going forward. Lee Christian – when present – said little to nothing. He might give an IT update here or there. Aaron Hartley agreed 100%, and Vincent pried best practices out of the other contributors as best he could. It was becoming the Vincent Scott show…just on a small stage. He was Elvis or John Lennon playing to a small, hole-in-the-wall nightclub.

And the real circus began.

Vincent would bring the results and sales goals to life through the numbers, he led conference calls, the company saw major lift in all selling metrics, and the disparities between Vincent and his "peers" truly surfaced. Hartley's managers started calling Vincent for help now that they knew there was this amazing resource out there.

Jordan Wallace – sniffing opportunity – started asking Vincent to visit Dallas regularly, so Vincent would pencil in trips when he did not have Elizabeth. What he found there was appalling: store employees had no knowledge of things they should have known for months, programs that were supposed to be instituted long ago were not and Hartley was seldom ever seen in the stores. He was always "working from home" and hard to get ahold of.

Vincent just took it all in stride and a day at a time. He kept up the daily calls, he led product-specific calls for training purposes on the individual metrics, he visited Dallas and boosted their morale despite constant payroll issues and inventory issues, and continued to helm his own market despite lack of traction on the 1099 contractors he was bringing on board.

Fortunately for Vincent, close friend and former co-worker, sales enthusiast and fellow verbiage scripter Jeff Mason had moved to Dallas with his family earlier in the year. Vincent used these Dallas trips to survey the Brink business thereby day but spent evenings with Jeff reminiscing about old times in the call center, laughing over sales verbiage, watching the movie *Cocktail* and drinking beer. It was a welcome escape from the debacles of Vincent's business and personal life.

In the face of the odd changes to their business, Vincent followed orders, but he did it on his terms. He hired 65 of the new 1099 contractors in 3 days for the 5 Brink-owned Minnesota stores. He never did anything on a small scale; it was all audacious and exaggerated and then he would talk about how easy it was to all the non-believers on the conference calls. What he was going to do after hiring them was irrelevant; they'd bring them on for training and see if these folks had any leads and they'd fly by the seats of their pants.

He tried to get his teams doing Outreach 200. He showed them how to cold call, drove around town to deliver phones and kept morale up as high as he could.

Saul, Terry and Vincent found themselves venting to one another daily; it was a support system built on "what we can do" and "what is the next game plan?" and "where is this business headed?"

One day, Wallace would call and say his existing investors were going to pump in more money to keep Brink going as is.

Then it was a new face from Texas named Alan Starr who was going to buy the Texas and Minnesota stores.

Then he was just going to buy Minnesota, but wanted some of Wisconsin. Then he wanted just Texas.

Then it was Moriarty who was going to buy out the stores. It was constantly in flux, the story changed on a daily basis as the weeks and months continued and Vincent did his best to shield the team from the uncertainty surrounding their entire organization.

And, as time wore on, the situation worsened; the Texas stores reached $500,000 in debt to Moriarty on the inventory purchasing orders that Brink was running through them – and Moriarty cut off their inventory ordering.

Wallace started using Minnesota credit and Wisconsin credit to buy phones for Texas, so Moriarty cut off that credit, too.

This meant that despite the explosive gains of Vincent's market, he could no longer order phones for his team. And, even if he could, the fact Vincent, Lee and Aaron were sharing results meant they were all feeling the pain that should have been reserved for Texas.

Wallace vowed to order product from another vendor, and it turned out they were getting refurbished devices that Wallace wanted them to pass off as new.

The lead generation platform was sputtering, as reps dropped the ball on calling and closing the leads, the support the host company promised faltered as they failed to deliver on most of their promises, and many stores in Texas and Wisconsin just ignored the initiatives that Vincent rolled out to improve them. Vincent did not have enough hours in the day to enforce every initiative in every store with little support from the Wisconsin and Texas leadership; thus he just kept going through the motions of daily calls, sending out communications to the company and whatever stuck stuck.

The Doug and Susie Wilson two-headed monster teamed up against Vincent on the 1099 topic, freaking out that this was not the way to do business. When Vincent wholeheartedly agreed but informed the two that he was going to find the perfect blend of following orders and running the business the way he saw fit, Doug Wilson called Jordan Wallace and told him outright that Vincent disagreed with Wallace's vision for the business. This led to a terse call from Wallace and Vincent had to spin his way out of the mess tattle-tale two-faced Doug created.

It was clear: Doug Wilson could not be trusted, and was only after his own interests and politics.

The next hit was when Volition Wireless – the largest Cellular Horizons dealer in the country and second to Moriarty in the Midwest – expressed interest in bringing Vincent and Saul Portman on board in larger capacities (certainly financially) than what they were manning at Brink. Susie Wilson caught wind of it and the conversation was immediately squelched. The top players in her district leaving certainly would not benefit her!

It was clear: Susie Wilson could not be trusted, and was only after her own interests and politics.

Wallace's stories kept changing about what was happening with the company, while he used Vincent to the fullest without financial compensation. The carrot kept being dangled, as Vincent would "become the President of Brink" in the new regime – per Wallace – but there were no actual signs this would be true.

Alan Starr phased in and out of the picture and was supposed to swoop in come November to save them all and bail out Wallace's finances…

Wallace kept cheating on his wife and going on trips with either her or Lyle… payroll was messed up every time it was run… inventory was lacking… and Vincent Scott realized this was not where he was going to be long-term. He just had to hold on to see what was going to be on the other side of the imminent inferno.

And the calls started coming to Vincent: the employees wanted to mutiny Jordan Wallace and go to his investors and to Moriarty and to Cellular Horizons to unseat him and have Vincent take his place.

They wanted Vincent to go to Moriarty and try to get him to start his own management company.

It was déjà vu all over again for Vincent Scott.

## "The Surviving Game" by Vincent Scott
## Remaining Motivated When Undervalued

People are the world's greatest resource - in day-to-day life, in relationships and in business. Unfortunately, however, if you have not already, you will encounter times when they are not cherished as the precious jewels they are in the work setting.

Maintaining motivation in the face of adversity, constant changes and corporate politics is difficult enough as it is, but when we are undervalued as employees, this becomes especially challenging. The warning signs are there: you bring your "A" game to every event, you under-promise and over-deliver and you shine above the rest... but those in the position to upgrade your position and pay do not seem to care. They either shower their attention elsewhere or they are otherwise aloof.

They may give you more responsibilities without additional pay or title. They may tell you that you are appreciated or give you paper certificates but let the months and years go by without ever considering you for promotion. They may string you along – taking what you contribute without giving you anything but the bare minimum in return.

Research shows that people do not seek out or stay at employers for money. The desire for financial gain is a component of why we work, but when it comes to career satisfaction we often just want to feel appreciated. We want to know that our contributions matter. Many of us want to get into a position where our skills can benefit the most people possible.

Unfortunately, there are far too many employers who are inept when it comes to cultivating, investing in and properly rewarding their greatest resource.

Fret not; there are ways to combat this.

First off, realize that nothing lasts forever. Poor leaders have a way of eventually being ushered out of the business one way or another. While this can take time, and will certainly not occur on your timetable, things change, and the trick is to be at the top of the list of prospects when they are looking for someone to replace shifting upper management. If someone else passes you during this time, you will only kick yourself later.

You are in control of your effort and your actions during times like this. Put your head down, escape into things you enjoy during your free time and make sure you do nothing to jeopardize your standing as an employee and leader.

Second, are you worried about the wrong people valuing you? Surely, someone values your work and contributions; it just might not be the ones you think you want it to be. Do you have a significant other and a family for whom you are bringing home the bacon? They value you. Do you have a team of subordinates or peers to whom you bring a great deal of support and knowledge and guidance and contribution? They value you. Do you have peers with whom you have a good working relationship, share ideas and support throughout your stay there? They value you.

So, you see, while those who control your paycheck have you down because they do not seem to know you exist, your home team does and you are making a difference for them. Don't let them down.

We often make our worst decisions out of emotion and fear; anything we do to take for granted the people who appreciate us and matter to catch the attention of those who do not will merely lead to later regret.

Constantly review your priorities to ensure the ones you are choosing and the ones getting bumped are the right ones on both counts. What are you working toward? What is your end goal? The present - while important - is a relatively brief moment in time and provided you are still able to work toward your ultimate goals in some way, it can serve to keep you motivated during these difficult times. Find an outlet. Find release. These things will help keep you whole.

Again, nothing lasts forever and all you can do is control what you can control; you can control your contribution and seeking solace in other outlets, but ultimately, these determining factors may lead you to diagnose a lingering dead end situation as one you want to move on from. You can do your best, but in the end you must make the decision - as the Clash famously pronounced - "Should I stay or should I go?" You may change your circumstances by taking your talents elsewhere. I would imagine this would be your employer's loss, but it just might land you closer to your destiny.

Ultimately, staying or going is your call. The grass will appear greener elsewhere, but – specifically in this day and age – you do not want to appear to be a job-hopper who leaves at the first sign of challenge. Paying your dues and seeing things through will determine your path; to grow as an employee and person you will eventually have to navigate through choppy waters.

Work hard for yourself and the people who do appreciate you and do what you can to block out the rest as you endure and press on.

Motivation comes from within. Even when we talk of someone motivating someone else, we are really simply referring to the internal spark someone manages to trigger through an action or inspirational word or deed. The lack of respect we are getting at work or in a relationship is causing us to feel defeated or worthless. This is why we consider if they are worth feeling this way over, we reassess our priorities, and we make a finite, firm decision on how to move forward based on everyone impacted by our decision.

Regardless of your decision, you will face new, unique challenges, but to remain motivated while undervalued it is imperative you find the value for yourself and are motivated by the ones who value you.

## On the Brink

A daily morning dose of 24 ounces of coffee and a 44-ounce Diet Coke works wonders for any human; Vincent Scott – already an energetic and self-starting individual can seemingly save the world single-handedly on the stuff – but every individual has limits. Even Vincent.

The good news was that his father was back on the basketball courts of hometown Mankato, popping 3-point shots over men half his seasoned age of 66.

The bad news, however, was coming in droves.

He was once again conflicted over Abby Winters, back in her life and bedroom, all so he could wonder how much he could try to forget and forgive and he could see the love of his life – Elizabeth – every day.

He had seen the political backstabbing by Doug Wilson of Moriarty and Susie Wilson of Cellular Horizons, all while being coyly used and abused by Jordan Wallace – absentee owner who was allowing inventory not to be processed and payroll not to be corrected at his employees' and customers' expense. These were the two biggest cardinal sins of commerce, and he was committing them daily. The only thing Wallace did right was tell the Wilsons and Vincent that Vincent was the only person he refused to lose in the debacle nearly upon them.

Vincent reached out over Doug's and Susie's heads to their bosses – Kent Smyth and Kurt Stillwater respectively – in attempts to pitch Scott Enterprises, LLC – a management company that would run with Vincent, Saul, Terry and the likely multitudes that would contribute, but pleas to Stillwater went completely ignored and Smyth politely explained that lack of success in pitching other management companies (Brink) led Moriarty to decide never to pitch them again. In fact, they were starting their own management company… Interesting.

What Vincent branded "1099-a-palooza" was a complete joke, but it was what he was told to do and he was going to do it better than anybody else. He had 75 of them hired within the first week; 10-15 flaked even before the initiation, others walked out mid-initiation when they realized the cattle call they were a part of and most were gone within the first two weeks. Several, however, did stay - for better and for worse considering their lots in this life.

Vincent was convinced that the only way to make this whole project work was to perfect the in-store process and then go outside the doors: door-to-door, business-to-business, lead generation marketing, events, etc. He was going to have to do it with a few of the old faithful, an undersized budget and a hiring frenzy of

1099 contractor flakes. The odds were against them and the situation grim; it was right up his alley.

Among the notables in this new batch of misfits: Mitch McConnell, the alcoholic B2B "manager" as he called himself who had 5 DWI's to his name, no driver's license, got rides from his sister to work and spent the first half hour of every shift in the bathroom trying to get last night's binge drinking out of his system.

There was Andrea Kessler, "B2B specialist" who moved from Indianapolis to take this job; on the surface, she seemed polished and professional, but it turned out she had quite a personal and criminal past and an unhealthy affinity for the male superiors in the Minneapolis market – like Terry, Saul and Vincent.

There was the gorgeous Camille Bright – who moonlighted at Hooters and charmed Vincent from the start and he believed she would be a rock star– who turned out to be all beauty and no work ethic.

What was impressive, however, was there was a core crop of these folks – a handful, in fact – that despite the lack of inventory, dipping morale and zero paychecks stayed on and showed up every day – because they believed in Vincent Scott and his management team and what they were trying to achieve.

He kept up his regimen of regular conference calls and store visits and daily sales reports, despite all of the obstacles being thrown at him every day. Despite not knowing where this was going and his awareness he was the first mate on a sinking ship, he peeled himself off the couch every morning or mid-morning to go through the motions. Sure, where he had started out full of piss and vinegar and visited three stores per day, he was now typically only able to view the disarray of one before turning back for home. But he was doing everything he physically could bring himself to do.

There was a calling tree between Saul Portman, Terry Bunche and Vincent; they took turns calling one another and talking about all of the different scenarios they may face – a potential future where power player Alan Starr would come in and save the day and they would get the prominence they deserved…whether they believed it or not. They were still searching for the blue skies; scrambling from cloud to cloud hoping to find it hiding there.

Vincent spent much of his time in the core Brink stores trying to feed off remaining morale and energy from his core players – Saul, Terry, De-Metre and Darryl – and they lunched together frequently at a deli in Eden Prairie.

Payroll continued to be screwed up, just even more widespread as time marched on. Reps and managers would be inexplicably missing large chunks of their commission checks despite the fact the stores reported the amounts they were due up the chain.

Inventory continued to be haphazard at best. The store personnel would consistently and dutifully place orders for what they needed; what they received was quite the different story. They were fortunate to receive new devices that they were running low on and store managers (and sometimes Vincent) spent considerable time stock rebalancing by driving store to store.

Terry, survivor of the Bruce Rollins era, frequently said, "I've seen all of this before with Bruce" and predicted doomsday for Brink Management Company. The inability to cover their debts or order product or pay their people would capsize the ship.

The conversations between Vincent, Saul and Terry reached fever pitch: Vincent was going to have to go for outside help to save the people. He could not put it off anymore.

Vincent requested a meeting with Doug Wilson at the Bloomington store near his house to brief him on all the woes the staff was facing with Brink. Doug accepted and Terry and Saul joined in so they could tell him firsthand what was happening on the front lines.

Terry, Saul and Vincent educated Doug with a strictly confidential briefing to confide in him their worry that they needed Moriarty to get involved in this impending doom. They gave him full disclosure on all of the warning signs Brink Management Company was showing and the day-to-day constant uncertainty. It was a plea for help to Doug on behalf of all their employees.

Vincent was not sure what outcome would come of it either way; Doug could breach confidence and report back to Jordan causing implosion. Doug could do nothing. Or Doug could get others involved in drastically overhauling this operation – with unknown results for the folks sitting in this back room in Bloomington. Nevertheless, it was the chance they were all willing to take.

Unfortunately, there was no immediate action. Doug committed to "looking into things" and that seemed to be that.

The next few months followed the same patterns: daily questions and concerns and chaos. Store employees quitting with no notice after not receiving paychecks – they'd just walk out. And who could blame them? Vincent back and forth between being with Abby in brief bursts and retreating to the Fortress of Solitude of his apartment at the first sign of trouble. Constant empty promises from Jordan Wallace to "build the business around Vincent" as Vincent continued doing more and more to keep the company afloat while it slowly descended into the chilly, gloomy, unknown waters.

Wallace's new response: he announced a conference call on a whim and committed to working 7 days a week, traveling to the four regions on rotation for the foreseeable future and helping out in every way – putting out fliers, working on the sales floor, cold calling to drum up business, discovering and putting on events, conducting training, etc. He sent an open schedule that he had the three Regional VP's fill out for him that covered every day for the final months of the year, where they wanted to schedule him to fill in.

That commitment lasted three days before Wallace ceased following the schedule and was MIA again.

Vincent's corporate credit card started being declined on a regular basis, as Wallace or Betty Bendis would charge inventory on it since they couldn't anywhere else. This meant he was picking up his own tabs on gas and recognition rewards to keep his team going, or being forced to pay out of pocket for customer appreciation events at stores. Furthermore, there was never any warning to when the card was at its limit or indication if and when it would become active again. He'd simply be in the process of making a gas purchase or gift card expenditure or lunch expense for him or his team only to find out this time it was solely on him.

But Vincent was hell-bent on going out in a blaze of glory, no matter what was going to happen. He kept bringing in 1099's, he headlined a breast cancer awareness karaoke event (stealing the show with his renditions of Frankie Valli's "Can't Take My Eyes off of You" and Marvin Gaye's "Let's Get It On") and parading around outside the downtown Minneapolis store (and his old employer's fortress) with a megaphone trying to stir up customers. His message: "Are you stuck in a wireless contract with an inferior carrier? I'll buy you out. Tell 'em Vincent sent you."

Needless to say, word of his antics made their way throughout that 45-story building of former friends and foes in no time, and his phone erupted with those cheering him on or thinking he was crazy, or both.

Vincent really started to feel the Brink world closing in on him – but he was thrashing back as best he could. He would joke that it didn't matter if they closed down every store in his jurisdiction: they'd have to box him into a corner in his last remaining store and take the keys away from him.

He would map out his day to hit 3 or 4 stores, but midway through the first store visit or second, his corporate credit card was declined for the fifteenth time or 1099's flaked or paychecks were not correct or inventory was not shipped at all or the company housing their lead generation program would reveal yet another thing they originally promised that they could not deliver upon.

For the first time in his career, Vincent would deter from his daily plan: he would forgo the third and fourth stores and either go home or pick up Elizabeth on his days with her and just retreat from this madness and lunacy. He would shut off his phone and accept defeat for that day.

He found himself unable to physically continue on those days. And, with his history of perseverance, this experience of having limits frightened him.

The following day, he would do everything he could to spring back up and go full throttle. However, far too often, his tie would be loosened by 11 AM and he would be done for the day in early afternoon – accepting the inevitable defeat of yet another day on the brink.

It was sobering for him to acknowledge this. Why was this happening to him? He was Vincent Scott – the unstoppable force who had been through hell and back. Unfortunately, hell had chipped away at his ability to once again completely sacrifice his body and mind for another undeserving financial exploit.

He was killing himself for a doomed small business with no support and no structure and no hope and low pay, no benefits and no glory. The greatest frustration and worst penance was that he knew he was destined for greatness but had no clear path to it. Quite the contrary; the path was shielded by haze and cluttered with pitfalls. And his motivation was now rapidly decaying; something he had never experienced before.

Susie and Doug Wilson – now under fire from their bosses for declining results thanks to Vincent's stores not having inventory, paychecks and morale – started throwing Vincent and his team under the bus. They would armchair quarterback which terminations he needed to make, tell him his managers like Saul or Terry were not all they were cracked up to be and hit him with all of these store improvements they recommended which required money that did not exist. Every chance they got, they'd come up with something Vincent or his team wasn't doing that they had recommended so they could take the heat off themselves and put it all elsewhere.

Of course his staff wasn't perfect; Vincent's own efforts weren't anymore. But how could they be at 100% when they were being mistreated, mispaid and misled?

Despite all of this, the results year-over-year were still somehow inexplicably improving, despite all of the obstacles in their way. But once Hermantown stopped selling 100 new lines per month and they had their slow period of the year begin, the averages Doug and Susie were accustomed to slipped dramatically. Rather than speak from experience from their nonexistent visits to the stores, they started looking for people to blame. Vincent and his defiant defense of his team was an easy target, and he became their fall guy.

Kurt Stillwater, Steve Flowers and Kent Smyth had no idea Vincent's stores were being hit so hard by lack of inventory, paychecks and morale; all they heard was that Vincent was foolishly hiring 1099's (as he was instructed to do), that Vincent was not adopting their recommended changes to the business and that Vincent was keeping around people that were being less productive without holding them accountable. Vincent was praised in the good times and now being blamed for the downturn.

It is difficult to come down on an employee for selling less when they have nothing on hand to sell and wouldn't get paid for it anyway.

Terry Bunche was a fall guy; they would say Terry did not know the systems as well as he should, his team knew he was not well-versed in them and the products which diminished his credibility and needed to be fired. Let's forget that he was the only reason Greenfield held on as long as it did, poured in 80-hour work weeks and was the catalyst for lead generation!

Saul Portman was a fall guy; they would say that if they called the store Saul wasn't there, when he was just running around picking up inventory so he could continue making money. They said his back room operation was a disaster. Let's forget that he had been with Brink since Day 1, opening multiple stores for Brink as they added more, had mentored countless reps and managers in the business and that he was the best salesperson Vincent had!

Sure – everyone had faults in this broken system. The problem was that no one had the incentive to give their all anymore, yet some were still trying. You cannot master everything; you gravitate toward what you are great at, and these folks were in their attempt to hold this thing together as long as humanly possible.

The job was providing drastic highs and lows at both ends of the spectrum – now on a daily basis. It was something Vincent had never encountered – feeling a brief bit of success or joy about lifting the company's revenue with his contributions across 4 states only to realize he would be paid less running the entire company than he made running Minnesota.

He contributed more quality and quantity than anyone in the organization, but the battle was uphill and it was losing. Managers and reps still repeatedly failed to log into conference calls or deliver on much of anything he requested, the state of the stores was declining rapidly on every level from cleanliness to operations to inventory to sales, and what stung most was he had been wrongfully fired from a job where he made lots more money and didn't even have to try this hard.

Where was the justice in this world?

His old department was trending for a finish of $26 million in annual billable advertising revenue dollars in 2011, compared to $51 million in Vincent's final year. Vincent's multi-million dollar worth was now evident on paper, yet he was tragically was peddling cell phones for a pathetic excuse of a dealer that was about to hit the wall.

Vincent had done nothing but suffer – for years – across failed relationships, failed business ventures and fighting for everything he held dear.

A letter from his government case worker Jon Jefferson revealed that they were – 20 months after his complaint – finally doing some semblance of their job and reviewing his case. However, they felt that despite the fact they had not talked to his witnesses or responded to his e-mails or phone calls and were sitting on hundreds of pages of documentation Vincent provided, there was not sufficient evidence to press forward with a case. In other words, because they had no angle – race, sex, religion – on his own behalf that made this easily winnable, they had no desire to pick up the tab for a case there was any chance they'd lose.

Abby continued pursuit of Vincent and vented her frustration that he was completely closed off to her emotionally; Vincent came to the realization that he had blocked out most of the past several years of his life and there were happy times they once had that he couldn't even remember.

Vincent was teetering on the brink of his own very existence right now; his Dad's death was always just a phone call away, the next catastrophic explosion in his life just an Abby Winters relapse away, and his career – once headed for a clear trajectory of greatness – was a joke. He felt like a joke.

But – no matter what – he still had some fight. It burned down deep inside and flared up when he manned near-empty conference calls with passionate words and speeches about greatness and shining through adversity. It flared up when he hit LinkedIn with a vengeance trying to drum up new contacts with whom to latch on to for his next career endeavor – whatever it may be.

## Vincent Does Dallas

With the Texas stores severely hemorrhaging money and never having turned a profit in their existence, Jordan Wallace enlisted Vincent Scott to make another trek to Dallas to investigate. Vincent's mission was to breathe some life into them per usual and potentially save Brink's Texas investment. He was there to report back to Wallace a specific, targeted plan to either save or scrap the Texas stores.

The visit was illuminating – to say the least – for many reasons. Hartley picked Vincent up from Dallas Love Field and took him back to the apartment. Neither was completely sure of the other; Hartley knew Wallace was no fan of his and that Vincent was seemingly his golden boy. Vincent knew only of Hartley what Wallace said about him and of their interactions in person and on conference calls. Vincent also knew what he himself was dealing with in Minnesota and the company as a whole; if Vincent could squeeze results out of the turnip of Minnesota against all odds, why could Hartley not show any traction?

Over meals and store visits together and apart, Vincent pieced together the backstory of Brink's Texas presence. He met Jared Cox – the equivalent of Doug Wilson for Moriarty, in title only, as Jared was actually invested in the business and support role he carried. He heard all about how Moriarty had pumped up Wallace's already healthy ego about opening new stores here for Cellular Horizons. Wallace foolishly bit, opening up 7 stores with no idea what he was getting himself into.

But most interesting to Vincent were the complaints from the workers: they never saw Aaron Hartley. There were basic components of the business – like the insurance options the stores were supposed to be carrying – that had not even been introduced to them. Stores were short-staffed, they were clueless on their compensation program and they had gotten no support from Hartley and empty promises from Wallace.

Case in point: Jordan Wallace had promised store manager Seth Kerr a marketing and events role that turned into a completely non-glamorous store manager role over one of the least profitable stores in town. There was no marketing and were no events to speak of. This was how Wallace wooed Seth away from a better job he had left to come to this disaster. More blue skies: bringing in overqualified people, selling them on an unrealistic pipe dream like it was right around the corner. Wallace had landed these marlins but they were waking up to the fact they'd need other waters to find their dinner.

The commission payout issues that plagued Vincent's stores hindered these stores as well, but Vincent's bravado and proven track record of success was a breath of fresh air to these people. However – could this man, no matter how great he sounded, save them from their horrible predicament?

On visits Vincent made to stores with Hartley, all he heard about was how Jordan Wallace had let them all down. After a handful of store visits, meeting clueless and/or jaded employees and realizing just how disastrous this market was – because of both Wallace and Hartley – Vincent had seen enough. It was the last full day Vincent was in Dallas.

"I can't take anymore," Vincent uttered, upon getting into Hartley's 2006 Camry.

"It's depressing, isn't it?" Hartley asked. "Yeah, I admit, I stopped giving 100% a long time ago."

This was evident.

"You know, I once believed in hard work, in reward and in a higher purpose in all of this. I know that for whatever reason, I'm here for a reason. But I have no idea what it is. This place is the pits," Vincent continued. "I hate not having all the answers."

"I know, man. My Dad owns his own business and was a self-made man. He's so successful and I've always lived in that shadow. I read all of these Steve Jobs books and I have always wanted to get to that point – where I'm really making a difference somewhere," Hartley responded. "I just feel so lost."

Hartley wasn't a bad guy; his heart was in the right place but he was not capable of putting forth the effort to get where he wanted to be. Vincent's issue was that he had never done anything but give the effort, fight the fights to take care of his people and do what he thought was right, but he kept getting beaten down by bosses or life as punishment for doing things his way.

These two men with completely different pasts, work ethics and paths were in the same role at this moment in time – and neither knew what to do next. Both held out hope for some outside force to come along and save the day, but as each day wore on that vision became less and less tangible.

"Well, we've got to come up with something," Vincent mused. "I can't take anymore of this shit."

"Let's go back to the apartment and get something to eat," Hartley – a slave to the pleasures of overindulgence – offered.

"That sounds good," a distracted Vincent responded.

His wheels were in motion. He was determined to crack this case.

Wisconsin worked because it had such a high penetration for Cellular Horizons – that was a given. Minnesota was now working because of Vincent Scott's leadership and the team he had assembled. What if…?

Hartley and Vincent had ordered the shrimp tacos from the seafood shop at the ground level of the apartment complex Hartley lived in and took their seats. Vincent flipped open his padfolio to a blank piece of yellow blue-lined paper and started scribbling in his scratching that typically only he could read.

"Here's what I propose," Vincent began. "We move my managers to Texas."

He looked at Hartley's reaction, which quickly changed from his typical uninspired stare to one of interest.

Vincent continued. "We've got Reggie Sherman, who is strong operationally, De-Metre Jones who can drive sales and Darryl Wilkinson, who is good at both. Your managers are a fucking disaster. We fire or demote all of them except Seth Kerr and have my guys all watch over 2 stores apiece until they can groom their own replacements to manage the store they don't want to keep."

There was silence for a moment as Hartley took it all in, and then he couldn't help but smile.

"Dude, I love it," Hartley responded. "But – what are you going to do for managers?"

"I'll be fine," Vincent responded coolly. "I'll still have Saul and Terry, can promote a couple of people to fill in for the ones I am losing and will make it through. I've built a workable bench roster and I'll be OK. The bottom line is we can't win if any one of us is losing. Moriarty will cut us off at the knees no matter where the debt's coming from."

"Wow, man," Hartley gasped, appreciatively as if he had just received his life raft in the midst of a raging ocean of doom, "I don't know what to say. Thank you. This is out of this world."

"Don't mention it," Vincent responded. "I'm actually excited to see how well it works."

"But there's one last thing – how do we get Wallace to approve it?" Hartley asked.

"Leave that to me," Vincent said dispassionately. "I'm his golden boy, remember?"

The two retreated to quarters shortly thereafter and Hartley watched television with his girlfriend while Vincent phoned Wallace and laid out his plan. Everything is selling, and Vincent sold that this was the only way to right the ship they were all on that was currently heading into rough waters.

"Jordan, Wisconsin is doing fine. They are profitable. Minnesota is good – finally. Texas is an absolute disaster – for a lot of reasons," Vincent pitched. "I know you're no fan of Hartley, and I can tell why. He's lazy and he does literally nothing to support these people down here. It took me all of one store visit to figure it out. But here's your easy fix: I can manage this market here. I want to move three of my managers – Reggie, De-Metre and Darryl – down here, fire or demote everyone here except Seth, and jumpstart this market. It's a no-brainer," Vincent said, strategically, making sure there would be no dissent on the other end, "and it gives me a foothold here with people I trust that can communicate to me what needs to happen."

"What do I do with Hartley?" Wallace responded.

"Personally, I don't care. He has given up," Vincent answered. "But if there is any value in him whatsoever, we'll see it when this plan comes to fruition. He sure as hell won't have any excuses to be unsuccessful – he'll have my managers. And I'd rather have him here than not since I can't be here every day."

"I don't want to hurt your market."

"I understand, and you won't. I will promote Kevin Salmon, Mitch Robinson and Walt Houston and we won't miss a beat."

"Are they ready?"

"We'll make them ready," Vincent answered quickly. Now it was time for the close. "Bottom line, Jordan, if you want to stop bleeding money in Texas, this plan gets you there. I will be fine no matter what team I have on the field. This is a can't-lose scenario."

"And it basically puts you in charge of the Texas market," Wallace chuckled. "You're a very smart guy, Vincent. Probably the smartest person I've ever worked with. I like how you are planting your own people down there. I love the idea. Fax me over the specifics and I'll meet with the investors."

"Consider it done."

Vincent hung up the phone. Victory. Confidence exuding from Vincent from open to close, he was satisfied that this would be another substantial way he could make a splash.

Between pitching this plan that would put Vincent in even more of a position of strength, having Hartley at his mercy and Alan Starr on his way in to this business that lives off Vincent's adrenaline, he was forcing his agenda and his way to the top.

Whatever new incarnation of the business they would head to, whether current investors kept Brink alive, Alan Starr bought the business, Moriarty bought the business or some unforeseen force entered the picture, they wouldn't be able to make heads or tails of what they had without Vincent Scott.

He had gone from rock bottom to an epiphany in sixty seconds.

The following day, Hartley dropped Vincent off at Dallas-Fort Worth Airport for his flight back to Minneapolis, Minnesota. Vincent led the company conference call from the airport, boarded and landed… it felt so good to be home.

As soon as he landed, he drove to the Cellular Horizons corporate office for a leadership training that his managers were already in. He received a hero's welcome.

Each moment of Vincent's life was lived in anticipation of the next – to capitalize, to put a perfunctory exclamation point on it and to put on a production. He walked into the training, exchanged nonverbal acknowledgments of his team, shook hands and bumped fists and then took a seat near the front. But most of his time there was spent scribbling notes that were to turn into his next big speech that would train, titillate and teach.

Everyone knew that now Vincent was here, this ho-hum session would become a training to remember.

The topic was leadership; one that Vincent Scott was very passionate about and familiar with. The seminar was conducted by Cellular Horizons' corporate trainer for the indirect group – Nora Justice – and several familiar faces were in attendance.

From Vincent's squad alone sat De-Metre Jones, Saul Portman, Darryl Wilkinson and Terry Bunche; Vincent was keen on enrolling everyone available in such a worthwhile investment.

Susie Wilson was there. Jerry Smalls – who had recently defected to Volition Wireless because they foolishly gave him a management position over their smallest store – was there, in his typical schmoozing way. Also there was Ben Kennett, whom Vincent had bested at Cellular Horizons Superstar, and there was the occasional pop-in from Kurt Stillwater, whom Vincent still wanted to impress in hopes of parlaying his success in the indirect channel to the corporate side.

Vincent – in control and high on the current upswing – enjoyed himself mightily, from the introductions to peppering his anecdotes throughout the conversation in appropriate times. Near the conclusion, while Stillwater was out of the room unfortunately, each leader was taking turns talking about their leadership experience and the philosophies by which they coach their teams, the Cellular Horizons structure and support and what they were going to do – differently or otherwise – going forward from this training.

The Brink team impressed. Each of them had something intelligent to say about what their core team was working on, circling the philosophies of Vincent Scott and his people/process-first mentality. It was quite refreshing and rewarding for Vincent to see his impact; that these good people were learning from him and were better leaders because of their time together.

Jerry Smalls sputtered, predictably, trying to brag about himself and then saying something overly flattering about Susie to suck up to her. Ben Kennett spent his time on his soapbox, negatively deraiIing the fact that he had already been in this exact training module before.

Vincent was appropriately the last to speak.

"First off, I just want to thank Nora and Susie for putting this whole thing together," Vincent began, always nodding to those in "power" in the room for posterity and points. "We can never have enough refreshers or reminders on why and how leadership is vital to our everyday lives in management," he continued – giving the training relevance and showing why he was worlds beyond what Ben Kennett could ever be.

"Leadership and management are two completely different things. A title gives you management. Passion, enthusiasm, the ability to adapt, the ability to empathize – these are what make great leaders.

"If I may, I have synopsized the principles we discussed today into a 5-bullet point list of how to lead. As for implementation walking out of here, I ask my team to hold me accountable to these principles, and they will be discussed and practiced every day going forward.

"The first step of leadership is building the relationships. You cannot waltz into any scenario and start barking orders, pulling rank and making changes. For any leader to truly lead, he or she must build those relationships – know your people. Show that you care about their place on the team. You cannot cast yourself as above anyone on your team if you want to be a part of it. Certainly, in times of accountability and discipline, you have to own that role, but number one is earning the respect of your team by being one of them, doing their job and showing them how to do it better. Once you have earned the respect of your team by giving them respect, leading by example and showing – not just telling – that you mean what you say, they will follow you anywhere.

"Number two: elimination of obstacles. This is different from being able to wade through the excuses, of which there will be plenty. It's like when you walk into a store for the first time – what do these folks tell you? They don't have enough traffic. 'Marketing sucks.' 'I don't get enough support.' Our goal as leaders here is to identify what's real and what's nonsense. From there, we eliminate the legitimate obstacles to their success. If they need aesthetic improvements around the stores, we take care of that. If they have not been trained on something, we train them. The point is to remove any legitimate barriers to their success so they have no excuses not to be successful anymore – and, through this process, they will realize that you won't listen to and don't care to hear their excuses... and they go away, too. They also see that you're willing to do what it takes to improve the territory. They see that you are working for them.

"Management boils down to two things: people and process. That's it. If you have the right people in place, following the right process, you will be successful. Don't get me wrong – things happen all the time that take you out of that utopia. People get burnt out, they leave, or we make bad hiring decisions – we're all guilty of that at one time or another. Fires pop up and things happen to take us out of our process; take us off our games. But sports stars in slumps don't change their stance, their swing, their stroke; they have to recapture the process that brought them success. Our jobs are no different. We must perfect our in-store process: make sure we are doing everything we can to close business when we see it and leave little to chance. We know customers likely won't come back when they say they're going to think about it, so we overcome objections until we close the business, or we know the specific reason why they didn't buy. We follow up and get a finite answer. When our in-store process is solid – and *only* when – we go outside the doors and drive more people in, because at that point more people need to hear our value story. Then we repeat. That's our *process*. Sure, we will make small tweaks here and there, we will perfect the process, we will add new things as there are new innovations in the business, but our goal as leaders is to get to that point where it's a fine-tuned machine that just needs a little maintenance here and there. *That's* leadership. And the process of how we select and train and groom our people will determine whether or not they reach the potential we saw on interview day.

"Number four: Do not get caught up in the day-to-day minutia. Our primary focus needs to be making the moves that positively impact the most futuristic interactions possible – no matter what that can be. A lot of managers are hesitant to pull their reps off the floor because they short-sightedly see it as losing money. But if you make a positive investment of time in a team member, they go out and actually start implementing what you discussed and it results in more money, wasn't that investment worth it? Just by them sacrificing that hour of maybe clerking out a phone that makes us $200 in profit that the customer probably came in and asked for, next time they'll go out and they will sell the phone, the accessories, the mobile broadband, and the television package – or they'll come close. You've improved *their* process. See, numbers mean nothing. They tell a story, but they don't define you unless you let them. Don't get so caught up in numbers that you forget your job. Again – if you have the right people in place following the right process, you will never have to worry about your numbers. They'll always be there. I've made a career on that statement.

"Finally, always be the ambassador of the business while ensuring your people are taken care of and their voice is heard. It's not about friendship. It's not about being a yes-man or a yes-woman. It's about communication; and sometimes over-communication. Be transparent as a leader; you are human, you will make mistakes, but your people need to see that you legitimately care about their needs and wants. Your company needs to see that you legitimately care about their needs and wants. You will often get caught in the middle and the trick is that sometimes it's an act, sometimes it's a balancing act, but don't let anyone see you bleed. Don't let negative effects affect you to the point where you can no longer lead or where your team sees your doubts or fears or frustrations.

"In closing, I'm honored to be here today. This is a topic that I'm very passionate about and I hope all of you are as well, because we have an important responsibility as we mold salespeople to their potential. We can coach and develop and help them put more food on the table; we can help them find a better life. I don't know that any of us want to be in the exact positions we're in five years from now, and that's the point. What are we doing to grow and develop as leaders ourselves? You can look at this job like we're peddling cell phones and handling customer complaints, or you can realize that each day we have the unique opportunity to learn how to run a business, how to build relationships and how to lead and develop sales teams. There are so many sales and business fundamentals present in every day. Seize them, for you will use them for the rest of your careers. Thank you."

Vincent Scott earned a standing ovation.

It was moments like this – scarce since his termination – that fueled his engine and kept him going. He felt he was making a difference for these managers, even if it was on a smaller scale than he desired at this stage in his career.

Directly from the leadership conference, after exchanging some pleasantries with those in attendance, Vincent was able to leave to pick up Elizabeth and be reunited with his heart. And, in the evening, Abby came over and spent the night. It was the family dynamic he had such a hard time letting go of.

In summary, the day was everything Vincent needed at this stage in the game. It stood for everything he wanted: family, career and potential. But it was always on the brink.

# Closing Time

Jordan Wallace called to reveal that he was working to transition Aaron Hartley out; the two obviously hated each other and spoke ill of one another every chance they got. Wallace disliked Hartley because he was lazy and could not produce results. Hartley disliked Wallace because Wallace was siphoning away the apartment that was part of his compensation; he was also always off on some adventure wine-tasting or skiing with his wife or a one night stand while Hartley's reps and managers were not getting paid. Both had ample reason for their disdain.

That said, Wallace now stated it was "99% done" that Alan Starr would take over and he promised that Hartley would be phased out and Vincent would report directly to Starr in the new alignment.

Starr loved Vincent's proposal to share his Minnesota management wealth with the Texas stores and Vincent's duties would be to helm both markets. Starr was looking to purchase Minnesota and Texas outright; he wanted a stake in Wisconsin and Missouri but that was not finalized yet. Vincent would be able to continue overseeing and managing lead generation for the entire group of Brink stores. Jordan Wallace would stay on as a partner and be able to oversee his other operations; namely Wally's Weenies and a new venture he wanted to pursue that would be saloon restaurants in North Carolina. He could be Berkshire Hathaway – in his words.

Thursday, October 20 saw some outstanding items come to a head. After completely ignoring his case and the witnesses, Jon Jefferson was dismissing Vincent's claim and issuing him a right to sue letter leaving him on his own to battle the complaint out in the lengthy court process. 21 months later – and no end in sight.

And yet the trials and tribulations and tasks did not stop. Vincent's phone was constantly erupting, be it from current jaded employees, former jaded employees wanting his lawsuit to eradicate the corruption, or from Jordan Wallace, laying out this blue sky future. His spin on this day was that Hartley would be offered a management job or removed, Alan Starr was buying out Paul Gemini and the other investors effective November 1 – or January 1 at the latest – while Lee Christian would be out or offered a manager job, Wallace would run Wisconsin himself to save on overhead, Vincent would run Minnesota and help Alan in Texas (as he was going to be a hands-on owner), and Jordan would work hand-in-hand with Vincent to package their business model and management contract and sell it to every Cellular Horizons store in the United States. They'd be millionaires.

Every time Wallace spoke, Vincent could practically hear Frank Sinatra belting out the classic "Blue Skies."

Wallace was actually in Dallas, flying back that night, and Vincent was flying to Dallas the following morning after dropping off Elizabeth to room with Hartley for a few days and further help the struggling market. It was discovered later that day that while Aaron Hartley was on vacation in Cancun with his girlfriend and Wallace was staying there, he wined, dined and bedded one of Hartley's store managers – Maria Marcos – and Hartley's cat of 2 years (who was even a point of contention in his divorce a year prior) fell 25 stories to its death when Wallace left the windows in the apartment open. Wallace offered to buy Hartley a new cat, but this was yet another dagger in their damaged relationship.

Buyout of Brink Management Company could not come soon enough, specifically for the folks who could really see the damage that was being done on a daily basis. The conversations between Terry, Saul and Vincent over lunch reached fever pitch: these guys were ready to bail on this business to do just about anything, and something drastic had to change now. Alan Starr couldn't come on soon enough.

Terry was getting no additional or real money to run the marketing for the business, Saul was overseeing multiple stores and seeing no advancement, and they continued to be haunted by payroll and inventory problems galore. It happened so often, with such deep impact and lasting scars that the once humorous punchlines about the company's shortcomings were no longer funny. They were on a ship being held together by super glue and duct tape, leaking at every seam.

Employee unrest was rampant, and it was all Vincent could do to drag himself out of bed – much less address everything going wrong in this business. The confidence was being replaced by doubt; the passion by apathy and depression.

Every day was the same: employee complaints and issues, inventory problems, payroll problems, a lousy paycheck to compensate for the work… and Jordan Wallace talking about pipe dreams.

"How's it going?" Wallace inquired on a call in late October as Vincent was calling him to pitch him on becoming President.

"It's going" Vincent responded. "I just wanted to touch base with you on some items."

"Sure, shoot," Wallace answered.

"Just in looking at the business right now, we have all of these different entities and we're out on islands," Vincent began. "We're all grappling with issues, but we all have some good things going on. Let's call it what it is: I'm making a lot of this stuff work, despite circumstance, despite issues and no matter what's being thrown at me. I got involved in Texas and you're seeing some improvements. I have led conference calls for every manager in your business, and you're seeing improvements. But these stores in Texas and Wisconsin – for the most part – won't do shit that I ask them to do. There is no accountability, and it's because there's no structure. You yourself said you have no idea what Aaron and Lee actually do and what you're paying for. Furthermore, I know this business is not your primary passion."

The sales mechanisms in Vincent Scott's brain never stopped.

"I'm willing to run this entire business, Jordan," Vincent said, slowing slightly to emphasize and enunciate this key point. "But I need you to give me that authority and ability. With me running Brink Wireless, it gives you the chance to turn this into a holding company, to explore these other endeavors and grow our long-term viability. I know what I bring to the table, but I can't serve you to my maximum capacity without the blessing, without the go-ahead and without the official authority. I am asking you to make me President of Brink Wireless and have all of these markets report to me."

There was a brief pause.

"Yeah, man, that definitely makes a lot of sense," Wallace responded. "I'm working on a lot of things, and I'll definitely talk to the investors and to Alan about all of it. We definitely want you to be a big part of the business."

"Great," Vincent replied.

"I also want to tell you about this website I'm building."

*Oh boy,* Vincent thought. *Here we go again. I bring up this groundbreaking innovation for what's going on right now in an attempt to save the company and salvage what's left, and here comes the blue skies on some topic that has nothing to do with us with some idea that will inevitably never happen.*

"What I'm envisioning is this one-size-fits-all hub for all wireless needs," Wallace continued. "Have you heard of Amazon?"

*Are you fucking serious?*

"Uh…yeah. I use it all the time."

"Exactly," Jordan Wallace continued. "Right now, agents like Moriarty facilitate the ordering of our everyday needs – stuff from phone vendors, accessory vendors, supply vendors – you name it. This website is going to enable me to broker relationships with companies in every facet of the wireless business, provide links to their merchandise, and make a cut of the profits. In essence, we will out-Moriarty Moriarty and then sell this all across the United States. And it doesn't just stop at Cellular Horizons – we could do this for every carrier."

"Yeah, absolutely," Vincent responded, emotionlessly acknowledging Wallace's latest purported multi-million dollar scheme.

Wallace went on to ramble about how he would charge, how much of a cut of the profits he would make, how they would be millionaires within a few years, and how Vincent would play a part in selling this all across the United States. It was a typical Wallace blue sky call. And – also in typical Wallace fashion – he was whitewashing the entire real issue: that the blue sky pipe dream Jordan Wallace had *originally* sold everyone on – Brink Wireless – was very much on the brink.

Vincent Scott was at his wits' end. Again.

As Terry Bunche put it, Jordan was great at blowing sunshine up everyone's ass, but where was the actual money? Where were the actual results and fruits of everyone's labor? Some of the Brink devotees had been there for four years – they were ready to see some money. They were ready to see some shade of blue in their grey skies.

Where was the real plan? Where was the structure?

And what was the lesson to be learned here? You can work for straight-laced, strict corporations and be treated like a number and mercilessly beaten to a pulp if you are an innovator and want to help improve the system. Or you can work on the dream and a prayer of someone else and be at the mercy of their lack of structure and plan and execution. Or you can try to go into business on your own and literally be just that – on your own and against all odds and hope to find people you can trust who will help you execute your vision.

Vincent still had visions of sugar plum roles with corporate Cellular Horizons in his head; he thought surely these folks would want to secure his talents on a grander scale. But no such call came.

Vincent even reached out to Chris Jeffries to pick his brain and see what he could or would be looking for in a potential management company… only to learn he was heavily considering leaving Brink because the ends did not justify the means. To his credit, Chris did tell Vincent he had thought several times about buying Vincent away from Brink to manage his own pocket of stores… he just never could have afforded it.

These two who had initially been such at odds were now on the same page and getting along. And the folks Vincent initially bought into – Jordan, Kurt, Kent, Doug, Susie – were all showing their true colors. They cared about their interests, but certainly not Vincent Scott the person. It was all about sucking him dry and using him until there was nothing left of value. And Vincent feared that day was on the horizon.

As October ended, the Chris Jeffries stores did bail from Brink Management Company, meaning even less bonus money for Vincent and that the question he asked upon hire – about how stores leaving would impact him – that Wallace dismissed saying he was only planning to add stores, was very relevant and detrimentally valid.

Vincent had been getting a bump in pay for his dealings with helping Wisconsin and Texas, but was pulled off helping Wisconsin for November – further reducing his potential paycheck.

October end-of-month commissions were wrong across the board – without explanation and certainly without quick restitution.

What you had at Brink was a bunch of guys who want to own a business because they think it is cool or it will get them laid, but – when it boils down to it – they have no idea what it takes to be successful and are either unable or unwilling to do the work it takes.

And – sadly – Moriarty was just a bigger version of Brink! Same cluster of young money at the top with no guidance or vision or ethics, or respect for the people under their rule. They were profitable because they had no overhead and everyone was replaceable. Sell a 20-year old who has no idea what he's worth that he can run a store, provide a shoddy customer experience but pay your employees nothing and you will make money. Unfortunately, for a 33-year old now-dimming sales supernova, this was not a suitable spot.

There was Jordan Wallace, who was *now* pitching a social media site for wireless that would unite everyone in the industry and he could package all over the country. "Have you heard of Facebook?" And he was serious. "We sacrifice for two years and then we'll be millionaires." And he was serious. "I'm just an ideas man. I don't want to actually run the business; I just want to start these things up and be a holding company and get paid while they do all the work." And he was serious.

Vincent's lead generation platform was delivering leads to his stores left and right; and they could not close them. The concept of how to reach out to these warm leads, how to manage the account and close the business was lost on them, no matter how many scripts or hands-on displays Vincent put on. Tragically, Vincent had his own job to maintain; he could not hold their hands and do all of these things every day, too.

The place was about to blow up into an inferno, and Vincent had to take matters into his own hands.

If being unemployed for a year had taught him anything, it was that his greatest resource was himself and that he had to sell that resource – by any means necessary. He took to LinkedIn even more ferociously, he started applying to jobs with fervor; the demise of Brink in its current incarnation was inevitable and there was certainly no guarantee that this blue sky utopia where Alan Starr swooped in to save them was actually going to happen. Considering everything else Jordan Wallace had sold them had been empty promises, Vincent could take no chances.

It certainly did not surprise Vincent when November 1 – his 33rd birthday – passed with no sign of Alan Starr's takeover. And as days upon days with no news piled on, Vincent needed to create news.

Vincent would do everything he could to conjure up excitement for his job or the potential future, and by 11 AM or noon he felt like someone took a crowbar to his face. These someone's took several forms: his inept 1099 folks (and – God love them – some of them actually lasted weeks and months and never made a penny working there), Doug and Susie Wilson in stereo surround sound Monday morning quarterback glory trying to pick apart his against-all-odds ragtag team, Jordan Wallace all of a sudden deciding he is not going to follow through on any financial commitments (like paying flier distributors after they did their job for a weekend or promised compensation plans for 1099's) – it was just too much.

Saul Portman was up front with Vincent about the fact he wanted advancement and was being pursued by another of Vincent's Brink predecessors; a gentleman named John Jenkins. On November 1 – Vincent's birthday – Saul called to put in his two weeks' notice; Jenkins wanted Portman to helm a Minneapolis portion of his operation for another independent retailer for a prepaid wireless carrier with the promise he could potentially take over the Chicago wing when it got up and running (which was Saul's hometown).

Vincent was grappling with these feelings and emotions and realizations that – from a career standpoint – were new and terrifying: he had nothing left to give this place. He was unable to sell Saul Portman blue sky bullshit; nor could he in good faith try to keep Saul here knowing full well this business was in utter limbo.

Vincent told Jordan Wallace of Saul's pending departure and Wallace asked if he wanted a package put together to try to keep Saul; Vincent asked to mull this before making a final decision.

On the one hand, there was a desire to watch this whole thing just implode and end. If Brink just hit that proverbial iceberg and finally was demolished – whatever the aftermath – at least this uncertainty and daily guesswork and putting out fires of ridiculous magnitude – would finally be over. Somebody would pick up the pieces and potential, and surely Vincent would be recruited to run the remains.

Vincent was the only glue holding it together, and even he was coming apart.

There was nothing to indicate career path here, but – to talk to Jordan Wallace – they were still going to sacrifice for a bit and then take over the world.

Vincent was certainly starting to lean more toward letting it all fall apart.

And he definitely was consciously making the decision not to continue over-working himself.

The next day when he returned to work from his birthday off with Elizabeth, he canceled the every-single-morning conference calls Wallace had appointed him to run for every manager in the company. He canceled them without consulting anyone else; he was tired of logging into these morning calls only to find that only one-third of those who were supposed to be in attendance actually were and to give speeches to people that didn't care when he no longer cared.

He was tired of talking people off the ledge.

He was tired of listening to Jordan Wallace's baloney and hearing how a new scenario presented itself every day or that his website that would cure cancer (to hear him tell it) was the ticket or that Vincent was taking over the company or would be reporting directly to the unicorn savior Alan Starr whom no one had even seen.

With Saul leaving, Vincent was transitioning Terry to run the downtown store and they finally got the blessing from Wallace to start a call center. The catch was that they had to hire them as 1099 contractors, put them in the abandoned bar/restaurant next door to the store (also in the Brink lease) and that they had to start with two and go from there. But it was something, and with Vincent's and Terry's expertise in the call center game, it was a project that gave them a little something to care about again.

Reggie Sherman – right around this time – was game to go to Dallas to helm a couple of stores, but Wallace dragged his feet and Reggie took another job as a loan officer – leaving the business. Tired of his people never being paid properly, running one of the larger volume locations but his inventory orders being constantly botched, Reggie was fed up; he was willing to embrace a fresh start in Dallas, but Wallace's unwillingness to focus on the details and the people was the final nail in the coffin for Reggie. He moved on.

But it took just a day or so for Vincent to realize that – no matter how this ended: win, lose or draw – he had to go out the only way he could go out – unbeaten. He could lose his people, his joy for the job and his inventory, but he would go out a champion.

The hits did keep coming, however.

Doug and Susie Wilson – who started to be largely silent from the peanut gallery – changed their tune into November and December and just started attacking sales results; these were sales results that were still better than year-over-year results and were certainly not going to get better when employees were not paid properly and inventory was not arriving in stores. With Moriarty cutting off ordering until Wallace would make a payment to bring Brink current, with Wallace often opting to order cheaper, refurbished devices and passing them off as new and with managers and Vincent spending way too much time driving around town to stock rebalance, they did not even have the product or resources to realistically reach their potential anytime soon.

It became more and more regular: Doug from the Moriarty side or Susie from the Cellular Horizons side would send out e-mails chastising results and asking why they were not where they needed to be, all while they copied their supervisors and Jordan Wallace. Vincent would be the one to respond – responding to all, subtly (and sometimes less-than subtly) chastising Doug and Susie by inviting them to actually do their jobs and spend time in the stores, making reference to the times he had gone to both of them telling them they needed support and help, and backing his team. Vincent said numerous times that if they had any issues with the results, his team was certainly not to blame but that he took full responsibility for what they achieved on the limited resources and insane situation they were mired in. It was his chivalrous way of saying, "If you want to attack someone, attack me and leave my team alone."

Vincent had privately given both Doug and Susie full disclosure – whatever was going to happen to Brink, with Alan, with Moriarty, with whatever was going to happen – needed to happen now. *Right now.* He and his team could not hold on anymore. It was going to get ugly really fast and he could not be held accountable for the ensuing explosion.

And they did nothing.

Vincent put a full court press on looking for new jobs and new connections. He had to finally accept that this might not end well for him and – fortunately – he had learned just a bit from his stint on the unemployment line of how to network and how to optimize his résumé to best cast his candidacy in the desired spotlight.

He pulled back from his tireless devotion to the work enough to keep his sanity. The best part of this venture was that he had his freedom, he was the law of the land and he really did not answer to anybody. (What were they going to do, anyway – fire him from this madness and put him out of his misery?)

But there was no direction, no guidance, no structure, no career, no future. Vincent spent more and more of his time he could with Elizabeth and – when she was not with him – pursuing other career alternatives.

Why would he or should he give so much of himself to the business anymore when the managers across the enterprise were not giving him the observation forms required, logging into conference calls, employees were not doing activity logs required of them, stores were not putting together their marketing plans, and – frankly – they were not getting the paychecks or inventory they needed to be successful to motivate them to do so? What was Vincent going to do – discipline and fire people that were not even getting paid properly? He was lucky the doors were open.

And – as Terry Bunche said frequently – the doors were only open because of Vincent Scott.

Terry and Saul still kept the triumvirate going; talking amongst themselves and reaching out to Vincent. Saul made clear he did not really want to leave and that he felt they were not finished, so Vincent did reach out to Wallace and sold him on putting together a package for him to make it worth Saul's while to stay. The verdict? Vincent sold Wallace on being able to make Saul a District Sales Manager, reporting to Vincent and running the now-vacant Bloomington location while doing all training for the market and doing some additional coaching opportunities for $1,000 more per month. It worked because it was less than Wallace would have paid to hire a new Bloomington manager and it appeased Vincent.

Saul and Terry were both looking into Alan Starr and his background – he had a successful career in the cable industry and marketing; this foray into the telecommunications industry was exactly what he wanted to complete the puzzle for himself and obtain an ownership stake in something.

If and when Alan Starr came on board – if Vincent was truly going to be prominently placed – this could go well for everyone. That was just a big if and – again – it had to happen immediately.

The potential of what could be done was huge; it just could not be done with Jordan Wallace at the helm. Wallace had made abundantly clear he loathed the cell phone business and wanted nothing more than to be Berkshire Hathaway, Amazon, Google or Facebook – or all of them wrapped into one – and every time it came down to execution on ideas and innovation or treatment of people, he failed.

Cellular Horizons was highly regarded in the industry, and Moriarty was purportedly their best, but neither was worth a damn when it really came down to it. They had both already proven they could not be counted on nor did they care about breaking political ranks when push came to shove. They were just like – practically every other company. Playing it safe and playing it political.

Vincent was also realizing that he could not always pin his hopes on potential. He had stayed in businesses and relationships clinging to hopes for improvement that never came. There had to be a moment to draw the line. Where was that line? Would he know it when he got to it, or had he already seen it and just been too foolhardy to acknowledge it?

And he again questioned absolutely everything: where did this experience fit into his life? Where was it taking him?

He was certainly not sitting idle; connecting with people left and right via LinkedIn in prominent places in Corporate America in Minneapolis. He set up several meetings with Directors and Vice Presidents in sales across the city with numerous major companies.

Vincent was going to run his team the best he could, control what he could control and look outside the business for his next opportunity in the event he needed it. This time, he was going to look out for himself.

Vincent found he was very able to push his agenda on Jordan Wallace, because Wallace knew Vincent was all that was holding the ship together. Wallace allowed Vincent to concoct a 30-60-90 day plan with Vincent as the #2 to Alan Starr once his takeover was complete and present it to Starr via conference call with Terry and Saul riding shotgun.

He had also had enough with the horrendous Texas team, ordering Aaron Hartley to put a plan in place to remove 5 of the 7 managers there.

It also seemed that Reggie Sherman quit too soon as his other position fell through once they ran his criminal background; to hear Reggie tell it, his ex-wife and he back in the day "liked to get drunk and trash each other's houses." To each his or her own; Sherman was a cranky old drunk, but would be an upgrade to the terrible Texas managers and it was now easy to get Reggie to come back and move to Dallas.

This enabled Vincent to drop the hammer on two deadbeat Dallas area managers and have Reggie watch two stores so he could get his desired compensation. It also kept Reggie away from the Minneapolis managers that he – for the most part – did not get along with due to his teamwork deficiencies.

Each day was pretty much filled with Vincent going as much through the motions – interviews, store visits, reports, uplifting calls and e-mails, taking part in store meetings and one-on-one's for development and coaching sessions – as he could while fielding calls from everywhere: Wallace pitching new blue sky scenarios or talking about his website that would revolutionize the wireless industry, Lee Christian and Aaron Hartley describing the decay of their markets and the differing sides of Wallace's story they were getting, and the store managers from across the enterprise relaying the latest business gaffes.

Hartley would whine, but he spent his time either "working from home" or simply complaining to the employees that were left while dropping the ball on calling new candidates Vincent had teed up for him to hire on his visits. Betty Bendis was quite disgruntled and running her mouth left and right, spilling things she overheard while Wallace was on calls with Alan Starr or Moriarty, such as impending doom for Aaron Hartley or pending dismissals for other Texas managers. All the while, she neglected to pay people properly or answer the ample e-mails sent her way requesting answers on payroll and inventory – two of the lifebloods of the business.

There were five sides to the story, and then there was the truth.

As November waged on, Jordan Wallace pledged that he was working with Moriarty to broker a relationship that would see all Brink employees transition to become workers for Moriarty effective January 2012. The relationship would net better pay, increased benefits and some stability. This story, however – like everything else at Brink – did not add up.

Alan Starr's role and the date he was joining the project was a moving target. To hear Jared Cox tell it, Cellular Horizons was terminating Jordan Wallace's license in a matter of days and Alan Starr was coming on board then. Wallace was going to be given the boot a la Dustin "Bruce" Rollins.

Wallace bragged he was selling his website idea across several different vendors; Lee Christian told a different story. His more likely version was that there were some folks listening to Wallace, but only to hear if he had a decent idea and if it was worth stealing. No one wanted to do business with him.

Wallace began claiming that the Minneapolis operation was no longer profitable, yet Brink was #1 of the Cellular Horizons dealers in Minneapolis. Per Jordan, Starr is buying in, then he's not, then he's dragging his feet.

One thing was clear: Jordan Wallace owed Moriarty a lot of money and the stores Vincent Scott and his team ran roughshod over were bleeding profusely.

Ahead of retail holiday Black Friday, Moriarty had to show Wallace they were serious and did so by flexing the inventory muscle: they cut him off completely from ordering anything in his Texas stores just prior to the biggest day in retail. Wallace scrambled to re-allocate funds, canceled some travel plans and went to his investors for more money to buy more time.

Jordan Wallace was not an irredeemable person. He got into this sales business for very similar reasons as Vincent Scott – it was a job with potential for pay and growth. He realized his charm worked on people and he got caught up in the euphoria of money and then power. As he got in with rich kid Lyle Caminiti it became clear he did not need to have a boss and he lived like a rock star for a couple of years. But the well was drying up and he was staring down the barrel of a gun about to take his head clean off.

Wallace was simply in over his head. He had started experiencing extreme anxiety, could not sleep and certainly could not figure out what to do. He desperately wanted to pawn this business off on Alan Starr, but it was depreciating daily in value and there was no way to mask that. Of course Wallace was no longer passionate about this business: it was no longer expensing his rock star existence.

What Vincent Scott understood – however – was that – one way or another – he would stay on under someone's umbrella, be it Alan Starr, be it Moriarty, be it Jordan Wallace in a late-inning comeback. He just had no idea when or just how much damage he and the business would sustain prior to the life raft. He also could not figure out if perhaps his time and efforts would be better spent working with a group of people who could actually do their jobs, rather than trying to latch on with Cellular Horizons or Moriarty; what he had seen of their employees thus far had not been promising.

Despite proving his sales mettle on Black Friday and a few other days by showing his team no one sold like Vincent Scott, Vincent's flame continued to flicker out. Wallace said Alan Starr's saving grace was 99% likely, but Vincent was 99% cooked.

He was sad.

No matter how this panned out, he felt his job as a dead end. He was setting up at least 1 to 2 meetings per week via LinkedIn by requesting advice meetings with new connections he made perusing Vice Presidents and Directors, but they were going nowhere.

"You're definitely going about this the right way," they said. "You're definitely on to something here," they said. "If this was five years ago, you would have companies lining up for you, but with the economy the way it is now, it's a different world," they said.

Heartwarming, but little consolation.

His stores were getting "like new" devices they were expected to pass off as new. Vincent's phone was exploding with people who were discombobulated over Wallace changing commission rules for months that were already over because he could not afford to pay them; Doug and Susie Wilson were always hovering with e-mails or with a lunch where they bullied Vincent with nitpicks about every member of his team. They rallied strongly for Vincent to fire De-Metre Jones and his assistant Bryan Venison for some fraud allegations at New Brighton that turned out to be false. In digging in, however, Vincent did discover that Venison was having sex with a 1099 in the bathroom and that he was activating store inventory on his personal account, resulting in immediate termination. And the mayhem never stopped!

Payroll was wrong. Every time.

Susie and Doug didn't stop with New Brighton: Terry Bunche couldn't complete his online training courses. Saul Portman was disorganized. And these were his "stars"! De-Metre was a walking sexual harassment and organizational calamity. Wallace was AWOL now that Vincent actually needed him for answers; the company cards were shut off pretty much every other day and there was no accompanying reason as to why.

It would have been one thing if some area of Vincent's life was providing him solace. He had Elizabeth, but only just over half the time. He would escape into their time together, but when she was gone – in those initial moments before he was able to close the chasm in his heart – he was an open wound.

It would have been one thing if the Emily Nance and Abby Winters decision was an easy one, or if some perfect brainy beauty with no baggage wearing a bow on top of her head would arrive on Vincent's doorstep.

Emily was in love with Vincent and would do anything for him… but Vincent would never feel the same for her. She was overly analytical and sensitive and needy of affection that Vincent could not provide. He cared for her and trusted her – but would never be in love with her, which was a prerequisite if he was going to retire his bachelor status.

Abby was inconsistent in her "love" and had been a no-show when it came to support in the past enough so that Vincent wouldn't let her close again. Not that Vincent had always made it easy, but – then again – he would search far and wide for just about any justification to avoid a relationship. He cared for her but how could he possibly let himself fall for her again when she'd surely pull the rug out from under him again as well?

It would have been one thing if Vincent could close the book on his previous employer. Then, perhaps he could sleep nights and stop dwelling on that dark past.

He had made the decision to look everywhere he could for better employment, but he was not going to walk away from Brink unless he had it.

He enjoyed the things that allowed him to showcase his talents: closing business occasionally on the sales floor better than anyone else could. A radio interview in hometown Mankato where he got to talk about a Cellular Horizons promotion and make a few subtle jabs at the competition. Black Friday was big.

But this place could not give him enough. He felt Abby and Emily could not give him enough. And the court battle and needed closure could not be resolved soon enough.

And he couldn't be with Elizabeth enough.

He stopped wearing ties. He stopped shaving and getting his hair cut regularly. He stopped giving his best.

Nevertheless, his 75% was better than most people's 1,000%. He was fried, but when he was able to will himself into a call or a store or a sales meeting, he was his old self – if even for a moment. He'd walk into the Mankato kiosk to the employees playing around on Facebook on their phones and a box full of fliers sitting there from the month prior and he'd blow his top and go put them on cars himself. He would give what he could when he could, but that was all he had left for Brink Management Company: sporadic bursts of his former greatness.

The days when he defied all logic and odds against a company that used and abused him and still sprung out of bed, loaded up on caffeine and led a department were long gone; he could barely manage to get out of bed and spent more days "working from home" drinking a few beers and listening to music to drown out the thoughts of despair in his head.

The reality was this: he had spent a full year and applied to a multitude of jobs to find *this* horrendous one, where people were not paid, stores had no inventory and the all-employee calls Vincent set up and wanted to perform with passion would net 9 of 120 employees. What on earth was his future going to hold now?

Sure, he wrote a book, but his search of 968 agents and publishers found him a terrible publisher that was not even paying him royalties he earned, marketing as they promised, featuring his book where they promised; is hard work and life really *this* hard and *this* thankless?

It started as a joke and gag from a conversation with Aaron Hartley, as his girlfriend worked at a creative marketing company that designed shirts and mugs, etc., but in December, Vincent ordered blue reminder wristbands akin to the LIVESTRONG bracelets that said "Blue Skies" for his entire management team.

He wore it daily as a reminder: if (as stated in a different Sinatra tune) he could make it there, he could make it anywhere. Endure.

The weeks to come were as hazy as the cigar smoke from regular outings Vincent started making with Terry and Saul to the cigar bar for drinks, smokes and eats. The list of unanswered questions grew and everyone was ready for the inevitable change — whatever it was — so they could accept it and move forward.

It was all a soap opera (and a low budget one at that — some of the actors were not very good). Jordan Wallace was trying to pawn off what he did not want — Texas stores — and keep what was making him a mint — the Wisconsin stores — in his conversations with Alan Starr. Moriarty was doing its best to push its own agenda by getting power over all the stores, putting the squeeze financially on their once golden goose Wallace and taking over in the most profitable way possible.

The sad fact in it all is that this was common: the flash in the pan. Someone buys into this business, has some quick success and everyone lauds them as a hero; shortly thereafter, they cannot sustain it or they take on more than they can handle, and when it goes awry everyone is looking for someone to blame.

Everyone blamed somebody else. Wallace blamed Hartley. Hartley blamed Wallace. Doug and Susie Wilson blamed Vincent or Wallace or the many other players in the organization, depending on who they were talking to. Wallace stopped speaking kindly of Doug Wilson as he saw him stay political and loyal to Mother Moriarty to the last as Moriarty started putting the screws to him.

Doug Wilson started to be conveniently quiet through much of this time. Aside from a lunch where he and Susie beat up Vincent on each member of his team, and a subsequent conference call where Steve Flowers demanded Vincent terminate De-Metre Jones, Doug was nowhere to be heard from. Questions to him regarding the state of the business were ignored. He had seldom visited stores before, but he completely stopped during this time. It simply added to the unrest.

Wallace called Vincent the first week of December 2011 and laid out three scenarios of how this would play out.

#1: They would shut down a few stores – likely two in Texas, and the kiosk in Mankato. Alan Starr would buy out the remainder of the business, giving his group 100% control. This would leave Wallace out. Lee Christian would be buying Wisconsin and already had a bid in.

#2: If the Alan Starr relationship was no longer salvageable after Moriarty tried to convince Starr that Wallace was trying to rip him off, they consolidate (closures), re-invest with their same investors plus 2 or 3 more, then operate further under the Brink umbrella.

#3: Wallace offered Vincent the opportunity to run stores as an owner/operator like Lee Christian was vying for in Wisconsin. He would order and pay a monthly dividend.

At this stage in the game, both the Minnesota and Texas stores were cut off on inventory completely. Wallace had not made a payment, so he could not order anything; he stated he was going to try to go through "someone else"… but this meant – inevitably – cheap, refurbished devices.

Brink itself would soon be no more; but a new manifestation was heading their way one way or another.

Vincent left messages with Alan Starr himself; after conversations with Saul and Terry it was vital that Vincent put in his pitch for his team. At this point, that was all that mattered.

Starr e-mailed Vincent that he would call him the following week. The call did not come.

All of this was occurring while Terry launched the 2-person "call center" and while the corporate cards remained shut off.

Everyone spent most of their time speculating or taking potshots at one another. Susie Wilson attacked results in an e-mail copying her bosses and Vincent retorted ferociously – inviting her into the stores to actually see for herself what they were dealing with and still posting year-over-year gains amidst. She actually waited for him to show up at the Bloomington store after he sent the e-mail to try to get his buy in back.

"Vincent, you need to align yourself with the right people," she said. "Obviously, things are going to change and you need to make sure your interests are aligned."

"Who are the right people? Jordan Wallace pays my bills… sometimes. Then you've got Moriarty, who won't return my calls or answer my questions. And you've got Cellular Horizons… not making a move as we are all about to hit the iceberg… and – in the middle – you've got all of this uncertainty. Who's going to be running the business tomorrow? Will I still be here?"

"I don't know, Vincent. All I do know is that when my boss tells you to fire someone, you fire them."

"That's just not how I operate," Vincent replied without hesitation. "DeMetre doesn't deserve to be fired. He brings value to this organization. He's not perfect, but how do you find a perfect store manager for $1,200 a month? Write him up, demote him – maybe. But I will not terminate him for what amounts to drama going on under his watch when I owe him the development to make him better. I'm not going to fire somebody I owe more coaching to, all while I'm barely holding this whole place together across four states now. I'm not going to fire somebody who's doing his best through utter madness of not getting paid properly, his people not getting paid properly and not having phones to sell to customers. It's not fair to hold him accountable for the sins of others he has no control over whatsoever. You want to hold someone accountable? Hold me accountable."

And that was Vincent Scott.

The fire was there, smoldering, hidden deep within, but it came out when his people were under attack. It came out when he could help someone be more successful and he was coaching. It came out when he was making positive changes to an organization. How dare these AWOL goofballs question him?

"I came to you guys months ago and told you what was going to happen," Vincent reminded her. "Why is everyone acting shocked now that it is upon us?"

"You didn't come to me," she said.

"I went to Doug, and you know it," Vincent retorted. "I've referenced that conversation many times to both of you. We told you what was happening and everyone has ignored it. My team and I are not to blame. Hell, we should be given medals for keeping the doors open."

Needless to say, cut-from-the-corporate-cloth Susie Wilson did not appreciate Vincent's cavalier approach to her attempt to woo him in to the web.

And his refusal to blindly follow Cellular Horizons' orders would certainly not play into his favor with the corporate team picking up his contract.

He had to throw bouquets to all crowds and he didn't like it. When trying to show loyalty to his people and going to Doug about Jordan Wallace's absurd ideas that were decaying Brink, he had gotten himself in a stir. But when these guys wanted him to bend over, he was just supposed to do their bidding willingly?

They wanted Vincent's allegiance because they knew they needed it; they knew change was coming and it was easier if they had their Moses.

Whether or not he'd live to see the Promised Land was still up in the air.

Christmas 2011 was fantastic; Vincent awoke Elizabeth with a kiss on the forehead at 7:15 AM.

"I love you, Daddy," she said, embracing him. "Merry Christmas!"

They opened presents and spent the time Vincent had up until 2 PM with his parents until he had to drop her off with Abby.

While in Mankato Christmas Eve, Vincent stopped into Cooke's Grocery Store, where he was employed from 1996 until his departure in 2001. In fact, there was still a place on the meat case where he had signed "Vincent Scott was here 7-29-01" for his final day.

Very few people from his era were still employed there, but most of those in the meat department where Vincent had finished his time there were still present. Vincent's Dad, Vince, Sr., was now doing deliveries for them part time as a retirement job and Vincent met his Dad's boss – a kid in his mid-20's.

When you are in a situation for however long you are in it, time seems like it's standing relatively still. But when you re-visit something or someplace from long ago, you certainly notice the differences; you feel nostalgic and sentimental.

Vincent had had a carefree existence there; his biggest concerns were where the party would be that night. He could work all day, carouse all night and come back and do it all again the next day.

Now he was a Dad, a wannabe writer and a vagabond sales manager – with still no clue where it was taking him or where he was going.

So much had changed at Cooke's, but so little had; the meat guys were still just dirty old men making fun of their former boss from years past. Other familiar faces were there; they just had less hair and more tummy. And there were still cute girls everywhere; they were just 17-to-21 and Vincent was 33.

One of the most challenging things to do when a facet of your life is going horribly wrong is to pull yourself out of it long enough to see the greatness around you.

The time with Elizabeth, with his parents, with his hometown that was now just a place to visit – it healed him, even if just for a moment.

Whereas he could not wait to depart Mankato 10 years prior, the last thing he wanted to do was go back to Minneapolis to the uncertainty and to dropping Elizabeth off with her mother.

The calls started up again promptly the following day: people wondering if there was any change, people wondering if they would have jobs in the new era, people wondering why Aaron Hartley was never around and impossible to get ahold of. It was an unrelenting disaster.

2011 closed with nothing but questions.

He knew that if the business was saved and everything came up sunshine and rainbows and unicorns that he could turn himself back to full throttle, but he couldn't now. And he couldn't have a lot of faith in these people who had caused all of this to begin with!

Their entire lead generation marketing program – squandered. The people just couldn't execute; that is what happens when you pay nothing. You wind up with bad employees. And not even Doug Wilson or Susie Wilson even understood the ingenious concept! They did not see the value in that, or in the call center; they thought the answer to everything was spending tremendous amounts of time sending "thank you" cards to every single customer because once upon a time a patron had a good experience with one. Doug went on and on talking about "being their wireless hero" by bringing up all of the different products they had, but he couldn't have sold his way out of a paper bag.

But it didn't matter: he kissed the asses of the brass at Moriarty, he did what they told him to do… and that is what too much of what Corporate America wants.

Jordan Wallace pledged he would grow the business; Vincent had 11 stores; then he had a hand in 33. Now it was 5. Tuncil, Rollins, and Jeffries – they were all gone – because this system broke them even despite gains they saw in morale and some financial areas with Vincent's help.

Vincent had interview blitzes scheduled, but how could he hire anyone into this mess? He did not even know what to tell them about what was happening or when it was happening, because he did not know it himself.

What was even the point in Vincent visiting stores? What would he do? Stand around? Would he coach? For what?

For a man of Vincent's intelligence, work ethic, drive and desire, this situation was sucking him dry. His immense talents were being wasted and he didn't know why. He didn't know what was next. He did not know why this was happening; he never thought he would be questioning everything but here he was again.

Not knowing your destiny and potential, while sometimes exciting in its unpredictability and freedom of choice, is also absolutely petrifying. But this was Vincent Scott we were talking about. His choices were the same as they always were: cowering in the corner and hoping something good happens, or getting out there, making noise, giving everything he could, taking ridiculous chances that make people think he is a lunatic and living without regrets.

He always chose the latter, so why should this time be any different?

# Moriarty

2011 officially closed fittingly: Vincent and Terry took Terry's truck to Mankato to box up the remains of the mall kiosk as that location closed for good. The writing had been on the wall and mall personnel had already alerted the employees that they had been informed of its closure, so it came as no shock as they had to deliver the bad news.

Every store in Vincent's jurisdiction – aside from Mankato – exceeded year over year productivity from December 2010, despite all of the issues they were grappling with and against all odds and reason. Take that, Doug and Susie Wilson.

Vincent spent New Year's Eve with Emily and came home to be there when Abby dropped Elizabeth off for New Year's Day.

Vincent could always tell when Abby was potentially wavering from Chris when she would linger while dropping Elizabeth off, or if – while he made exchanges at her place – if she would keep the door open for longer than fifteen seconds and probe him on where he was headed or ask how he was. The problem was he could seldom resist it.

This was one of those times when she lingered.

"So…how have you been?" Abby inquired.

"I'm fine, Abby," Vincent responded curtly to keep the conversation as brief as possible.

"I haven't heard from you lately."

"Why would you?" Vincent responded, making sure that Elizabeth was at least only halfway paying attention.

"Well, I thought something was going on with us."

"Abby, we spent some time together and then you tried to throw Emily in my face, all while you have this thing going on with Chris. I bet he's at your place right now – right?"

She was taken aback. "Yes, but, we're just friends."

"Yeah… so are Emily and me. I know how that song goes."

"He's only at my place right now because I'm playing taxi for him."

"After New Year's Eve – how cozy."

"It's not like that."

"So what's it like?"

"He was depressed last night and just wanted to hang out. He slept on the couch."

"Great – that's how it always starts, and continues, and pretty much repeats – isn't it?" Vincent retorted. "I was depressed for a whole year and never once heard anything from you except when I'd get a job."

"You're the one I want," Abby said.

"Really," Vincent replied. No matter what Abby had put him through and continued to put him through, despite the lawsuits and the lies, he still had this undeniable spot for her; not a soft one and not always in his heart. The physical attraction was intense but he also hated seeing her with anyone else.

"Yes."

"For now – right?"

"No, for forever."

Vincent laughed. "What are you talking about?"

"I want to marry you."

Vincent shook his head. "Abby, I know how this game works. And I'm not playing this time. Happy New Year."

He ushered her toward the door. She said goodbye to Elizabeth and was on her way, leaving Vincent confused per usual in her wake.

*   *   *

The phone rang and Vincent answered it.

"Hello?"

"Vincent," came Terry's voice on the other line.

"Yeah, what's up?"

"Our jobs were just posted online."

"What do you mean?"

"Moriarty posted sales rep and store manager jobs for all of our stores on their website today."

Vincent paused as his brain processed the information.

"Sales reps and managers," Vincent repeated. "Well – there you go. There's the answer. That's their play."

"But what does that mean?"

"I'll tell you exactly what it means," Vincent responded. "They are going to pick and choose who they want for your jobs. They are going to make you apply for your jobs, interview for them and then they'll pick and choose who they want."

And he was right. Doug Wilson returned a text message from Vincent for the first time in weeks to let him know that his reps and managers – if they wanted to work in the new Moriarty regime – should go ahead and apply for their jobs and participate in interviews with Moriarty personnel.

A conversation with Jordan Wallace took it a few steps further.

"Yeah, not only are they taking over, but they are only buying the management contract," Wallace informed him. "They will replace Brink, while we still technically own the stores and sign over all decision-making power to them."

"What can you do about it?"

"Nothing, man," a defeated Wallace responded. "I can't order inventory, I can't pay my people. They boxed me into a corner. They told Alan I was trying to rip him off, so he's pissed at me and won't return my calls. He will be buying Texas at a reduced rate. The original investors and I will still own the other stores with Moriarty managing them."

"I thought Lee was buying Wisconsin?"

"Lyle reneged on him."

"Even though he already took out the money?"

"Yes."

"Wow."

"Yeah – this whole thing is an ugly mess. But it's about over."

Vincent had to ask the final question.

"What about me?"

There was a pause.

"I don't think they're going to offer you anything, dude."

\*     \*     \*

"Hello?" Doug Wilson's voice sounded on the other end of the line – actually accepting a call for the first time in a while.

"Doug – what's going on?"

"What do you mean?"

"Well, I just got off the phone with Jordan," Vincent responded. "I've got my people applying to jobs like you requested. What's happening with me?"

"Well, uh… did you ask Jordan?"

"I did. He said to talk to you."

"Okay…well… let me talk to Kent and with Jordan and I will follow up."

"Fair enough, Doug," Vincent responded. "I'm a grown-up and a single Dad – if you're not bringing me on, please just let me know so I can plan accordingly."

"Sure – absolutely, Vincent. I'll call Kent right now."

Doug Wilson did not follow up.

After everything Vincent had done for these people – this was the slap in the face he was getting.

Would it have been better if he had just rolled over and fired people at will in the name of Cellular Horizons? Probably – but that wasn't Vincent.

These were the consequences of playing the game his way: the love of his people and the ire of the powers that be.

More facts were revealed in the days to come: Jordan Wallace was over $1 million in the hole with Moriarty's account.

Vincent was not one to take it all lying down; while there was a dying breath remaining in his Brink career, he'd breathe it. And he'd breathe it fully.

He fired off an e-mail to Kurt Stillwater, Steve Flowers, Susie Wilson, Doug Wilson and Kent Smyth straightaway:

"To all:

Jordan Wallace informed me earlier today that he does not believe Moriarty has me in the cards for the future of the stores I have devoted my life to for the last 11 months, in the aftermath of the current transformation.

On February 7, 2011, I signed on to this Mission: Impossible that is Brink Management Company, sold that I would make three times as much financially as I did. My managers told me after I had earned their trust and respect that they assumed I would take one look at this utter mess and leave after 2 or 3 weeks. I hung on for so long despite everything because I believed in this product, this business and what we would (not could) do if we had the structure.

Month-over-month, we had an immediate 59% increase in gross profit my first month on board. We did 30-to-150% category increases in every single key performance indicator from mobile broadband conversion to accessory conversion to insurance conversion, etc. overnight, and I wish I had a job interview now for every night I was up sending and checking work e-mails and compiling our sales numbers and spreadsheets for 33 stores at 3 AM. We did 150% increase year-over-year on new lines for my territory. At Susie's prodding, I entered and won Cellular Horizons Superstar locally and won the whole thing in Chicago. I made a dozen training videos for my folks, put on sales training clinics, and accepted Doug's gracious invitation to sit on a panel of experts at one of the few Moriarty conventions I was allowed to attend where I was arguably the top contributor of the event.

Very quickly, I created scripts for every scenario, every situation type, fact-finding, closing, you name it, plus an observation form, and observation form system and requirements for each store manager. I conducted anywhere from 1-to-10 conference calls per week for as many as 33 stores and 120+ employees as I got "promotion" after "promotion" within Brink because of the amazing kickstart effect I had on the Minnesota stores. I co-created and personally executed an automated marketing service that generated hundreds of leads, 30 new lines, 10 television sales, etc., for 33 stores over the course of just a few months. We started a call center to reach out to existing and new customer leads. I built social media presence for our stores, generating over 5,000 followers and sending out regular messages. I designed our own marketing pieces and promotions, which fed into our lead generation and translated into dozens of sales.

I held this team together through having no inventory and regularly massively incorrect paychecks, being forced to hire massive numbers of 1099 contractors, robberies, Bruce Rollins, and constant uncertainty.

Despite coming in to a situation with zero process and a lot of dead weight, we drastically revamped the business, as I even created my own hiring forms and process.

In the hopes that these items help others, I am providing some of the tools I created during my time here, attached to this e-mail.

Looking back, I know I did everything I physically could... and then some. I could not have made it without my management team, and I would be more than happy to sit down with whomever will be selecting new teams to let them know who needs to stay and in what capacity. We did everything we could to make this work under the unbelievable circumstances.

Thank you so much for support you have given and allowing me to be a part of this team.

I trust that all of you have ample contacts in the Cellular Horizons and Moriarty worlds; the prospect of getting back to 3$^{rd}$-level management interests me greatly. Surely, as you all know my talents, tireless work ethic and unparalleled results of success, your assistance can guide me on my career path at this time. Certainly, my extensive background in sales leadership, telecommunications, writing, call center, advertising, and retail can be of service in this business. Your assistance would also be very much appreciated.

Thank you in advance for your time and consideration, and all the best.

Vincent T. Scott"


Doug Wilson had committed to talk with his boss Kent, yet calls days later Vincent heard from this team that Doug and Kent were driving around to the stores in Minneapolis together and still no call had been received to make any sense of this madness. They were scouting the locations, meeting people, laying the groundwork for what was to come but Vincent's place in the kingdom he resuscitated was yet to be determined. No one was in any hurry to determine it, either.

Vincent scheduled a meeting with his team. No matter what was going on currently, nothing could prevent him from meeting with them.


\*      \*      \*      \*      \*

The faces were glum in the back of the Golden Valley Cellular Horizons store as De-Metre Jones, Saul Portman, Darryl Wilkinson and Terry Bunche sat waiting on their current leader.

This was different than any meeting Vincent had helmed before. In the past, he was a kamikaze sales leader – living every day to the fullest and not holding back. He once had to be gunned down in cold blood to eliminate the threat he posed to an unethical boys' club of secrets and lies and retaliation and commission scams.

This time, he was wasting away with a big title and a small paycheck for a Wild West-style retailer for a major company – thankless but pure. He wanted this more because he saw the potential, had the freedom to operate by his normal protocol and he just could not will them to the win. He was reduced to just trying to limp to the finish line.

"Team, good afternoon," Vincent said. He walked into the room wearing blue jeans and an untucked black shirt under his black leather jacket – certainly a far cry from the slacks and ties from the majority of his time there.

They acknowledged him. He placed his stuffed padfolio on the table.

It was a foldout table with folding chairs – a far cry from the massive sales offices and auditoriums he had spun his magic in prior. These were just normal, hard-working people – wanting to make a living, wanting to be inspired and wanting to work together. They had seen a beacon of hope from Vincent Scott. They wanted to hear what he would say and see what he would do next. They had followed him this far – partly because they had no choice and did not know how to look elsewhere. Partly because he had this uncanny ability to make them want to.

"As you may or may not know, Moriarty Wireless is in talks to buy out the management contract on the Brink Management Company stores. This would mean the ownership would not change hands; however, the deal stands to give Moriarty complete control over all decisions – including staffing.

"If you are interested in continuing on with Moriarty, I have been asked to ask you to apply to the openings on the Moriarty website and have all of your reps do the same. Some of you already have.

"As for me, I have been given no reason to believe I will be brought on."

The glum looks turned more to shock, as De-Metre and Darryl were taken aback by this news. Saul and Terry – already knowing this for the most part – were less so.

"So this – in essence – is the end of the line for me as the deal could be done any day now and I wanted you to hear the news from me while I'm still in the position to give it. It has been a great privilege to work with you guys. We are a great team, and you have the tools to finish the journey. This is a win for you; Moriarty can afford to give you the structure, the pay and benefits you deserve. I just want to say I appreciate everything you guys brought to the table. Don't be strangers!

"Is there anything else you guys want to discuss?"

The assemblage was silent for a few moments as they looked around at each other.

"This is bullshit," Darryl said.

"Agreed," De-Metre stated.

"It's life, gentlemen," Vincent responded. "We accept it and we move forward. I've been down before; I know the system. I'll bounce back. I wish we could have finished the journey together but I took you as far as I could."

They talked a bit more as a group and then started to break apart.

"So what are you going to do?" Terry asked, stopping Vincent en route for the door.

"What do you mean? That's it for me."

"No it's not," Terry said. "That's exactly what they want you to do. If you blow up, if you disappear, if you go nuts – that's how they'll justify not bringing you on."

"I'm not going to do anything crazy," Vincent answered. "I'll stick around until the day they drop me from the payroll. I just want to say goodbye first this time. This time I'm leaving on my terms. I didn't get that chance last time."

"This isn't over yet," Terry continued. "It's not over until the transition happens. Who knows what the hell is going on. You know Wallace isn't going to tell you the truth. You know Doug and Susie are just patsies. You need to get to Kent. You need to get to Stillwater. You know these guys can't run this place without you."

"That's done, man," Vincent responded. "They won't respond to anything I send."

"Then stay on their radar," Terry said. "You had interviews scheduled this week, right?"

"Yeah, I'm going to cancel them."

"To hell with that," Terry continued passionately. "Do them. Make recommendations to these guys as to who stays on and how you'd line this thing up. These doors wouldn't be open without you. We wouldn't be here without you. If they are going to take you out, let them, but go out 100% on top. Then they'll look like fools for taking you out because you didn't give them an excuse to."

Vincent listened and he truly heard; as much as he hated it, Terry was right. These were his stores until someone took the keys from him. The staffing was still his call; the entire operation was still his call until Brink Management Company was dissolved, Moriarty took over and Vincent didn't have a job.

It was the only way to go out. And it might just save him yet.

"I'll do it. But – for the record – just for once, I'd like to not be the martyr and reach the Promised Land."

Vincent went through three long, solid 12-hour days of doing nothing but interviews. He sent off his elaborate proposal for how the stores should be run and staffed. He forwarded the résumés for candidates he would hire to Doug, Susie and Kent.

It was revealed that Mark Sturgis was the VP who would be helming the brand new management company facet of Moriarty Wireless.

Store visits by Doug and Kent revealed just how little Kent knew about what was going on in the stores and Vincent's contributions and just how little Doug knew about what was really going on in the industry. It left a lot of egg on the faces of Doug and Susie, and made clear to the current employees of Brink that Kent was here on a fact-finding mission to learn what they didn't know. To hear Doug or Susie tell it, the stores were filled with employees and managers not doing their jobs and Vincent was part of the problem. The visits and the employee testimonials told quite a different tale.

Some stores were getting down to 1 and 2 phones in inventory – not brands, mind you, but actual, physical phones to sell. Store managers were driving to each other's stores to stock rebalance where they could but when the market as a whole had the combined inventory one store should have, this was near impossible.

Shortly thereafter, an interview roster was announced for all of the existing Brink employees. Vincent's name was not on it.

Vincent never received a response from anyone regarding the recommendations he made to the Moriarty team assembling a new market. Not even thanks.

Vincent was still not completely defeated. He left messages with Kent Smyth and Kurt Stillwater. He e-mailed them again. He simply wanted to be allowed at the table – especially after everything he had given these people.

They were assembling their "dream team" and – if that was truly the case – Vincent should be the first drafted. Everyone knew this. And not taking him along for the ride was inexplicable.

213

It did actually come as a massive surprise when Vincent received an e-mail from Mark Sturgis inviting him to meet during the interviews Sturgis, Susie and Doug would conduct the following week as they selected the team that would be in these stores come February 1. All of Vincent's noise at least got him a meeting, even if it was to tell him farewell.

Abby tried a couple of times to invite herself over to Vincent's apartment and he did not accept. He asked her the status of her and Chris, to which she responded that they had been fighting.

But when Vincent had to drop Elizabeth off at Abby's, Abby invited him to stay for dinner. With his 4-year old princess begging him to stay and that inviting look from Abby he had seen so many times, he did not relent this time. Everything around him had stripped him of whatever willpower he had left.

After Elizabeth went to sleep, Abby started overtly coming onto Vincent; sitting on his lap and kissing his neck – but he tried to remain strong, pushing her back. He stood.

"Abby – stop it," he commanded.

"Why? Don't you want me?"

Now there was a question. He fought back his impulses.

"Abby, it's not that simple. We've done this before with catastrophic results. I'm not interested in that happening again."

"But I'm different now," she said.

"I've heard that before."

"If you didn't want to be here, you wouldn't be."

"You're right, but you know I'm not going to turn away time with Elizabeth. You asked me to dinner right in front of her. Dinner's over."

"Can't you see we're meant to be?" she continued. "It's always been you and me. Whenever things go bad, you're always the one I turn to. You always come through for me."

"Yeah, I've noticed that. Now I just need to find somebody who will actually be there for me."

"I can do that. I'm in love with you, Vincent. I always have been and always will be."

"Abby – I don't know what to say. I don't think you even know what love is."

"Stay with me."

She started kissing him again. He moved his face away so their lips' paths would not cross, but she pulled him to her and he could resist no more.

The next morning, Vincent headed downtown to meet with Walt Jameson, employment attorney referral from a friend. He agreed to draw up the paperwork for a lawsuit and an attorney-client agreement as he committed to suing his previous employer out of his own pocket, which would be a $7,500 retainer down payment against what could cost him tens of thousands.

And the following Monday, January 9, Vincent was slated to meet Mark Sturgis. He did so at the Renaissance Hotel in an immense meeting room they had rented out for three days.

The table was made of oak and there were 20 plush, swiveling chairs. Only Sturgis (who stood upon Vincent's entrance), Doug and Susie utilized them, all on the far left side as Vincent entered. Sturgis sat at the head of the table on Vincent's left while Susie and Doug sat across the table from Vincent. It was the first time Vincent had seen them in the flesh in several weeks.

Vincent carried his brag book and padfolio in with him, setting them on the table.

"Hi. I'm Vincent Scott."

"Mark Sturgis. Good to meet you. Thanks for coming."

"Wouldn't miss it," Vincent replied. He walked around the table to shake hands with Doug and Susie. Kill them with kindness to the last.

"Doug, Susie – how have you been?"

"Good, how about you?" Susie answered awkwardly.

Vincent was not going to play into their expectation. He wouldn't play into anyone's expectations.

"First off, I just want to thank all of you for taking the time out of your busy schedules to meet with me. I want to let you all know that I want to do anything and everything possible to make this transition as smooth as possible for everyone," Vincent announced.

"I appreciate that," Mark stated. "You're here because what you have done for Brink, for Moriarty and for Cellular Horizons is undeniable. I've been in interviews all day today hearing many of the things you have contributed. The people we have met with today think very highly of you and I know you have done a lot for all of us. I definitely wanted the chance to meet with you."

Mark asked tough questions, like why Vincent did not terminate De-Metre Jones. Vincent told them why: because the issue was with De-Metre's greenness in the manager role and because of a rotten Assistant. He had fired the Assistant, recommended De-Metre stay on as a sales rep in the new regime and added, "I forwarded the résumé of the candidate I recommend for the New Brighton Store Manager to Doug and Susie last week."

Susie clearly had some pent up angst.

"Vincent – for the last few months, it has felt like it's you against us," she lamented. "It didn't use to be like that, and it's palpable. I can feel it when I'm on store visits; your managers are very cautious around me. Why have you guys been against us?"

"Susie, I wholeheartedly respect the relationship our business has with Cellular Horizons. As you've said to my managers – your name is on the door," diplomatic Vincent explained. There he was – selling again.

"That said, we noticed last summer that this business was not headed where we were promised. We noticed last summer that we were being mismanaged. My first priority is to the people I am paid to support and – because of that – I chose to come to Doug about the ways by which Brink was failing our people even though Brink signs my paychecks. After that happened, Doug told Jordan Wallace exactly what I said, so admittedly I have been guarded since then.

"But I understand why Doug did what he did," Vincent continued with the spin doctoring. "His job is to support the dealer, and he did. But you must understand that from that point, I had to act on my people's behalf and make decisions and ask questions in their best interests. With the results we have somehow managed to produce over the past year, despite no support from Brink, despite not getting paid and not having inventory and wondering for the last three months when we were going to lose our jobs or if we would have jobs tomorrow, and the fact not a single one of these people have quit on me, I'd say we did pretty well.

"However, in closing, I apologize. If there is any sense of us against you, that was never my intention and I take our partnership very seriously. I have done nothing in recent weeks but talk to my team about how good it is that you are rescuing them. I have done nothing but try to help you as you take on these confused, worried employees, even conducting interviews and making recommendations based on my construction of the team that's here. And I am here to help you in any way I can."

That answer left Susie speechless: quite a feat in itself.

Vincent was able to summarize everything he wanted to summarize; he said everything he wanted to say. There would certainly be no regrets and nothing left on the table.

Jordan Wallace called Vincent later in the day.

"What did you say to Sturgis?" Wallace asked.

"What do you mean?"

"He said that was the best interview he has conducted in his entire career," Wallace marveled. "Don't get me wrong – I'm not surprised. You were the best interview I've ever conducted. But he said he expected you to walk in and be an arrogant jackass, but that you were humble and endearing. I think he's going to offer you something."

"That's interesting."

"Yeah, man, but I'm already working on my next project."

"I'm not surprised."

"I've got a couple of things going right now. Have you heard of P90X?"

Jordan Wallace went on to change the subject to talking about a workout program regimen he was going to package and sell across the country. He also talked about his website that he was going to package and sell to retailers across the country. He also talked about a fruit smoothie pyramid scheme he wanted Vincent's help on. As usual, there were no salaries, and they'd sacrifice for a while, but then they'd be millionaires.

Where had Vincent heard this before?

Vincent smiled, as it seemed very soon he wouldn't have to hear it again.

Wallace claimed he was also going to make one last ditch effort to unload the business to someone other than Moriarty; flying to Las Vegas to pitch it at a wireless conference to other Cellular Horizons dealers.

The hand had been dealt and played, but Wallace refused to leave the table.

Fortunately for Vincent, he no longer had to play this game.

He had a phone interview the following day for a leadership role with a pharmaceutical company, a face-to-face interview with a major cable provider and now would be asked to join Moriarty.

He could finally breathe again.

Abby came over for a while that night, but left stating she did not feel well. Vincent text messaged her the following morning to make sure she had gotten home and to work alright since he had not heard a peep from her.

In her response, she said she thought it all over and wanted to just be friends.

Vincent had not even put anything else out there; he had succumbed to her advances and considered how on earth they could actually make it work this time for yet another time, but given it no further real concrete thought.

Obviously, something was up with her; Abby forced her way back on Vincent's radar. She told him how much she loved him. He actually let himself contemplate it. And then she says she wants to be just friends. He had enough going on to pursue it any further and had dealt with the ups and downs of this relationship long enough not to be overly surprised.

A text message that day from Emily inviting him over because she "only slept well when he was there" was an invitation accepted. A night with her and a bottle of Smirnoff were the only thing that could drown out the confusion in his head.

Vincent's phone interview with another potential company turned out to be a dead end; it was explained that they really wanted someone to already be in the business. So – knowing that he was not in the business – why on earth did they talk to him in the first place?

He had a meeting he had set up through LinkedIn with a Regional VP with Carter Telecom – a name in the cable and telecommunications business – where the VP pawned him off on two sales managers. What was this – they wanted to bring him on as a call center business to business rep? A role he had managed the managers of 5 years ago?

This was the job-hunting game at its best; his credentials either meant nothing or he was told he was over-qualified. No matter where he set his potential sights on, he'd have to start all over in their organization, even if he could have run the place.

At least there was Moriarty. It would hold him over until he landed something better.

Wallace kept calling throughout the week; it was the most Vincent had heard from him in a while.

"There are 100 million obese people in America," he preached. "We only need to sell 9,000 weight loss packages to make $75,000 per month. That's a million dollars."

He was also looking at using the space for the Mankato mall kiosk to create an upscale clothing kiosk. The real bonus was that he was going to be kind enough to let Vincent co-own, operate and staff it himself!

The next conversation it was selling travel packages across the country to business executives.

Then it was donating clothes to children on the behalf of patrons at featured clothing outlets.

At least that one wasn't half bad.

Rumors swirled, but nothing was confirmed about who was staying and where they were going.

Terry was still in Vincent's ear about teaming up with him and Saul to start Scott Management Solutions and set up "pods" of small business CEO's that would work together to generate leads and share ideas and form newsletters…

Vincent just wanted a steady paycheck he could count on and a role that would allow him to flex his management muscle. He wanted a consistent, steady relationship that actually made him feel good about himself. Why was this seemingly too much to ask?

On the morning of Wednesday, January 18, Mark Sturgis conducted a call for all Brink employees.

The finalization of the deal with Brink Management Company was front and center; the terms, the next steps and how the plan would play out.

Jordan Wallace, Doug Wilson and Susie Wilson were on the call. Kent Smyth was on the call.

Vincent was mentioned at 10 minutes, 11 seconds into the call for "doing great continuation training" for the district. He was not mentioned again.

Vincent spoke at the end, touting this as a win for the employees, thanking the employees. Diplomatic to the last.

But it was made clear: Doug Wilson would reveal the rosters for the stores and everything would take effect February 1. Vincent would have nothing to do with hiring or selection. He could only sit and wait for his job offer.

Vincent picked Elizabeth up from school that night, and Elizabeth told Vincent that "Mommy is going to marry Chris."

"Yeah, I'm sure she is," Vincent responded, thinking little of it.

But when a friend and former co-worker called him that night and asked if he had heard the news, it was confirmed: Abby Winters was engaged to marry Chris Hurst.

Vincent did not sleep overnight.

He stayed home the following day with Elizabeth since he really had nowhere to go or be. They played, he cleaned the apartment – anything to take his mind off of everything in flux in his life.

Terry Bunche called a few times. Nothing from Doug Wilson.

The silence was deafening on all sides. Where was Vincent's job offer? Where was any news whatsoever?

Abby did call later in the evening; she had gotten a call from Walt Jameson, Vincent's attorney, to gather information about Vincent's case. She was scared about how it was going to impact her job.

"Do whatever you want to do, Abby. You typically do."

"Vincent, I know what they did to you was wrong. Everybody does. I just don't want to be a target."

"If they wanted you gone, they would have taken you out already," Vincent said. "Don't you see that?"

"I just don't know what to do."

"Well – like I said – do whatever you choose to do. I don't care anymore."

There was a pause.

"I also have something else I need to tell you."

"I already know."

"What do you mean?"

"Oh, because you didn't have the respect to tell me previously, our daughter already told me that you're marrying Chris. Congratulations."

"Oh… I'm sorry. I didn't intend—"

"No, you didn't think. You never do. You never think about anyone but yourself. But you're not my problem anymore."

Vincent hung up. He ignored the ensuing rings.

Confirmation hit like a ton of bricks. But he could not talk to her right now. He had to absorb the punches and let them soak in so he could go numb again.

A few vodkas in, Vincent sent a text that night saying, "Don't marry him." Abby called again, but he again did not respond.

The Moriarty news was actually starting to come in now; Reggie Sherman – toiling away in Texas running two stores – was not being brought back. He had tried to unseat absentee leader Aaron Hartley, who was actually friends with Jared Cox, and it served as his undoing in the new regime. People who could bring dissent against these terrible Moriarty and Cellular Horizons practices were not welcome here.

Hartley was also given the boot.

The Abby thing still had him floored.

But it wasn't like Vincent could or would commit to her, right? So no matter how weirded out he was… he could not do anything to stop this man from becoming his sweet princess's stepfather. This man who was always Abby's go-to move when he didn't commit. This man who flaked on her every time something bad happened and she came running to Vincent. Faced with choices Vincent had faced with Abby before, Chris always did the least admirable thing. And now he'd be in Elizabeth's life forever.

Chris and Abby were going to be husband and wife.

More Brink contemporaries called; Saul revealed that Doug told him they were moving Saul back to the lower-volume and less predictable downtown location where he would make considerably less money and he would be losing his District Sales Manager title. The crown jewel of the Minneapolis stores – Bloomington – would be given to "an all-star" they were bringing in from Moriarty corporate that would know nothing about the location. Brilliant.

De-Metre was being demoted to sales rep and would work for Saul. Interesting – of course – that everyone wanted De-Metre fired so badly weeks prior and now he was being offered a job in this new program.

Doug and Kent were visiting stores together all day and spreading cheer.

Wallace called and was still talking up his revolutionary P90X program. When Vincent pressed about any news about himself, Wallace said he had called Mark Sturgis 4 times that day and not gotten a response.

Vincent got a call from a contact he had made on LinkedIn who was a Sales Director for a business supplies company. Even after reviewing Vincent's résumé, he was interested in Vincent as a possible sales rep.

Vincent put Elizabeth to bed, and could hear her singing and talking to herself from his perch on his computer chair.

There was a vodka and diet soda at his side and pictures of Abby, him with Abby, and pictures of Elizabeth with them on his computer screen.

Pit in his stomach, he was plagued with thought.

*Should I call her? Should I try to keep her from moving forward with this?*

*Why do I care?*

*I love her and I hate her. Could I ever live with her? Can I live without her? Could I ever forgive her?*

*I had the chance… and I was hesitant and reluctant. For good reason.*

*She's never been there for me. She isn't here for me now. And she only wants me when she splits with him or when the chips are down. She told me two weeks ago that I'm the one. Now she's getting married October 6…*

*So why do I give a damn?*

*It can't just be about Elizabeth; I've lived without her for 4 years…*

Vincent Scott had no idea what to do. About anything.

He went to lay by his daughter. His love. His sole salvation.

## Curtains

On Thursday, January 26, 2012, a full 734 days after being banished by his previous employer, Vincent Scott awoke, showered, dressed and set about his day.

He dropped the love of his life – Elizabeth Scott – off at her preschool.

He headed to the office of Walt Jameson, signed a letter of engagement, committing to the firm and handed over a check for $7,500 retainer.

He made the drive to the downtown Minneapolis office in the wake of the Moriarty transition with no knowledge of what was going to happen, what his next move would be and the realization he could not even hold on to a job that was beneath him despite exhausting every ounce of himself for it. But the days were ticking down and time was drawing closer to a conclusion: one way or another.

And despite the horrifying relationship past with Elizabeth's mother – Abby Winters – the book was being closed on any hope they could reconcile, as she was marrying his second fiddle: Chris Hurst.

Or maybe Vincent had always been the second fiddle.

Terry Bunche and Saul Portman were there, and it was fitting; these three had been part of a support group that made it through their team not getting paid, not getting inventory, not getting support, not getting leadership and not getting guidance and they would learn the fate of their band together.

The three sauntered across the street to a local sandwich joint where they indulged in a breakfast sandwich and their morning caffeine. And it was surreal: Vincent sat there staring through the window at the 45-story citadel where he had become a legend. Also inside that building was the other puzzling character of this play: Abby Winters, who was moving on with her life. Finally, across the street on the side closest him was Cellular Horizons, Vincent's latest failure.

Even with all his abilities, his efforts, his blood, sweat and tears, he could not make Brink Management Company work. And now, he had nothing left in the tank.

Terry's phone rang.

"It's Doug," Terry said.

"Answer it," Vincent responded, numbly. The fact his subordinate was getting a call before him did not bode well.

Again, the knockdown punch was inevitable. But the Moriarty players had lied; Vincent was supposed to be the first person they called.

Terry nodded, he acknowledged, he thanked. The whole scene was a blur to Vincent. He just wanted the punch to come.

Once the call concluded, Terry looked up.

"So, they want me to go back to managing Eden Prairie. No more call center. What a slap in the face," Terry muttered.

"At least you have resolution," Vincent responded. "At least you have a job."

"Vincent, you know that no matter what happens, we're here because of you. We're still fighting because of you. Moriarty can't take that away from you. Cellular Horizons can't take that away from you."

"They'll sure as hell try," Vincent said. He then looked away – outside the restaurant window again.

"And here I sit – it's funny in a sick kind of way," Vincent continued. "Surrounded by my most significant failures in life."

"Come on, man," Terry interjected. "Don't beat yourself up – it's not that bad. We wouldn't be here right now if it wasn't for you."

"Exactly," Saul chimed in. "Nobody gave this market any chance at success until you came along."

Vincent took a sip of his diet cola.

"We have great service, solid products and a winning team, and we can't even make it work because we don't have the support to do it with," Vincent said. "It's so frustrating – not being able to carry out your role because of so many factors completely out of your control. For some reason, I just always thought we could somehow win. Hell, look at what we've accomplished with zero budget and zero leadership just up to this point."

"Absolutely," Terry responded. "We've come this far on your back."

"One way or another, we'll figure out our next move soon," Saul added.

"And then there's Abby. For whatever reason, I thought we would figure it out – that we had time, the door was open and we'd figure it out. We were engaged, we drove each other mad, cheated on each other, had restraining orders against each other, we've battled in court five times… I had her exactly where I wanted her in court, but couldn't bring myself to finish her off. She's like my kryptonite… and I can't stand the thought of her with someone else. I've always been the guy she's turned to when she needed anything and I've always been there for her. I've just always believed we would eventually grow into the people we wanted each other to be… the door was open and now she's closed it."

Vincent took another pensive sip of his drink.

"It's not over 'til it's over, man – you know that. On either front," Saul offered. Vincent shook his head.

"Every time we come back together and try, something happens and I run for the hills," Vincent continued. "Sometimes I look for excuses to run. Sometimes she hands me the reasons on a silver platter. But I run every time."

The conversation was interrupted with Vincent's phone ringing. He fished it from his pocket and looked at the Caller ID.

Susie Wilson. *What the hell did she want?*

"This should be interesting," he observed.

"Hello?"

"Vincent, hey, it's Susie."

"Wow – yeah, long time no talk."

"Yeah, I know. I know this has been a crazy situation and I'm sure you realize why I had to stay quiet through all of it."

"Sure," Vincent responded. She had stayed quiet because she was trying like hell to unseat him.

"Well, I just wanted to say I heard the news and wanted to reach out to you and say I'm sorry to hear it and it's really been a pleasure working with you," Susie said. Her attempt to sound genuine was not having its desired effect.

*What news?* Vincent thought, and wanted to say.

"OK," Vincent said. Susie had to break the silence.

"Do you have any idea what you're going to do next?" Susie continued.

"Yes I do," Vincent answered. Again, there was silence because Susie had to scramble to think of what to say. Vincent was not taking this as she anticipated.

"Well, I have no doubt you'll succeed in whatever you do, Vincent," Susie continued.

"I have no doubt of that as well," Vincent said back, coolly.

"You know, I have to say, you're handling this very professionally," Susie commented, as if she wanted Vincent to blow his top or lose his cool.

"How else would I handle it, Susie?" Vincent asked. "I am a professional."

"Well..." Susie stuttered slightly. "I wish you the best, Vincent."

"Thank you," Vincent responded. "Goodbye."

He hung up.

Not only had Doug Wilson not contacted Vincent to break the news to him like a man, but Susie had called him just to get the satisfaction of seeing Vincent "defeated."

But he had not been defeated. He had played his heart out. The game was lost, but the season was not over.

"What was that?" Terry asked.

"Susie, calling me to tell me it's been a pleasure working together and she 'heard the news.'"

"What news?" Terry inquired.

"Exactly," Vincent said. "The fix was in from the start. And I'm going out in a blaze of glory. Let's go."

The three walked back across the street to their store. It was *their* store. They were the ones who had turned this into something; not Jordan Wallace, not Doug Wilson, not Susie Wilson. Vincent was proud that this team had withstood everything up until their forced dismantling.

En route, Vincent made a call to Lee Christian – one of his few real confidantes in the business.

"Hey, Vincent – what's up?"

"You tell me. Have you heard anything new lately?"

"Like what?"

"Well, I just got a call from Susie Wilson to offer her condolences on Moriarty not bringing me on in their new regime," Vincent scoffed. "I presume today's D-Day."

"Yeah," Lee responded. "I got laid off today, too."

"Well – it's been fun, my friend. I guess Jordan will be calling any minute to talk to me more about our next money-making scheme."

"Just be careful, Vincent. He told me today he's known for weeks that Moriarty wasn't bringing you on; he knew and let you believe that they might."

Vincent stopped dead in his tracks. His mind raced to their conversations.

"Interesting, but not surprising. Well – stay in touch, good sir. Let me know if you hear anything new."

"Will do, Vincent."

As Vincent's 100-words-per-minute lightning fast fingers leapt into action penning a eulogy to their project, his phone continued to ring throughout the hour to come; Darryl Wilkinson was being brought on board to stay on with Golden

Valley. De-Metre Jones was being demoted and sent downtown to work for Saul, while another hand-picked Moriarty clown would step in to manage New Brighton – *not* the one Vincent had recommended during his 3-day interview blitz but someone Vincent had once interviewed and disqualified.

The management team was mostly staying together, but Vincent was being kicked off the team.

Vincent's closest advisors – Saul and Terry – were being punished, and, while they were the best managers he had, were being banished to the worst stores.

Moriarty was showing them who was boss.

It made sending the final kiss-off all the more satisfying, but bittersweet; Vincent had given all he could and it just was not enough. Like with past loves. Like with his last employer.

He re-read his work just once. Terry read it.

He pressed the "send" button and felt it signal the official end of this thankless experience as it hit like a thud in the inboxes of everyone he had ever encountered since starting with Brink; Wallace, the Moriarty brothers and board members, Mark Sturgis and the Wilson two-headed monster, plus Hartley, Christian and every rep and manager in Brink Management Company, Kent Smyth and Kurt Stillwater. The recipients counted in the hundreds.

"Good afternoon, all.

One year ago, I signed on as Regional Manager of Minnesota for Brink Management Company. Sold a dream and walking into a situation with no structure, no support and virtually no hope, I banded together with a core team of people who has gained my utmost respect over the last 12 months. Today, I thank them wholeheartedly. Neither I nor we would have made it to this point without you.

Two weeks ago, after e-mailing and calling everyone I knew at Cellular Horizons and Moriarty, Mark Sturgis finally agreed to meet with me. No one else has even acknowledged my existence. Per Jordan Wallace, this meeting took place simply because there was fear I would do something detrimental to the stores I love were I not granted a meeting. It is a pity; all I was after is to be something other than Moses leading his people to a Promised Land he is forbidden to enter. Considering what we have accomplished with no structure, support or help, I was elated to imagine what we could do with the power of an agent as revered and heralded as Moriarty. I would have also thought that my leadership and contributions over the last year would have warranted consideration and appreciation. Not so.

Over the last year, our results in Minnesota skyrocketed. We were praised. We had a mid-year review with Jordan, Cellular Horizons, and Moriarty where our 150% year-over-year increases were lauded. Jordan Wallace "promoted" me three times, and I was running sometimes three conference calls per day for every store of the 33 in his jurisdiction. Times were high, our key performance indicators bested those of Cellular Horizons and Moriarty corporate doors in pretty much every area, we beat our year over year averages even in our toughest and most impossible months, and things were looking really good. We developed lead generation, marketing programs, Chamber of Commerce teams, you name it. I won Cellular Horizons Superstar, made 20 sales training videos, wrote scripts, made an observation form, developed appraisals, and ran the marketing for 33 stores.

There is some rumor that I was in support of 1099 coming to the company, which is simply not true, and I am copying everyone I know on this correspondence because you can ask anyone: I was expected to change all our stores completely to 1099 as Texas did, and I flatly refused. It was not in the best interests of my team. Doug Wilson has quoted that 'Jordan, Vincent, Aaron and Lee sat around and agreed on this.' Not true. I was given a directive. I hired 70+ of them, because I follow orders, and it did not work. In fact, when I went to Doug Wilson and told him that this would not work, he called Jordan Wallace and instructed him that I was not supporting him and his initiative. This caused unrest between Jordan and me, and was a first warning that I not go to Moriarty or Cellular Horizons with my or my team's concerns.

When Hermantown stopped posting 100 new lines per month and our average inevitably dropped, our results came under fire, despite huge growth and record numbers in nearly every other store and despite employee losses and morale drop due to constant payroll and inventory debacles. Doug and Susie: you asked me repeatedly in my 'interview' with Mark Sturgis and you about why it has been 'us' against 'you' and I told you then and I stand by it now that I have done nothing to create or foster this sentiment. Ask anyone. When our results started being attacked, despite having no inventory, our company direction being to hire nothing but 1099's, and having no idea day to day if we were going to have jobs by which to support our families, we were shoved to an island that we could never return from. Neither we, nor I, created a rift. And I will be damned if I am going to allow Monday morning quarterbacks to attack my team.

My team came under fire. I was told to terminate people that did not deserve to be terminated (and who, apparently, are now going to be offered jobs!). My management methods and the methods of my team came under question. My decisions came under question. But, standing here now, no one can or should even have the audacity to question the way by which I ran my stores. If it had not been for me, these doors would have closed months ago. Ask anyone. If it had not been for me, key team members would have left months ago. My MVP, Saul Portman, practically left three times, yet each time I secured him, and when he went to Bloomington, their GP and new lines hit new heights despite still not having any inventory or direction or structure. People like Terry Bunche, Saul Portman, Darryl Wilkinson, De-Metre Jones and Reggie Sherman stood by me and I stood by them, and we truly made a difference in an impossible world. NO ONE can take that away from us.

I went to Doug Wilson and Susie Wilson every time I had concerns with our lack of direction. Over 1099, over the inventory problems, the bi-weekly payroll problems, and the overall mismanagement of Brink. Not only was nothing done, but it was reported to Jordan Wallace. So, I ask you all now: what more should I or could I have done? Who else was I supposed to turn to? I followed the directives of my supervisor, all while fighting to serve and protect the people I was paid to serve and protect. If anyone wants to second guess that, shame on you, for you could not and have not lived a day in our shoes.

Three weeks ago, I called Doug Wilson and told him: I'm a single Dad and a grown man. If you do not have a place for me, just tell me. He fumbled for words, said he understood and would call Kent Smyth and call me back. That call never came. And it is not lost on me that Kent has been in town three times since that time.

Two weeks ago, in my 'interview' I was told that I would be the first person reached out to by Moriarty when a decision was made on what role, if any, I would play in the new schematic. Then, I was called by Susie Wilson moments ago, as she told me she 'heard the news' and that she wishes me luck. What news?

There was no news. So, the fix was in, and no one has the courage to tell me. Me, the one who worked 70 hours per week and killed himself for a project that had no chance of success, no support and no thanks.

Now I am told that Jordan Wallace has known for weeks that I was never going to get a job offer, but that he never told me. Even now, neither he nor anyone has told me anything. No one at Moriarty has reached out to me. No one at Cellular Horizons has reached out to me.

And you wonder why I consider myself a man against the world. You wonder who made it 'us against you'.

I think it is important for everyone to know exactly who they are dealing with.

I think it is important for everyone to know that the things this team and I did and fought for and fought through and contributed over the last year are things that no one else could have done. That is why we have been painted as renegades by those who feel threatened by us; because Doug and Susie never took any time to get to know this team. They were not in our stores. They have been to some of our stores maybe once or twice in the year I have been here. Unless they have 365 stores in their jurisdiction, this is simply letting us down and not doing their jobs. Their "store visits" consist of meeting each other at a store to go to lunch together on their companies' dime.

I did fight and will fight for anyone and anything I believe in. I believe in this team. It has been an honor and a privilege to be a part of it.

The shame in all of this is that the people who did the least in all of this never had any threat to their $100,000+ per year paycheck. The rest of us had no such luck or people in our corners.

I even did an interview blitz as an unsolicited service two weeks ago and sent a note with full recommendations on who should stay and who should be brought on, and I did not even get the courtesy of a response.

I have known for quite some time of some personnel changes that needed to be made, but I was not about to sacrifice what results we were managing all while bringing some new unsuspecting victim onto a ship as doomed as the *Titanic*.

Brink Team: This is my last act as your leader. Fight the good fight, hold your head up high and do what you believe in. I believe in you, and I thank you for believing in me. Have no doubt that we did the right things and we did everything we could. If someone else cannot see that, it is their loss. Not ours. Everything happens for a reason, and we will all live to fight another day. Never compromise yourselves, live without regrets and know that I am proud to have known you.

Susie: you stated when you called me moments ago that you were surprised I was being so professional. What did you expect? I am a professional. The unprofessionalism that I have witnessed throughout the past year and through this transition and the lack of basic human respect absolutely shock me, and I have nothing more to say.

All the best, and sincerely,

*Vincent T. Scott"*

 

    Vincent shook Terry's hand. Vincent's phone began to literally erupt as his team read the e-mail. It was set off instantly by calls and text messages praising his exit, wishing him well, calling him hero and telling him to call when he could.

    "You've got to stay in touch, brother," Terry said, embracing his fallen leader.

    "We'll see each other again," Vincent responded.

"Dude, seriously – you're an inspiration," Saul said, shaking Vincent's hand and hugging him.

And now, walking out onto the exact same street that greeted him with unemployment the last time, physically and metaphorically at another crossroads of his life and surrounded by his greatest failures with every facet of his life in question and no prospects to speak of, Vincent Scott was the salesman against the world.

# Abby

"Hello?"

"Hi."

"Vincent? Is everything OK?"

"Yeah, I'm fine. I want to see you. Come down."

"What?"

"You heard me. Please come down. I'm outside... outside my store," Vincent concluded.

She paused before agreeing. "OK. Give me five minutes."

In a scene of poetic imagery, Abby emerged from the building where she had first met Vincent Scott; she stood across the street – seemingly worlds away in that protective force field Vincent could not cross over to.

She was beautiful.

Vincent realized he didn't let himself look at her in that way anymore. He didn't really allow himself to look at her much at all; *really look*. He had been so lost in his anger and hatred for so long that – until now – he hadn't truly looked at her like he did at this instant.

It was in moments like this when Vincent found himself wondering why they couldn't make it work. Their past had been a battlefield, she had cost him a small fortune, but he could not bear the thought of this woman with anyone else.

Abby crossed the street to Vincent. It was cold and she wore a long brown overcoat over a purple shirt. Vincent wore his black leather jacket; his tie loosened after an eventful day.

"I don't really know what to say," Abby began.

"Start with how you could tell me two weeks ago that you're in love with me; that I'm the one. And now you can be engaged to marry someone else."

"OK – that's fair," Abby answered. "Vincent – it doesn't ever work between us. And I don't have the ability to wait around for it to."

"But to marry someone else and close off all hope? I don't know... I know our relationship has been insane but I guess I just didn't see this coming."

"Is that why you have a problem with it?"

"No matter what you've ever been to me, you are more than just Elizabeth's mother – you know that," Vincent said. "Are you in love with Chris?"

"I love him."

"So – that's a no. Which makes this even more perplexing. How can you marry someone you're not in love with? Did he change his stance on wanting kids?"

"No."

"Then – please – enlighten me."

"Why do you want to have this conversation now, as opposed to anytime in the last six years?"

"Because it's always been complicated. But now I feel like I have a gun to my head."

"And that's not what I'm after."

"What is this – did you get engaged to him to force me to act? Get attention? What?"

"No, Vincent. I want to be married."

"Sure – I get that. But why the urgency?"

There was a long pause. The two looked at each other and were flooded with the conglomeration of feelings that had existed between them for the last several years.

"I— " Abby began.

"Look... I don't know what we're doing out here. I know why I couldn't talk about this before... why I could never talk about any of this before. I have a lot to say but I didn't want to have a knee jerk reaction to your engagement. I thought I could just bury my thoughts and feelings but – for once, I can't."

He gave a slight smile and continued.

"I do love you. I always have. And maybe that's weird considering we fought like hell for years and we did everything we could to hurt each other or one-up each other in court and in dating other people... suffice it to say, we have never had a good relationship. I don't know if I ever gave you a fair chance, because I've always thought I was supposed to hold out for some relationship that just blew me away in every way and didn't require this much work. I've had girls in my past where I thought we had something special but I realize now they weren't real; we never dealt with real issues like you and I have. There was no substance and they always let me down and it was unfair of me to expect you to be like the perfect, unrealistic image I had of others or that I held you to.

"If this is the end, and you choose to marry Chris, congratulations. I really mean that. I've thought about so many things this past week; I tried to ignore it all but for once I'm going to let it all out in the open. I wonder if you used me to get him to commit, or if you committed to him because you finally gave up on me.

"You say you don't fight with him. When you're with me, we fight because we're alive. Then I'm at Ted's the other night and a scary movie is on TV and I'm thinking you and I should be watching it while your pets crawl all over me after we put Elizabeth to bed.

"*I do* want to need you; I just don't know how to let myself – with you or anyone.

"And I know I've held you to a different standard than anyone else – even myself. I know you ran back to Chris every time things blew up with us, but I had girls, too, so it's not fair to hold that against you. The last five years have been hell for me, but they haven't been easy for you either – I get that now. Neither of us has done a perfect job of being there for the other. We've both said and done things that we can't get past. But maybe that's the point; because we're different people now than we were five years ago. But we still love each other, and I believe we always will."

Vincent stopped momentarily as he looked at Abby. She was speechless, taking it all in, and tears started to well up in her eyes.

"I can't propose to you today. But what I can do is commit to figuring this out. We owe that to ourselves.

"My first offer on the table is a date. Valentine's Day at any place you desire.

"I want to take you and Elizabeth to Disney World this year.

"And I want us to go to counseling. We've talked about it for years and it's past time."

Vincent paused again to let it sink in.

"I know you probably think I'm just saying all of these things because you're engaged. Maybe that's partly true; I was warming up to these ideas and they were in the back of my mind, but the thought of you marrying someone else destroys me. I can't give you the ring today, but I can tell you that what we have is worth figuring out – once and for all."

Abby looked down and dabbed at her eyes. Vincent moved a little bit closer.

"And if you choose him, so be it," he continued. "I'll accept it and I'll be happy for you. Love is wanting someone else to be happy even if it makes you miserable. But I want you to tell me to my face that he's your choice and that things are finally, 100% over between us. We've done this dance for 5 years and the music's over.

"I can't guarantee anything, but I know we keep ending up back in this place. And I know that I hate fighting with you. And I know we love our daughter.

"And – for once – we can both know that we're not doing this because of her.

"When it's been you up against any other girl in the world, they have never stood a chance. All roads lead back to you and me. Maybe it's time we got it right."

Abby was crying. Vincent stood in silence for what seemed like an eternity to hear what Abby's response would be.

"Vincent…" she began, only to not be able to finish.

She hugged him. They hugged for minutes in the chilly evening of Thursday, January 26, 2011.

"Vincent," Abby continued as their embrace concluded, the two looking into each other's' eyes and tears streaming down her face. "I have cancer."

# "The Surviving Game" by Vincent Scott
## Hodgepodge: Important Ingredients to Success

To achieve your definition of success through all the experiences and challenges you will face, you must consistently remind yourself of priorities and the positive pieces of your life. That becomes increasingly difficult at times, specifically because there is not only one path, there are unexpected twists and turns and you will not have control over far more than you'd like. But what you do have control over is quite significant: who you surround yourself with, how you live your life and treat others, what you do with your talents and how you set yourself up to win in this interesting world.

### Faith, Family and Friends

At various times in your life, you hold beliefs that are likely very near and dear to you. These beliefs have substantial impact on how you live your life and what you find important.

So much of life consists of uncertainty and sacrifice and pain and doubt and you may wonder at times if and when it will ever pay off. That's where faith comes in. When everything else is stripped away and hope seems lost and doubt is prevalent, faith is what remains.

So much of life is spent wondering who we can trust and believe in; we will spend time feeling alone and isolated. We are abandoned, we realize our true allies; we go through thick and thin with these people. This is family. These are friends.

Faith isn't necessarily in a deity or an ideal, it is in something intangible that brings you strength. Faith is believing in something bigger than ourselves, be it a god, an afterlife or a higher calling in the universe.

Family isn't necessarily a blood relative, it isn't necessarily a parent or a child or a sibling. It's who you unconditionally love, who you let in to your inner sanctum to see the real you, who you are there for, no questions asked. It may be 1 person or 10, but these are the people who support your fortress when it is in danger of falling down.

Friends. Your list will erode, evaporate, dissipate greatly over the years. At first, you may even think this is a bad thing, but it is quite the contrary. The dead skin, dead weight, unnecessary fat has been shed and the bonds that endured and survived are the fittest.

Judge people by their actions, not their words; how they have behaved in rocky situations and if their words have held up. Judge situations and things by history and odds, not knee-jerk reactions. If someone has always been there for themselves and not for you; if someone has failed you every time you have been in need – these things will never change.

If you have people in your life that bail on you when you actually need their support, only come to you when you have something they want and have never given anything to you without hope for receipt, they are not your friends.

There are no free rides in life. We are entitled to the pursuit of happiness, not happiness.

Those who do the most, invest the most and pledge the most of themselves will ultimately get the most; just not always on their timetable or the means by which they anticipated.

And it's not about financial reward, about power, about fame. It's about freedom, about knowing who you can trust, and about getting up every time you fall down or are knocked down.

It's easy to complain or point fingers or play the blame game. It's more difficult to look inside, evolve, and become the person you are meant to be.

People often mock the rich and famous or the people they don't understand because it's easy to sit on their couches and curse them from afar, but these mindsets come from their vast insecurities they are unwilling to claim.

In life, we have all been bestowed talents and gifts, whether we choose to use them, give them, show them or not. We will all be judged, whether you believe in a god or not; we are judged by time, by history, by memories. They are not all fair, they are not all kind, but in death, that journey is over.

That is why life is the ultimate gift. Some squander it like the paycheck they rush to spend. Some invest and hold on to it for far too long, never truly experiencing it.

How will history and your actions and your life define you? And how will you define them?

Time won't tell. Your actions will.

To truly capture success and happiness, you must first acknowledge that your definition of those things is different from everyone else's in the world. Your goals, desires, talents and abilities are unique to you and you alone hold the keys to unlocking your potential.

It does not matter if no one else understands what you are after. All that does is that you know what you want and are fighting to get it.

You see, others fall and stay down; they look for reasons to stop trying. That is why they fail. Should you want to obtain your goal, the last thing you want is to "fit in" or be "average" or "status quo" because you will wind up just like them: a failure or underachiever.

What do you have more of: fear of failure or desire for success? Whichever tips the scales in the balance of your life is what you will inevitably find.

Journeys – of life and in life – are the true rewards, not the destination. That is why there are no shortcuts. Live a good life and take care of those you care about above all else. Leave the past in the past, take the lessons forward and embrace each new day if it comes.

There will never be an eternal, uninterrupted, prolonged peace and happiness. Seize the good moments while you have them and while you can. Fight to keep the people and things in your life that matter. Invest positively in your life so that future dividends can be realized and longer states of happiness enjoyed.

The older and more experienced you get, the easier it is to absorb the shock of the bullets from daily life. They will still sting and pierce the skin, but they won't reach the heart.

The more you know about the world, the more terrified you are of it and scared for its well-being. But you can make a difference in it: one action, one person you touch, one contribution at a time. The ripple effects your actions will have on the others who follow suit and continue to impact others can be monumental.

That said, it is faith, family and friends that pull us through the ups and downs, trials and tribulations and the wins and losses of living.

## Handling Criticism

We've discussed handling rejection in sales and searching for jobs, but one thing we never delved into fully was how to handle the critics.

Everyone has an opinion and believe me – you'll hear plenty of opinions about everything: the weather, the job market, jobs, relationships, people – you name it.

As we have discussed, there is such a thing as constructive criticism: advice or feedback that you can utilize or mold into concrete ways to alter your process. Learning how to accept constructive criticism as just that can take time because we have to first be able to acknowledge the person is likely trying to help or has a valid point. Accepting our own faults is not easy but it is imperative if we will grow and improve and jettison our comfortable ways of failing.

Nevertheless, there are a lot of people that hate or destroy or tear down for no reason other than to bring you down. There are plenty of people who are unhappy or lazy or less fortunate who would love nothing else than to see successful, happy people be less so. If you lend credence to their words and actions of hatred toward you, only they win.

Consider the source: you should care about the thoughts and feelings of those who have your best interests at heart. If someone really has no presence in your life or brings no value to it, their opinion is just as worthless.

Don't get me wrong: their words will sting and their hatred will affect you no matter what you do. Often, it can come out of nowhere; unprovoked and unwarranted. But it is what you do in reaction and in response to this hatred – like your reactions and responses to many things in your life – that will become part of your reputation and will define your character.

Think through the place this criticism belongs in your life. If it has no place in your reality, make sure it has no place in your mind.

### Financial Freedom

Like it or not, we need money to make it in this world. It pays our way through shelter and food (needs) and entertainment and experiences (wants) alike. That said, unless we are prudent about finding it, accumulating it and holding on to it, the financial aspect of our world can be quite agonizing.

**Never live outside your means – not even just a little bit.** With all of the innovations coming out, the phone we've just got to have, the movie we've just got to see or that expensive restaurant we love so much, this can be quite tempting to ignore. Let's face it: everyone wants to be financially well off – and you can be! You can be successful in this realm just like any other realm if you pay your dues.

When you are just starting out in the workforce, it is smart to start good spending habits. We need food, clothing and shelter; transportation to get to and from our job and other hotspots in our life is a must and there will always be unforeseen circumstances. Living paycheck to paycheck might sometimes be reality but stockpiling any additional harvest we can for those times our engine explodes or tire goes flat or we get a speeding ticket or other unsavory moments of life happen will ease future financial pains.

Money is one of those things we rarely have enough of in our own mind but we can certainly take positive steps to have a bigger sum. Even in years that were financially rewarding for me, I lived with far less than I could have had. I did this so I was always protected against any potential down side, was always able to have what I needed and was able to get much of what I wanted.

Consider carefully any extravagant wants you have and decide how important they are to you. If you are pursuing them to keep up with the Joneses' then stop jonesing – it's far more important to you and those who depend on you that you keep ahead of the Joneses' in another area: that of financial freedom through making good decisions and saving for the future.

When able, invest, and make it a point to regularly deposit your money in accounts that will yield a profit. When you can, see a financial advisor; you pay nothing for the initial consultation and if you find someone who has done well by someone you know, even better.

**Never loan money you are not OK with never seeing again.** People may mean well when they borrow from you, but when they are scratching and clawing to get back to some semblance of even, keeping up with the Joneses' is going to be a lot more important to them than paying you back. Trust me.

## Change

The word itself invokes visions of changes we have seen in our own lives. It can inspire, force adaptation and evolve the very way we think. It can also instill fear, trepidation and nervousness in even the most unshakable souls.

No matter how you slice it, change is inevitable in life. Sometimes the only constant in our lives - business and personal - is change; the seasons change, our outlooks change, relationships change. The approaches we take to things evolve based on experiences. As we grow older or witness or endure more things, our mindset, our application and our demeanor change as well.

In sales, the very concept of making a change is the entire foundation on which the profession is based; a salesperson's entire plight is determination of needs and weaknesses and holes in their potential client's current strategy (or, sometimes, lack thereof). The great salesperson is a listener; asking the right specific questions to best and most clearly ascertain the situation of their client so they can make a tailored, personalized recommendation that cures whatever ails them.

But, in the end, they are merely doing everything in their power to make the client's fear of change be outweighed by their fear of what happens on their current trajectory of standing pat.

They are selling change and the benefits of it.

People often resist change because they fear the unknown. Never mind their current diet or current work ethic or current bad behavior is leading them down a dark and treacherous path - they are mired in comfortable ways of failing! People do not change because they fear the effort and potential failure of the change more than they fear their current destination.

It's why people refuse to acknowledge health problems and continue smoking or drinking in excess or eating terrible foods. It is why people play it safe, why risk-takers are few and far between and why a lot of people are simply unhappy.

In my life, I have chosen change and have been forced to change; these decisions or situations were seemingly very difficult at the time, but we have to make decisions with clear definition of purpose in order to have positive growth in our own lives.

As I pointed out before, evolution of character, lifestyle and outcomes are all inherently based on making change. Change sounds scary, but so did going to war for those who have fought for freedoms or explorers who set out to discover new worlds. So did founding new countries, revolting against dictators or forging new destinies. So did sending a man to outer space. So does standing up to oppression or corruption. But if the right spirit, dedication and commitment lies behind that force of change, it will beget positive results.

People must let go of their fears, lest they will live a life of regret.

The real reason people fear change is their fear of the unknown and their willingness to settle for what they have. However, just as negativity can lie in the unknown, the answers to your wildest dreams are out there as well. It is far better to live a life of learning and no regret than to lament the decision to never chase after your dreams.

No matter who you are or what your calling, there has been an instance or hundreds which lifted your spirits to a plateau not previously thought possible. These are the inspirations, the influences and introspective energies that help us transform ourselves into better people. Their effect on us is often inexplicable but undeniable as they make us feel things - good and bad, powerful and riveting - and they are often the spice of our lives.

Much change is completely out of control, meaning our ability to adapt to it will determine our success. If we accept change and move on, we are far more likely to be at peace than if we complain or resist in these scenarios.

Parents are substantial influences in our lives, for better or worse. The friends, the teachers, the coaches, the mentors, the co-workers and significant others - they all come in and out of our lives (and sometimes back again, though few stay) and they give us things, take things, contribute things and teach us things. Then there are the countryside drives, the wind in our hair, the fact that just one song can encapsulate every emotion or memory we have attributed to it and be released simply by pressing play, and the hand of our child's in ours. Each of these things mold us into who we are constantly becoming in the ever-evolving process of life.

Life has a way of beating us senseless and refusing to relent just because we cry, "uncle"; occasionally, just for sport, it will even extend a helping hand only to sock us again when we try to get up. It typically stops just short of giving us more than we can handle, however, and, like the blacksmith forging a blade with scalding fire it sharpens us, strengthens us and instills in us the fortitude we need on our quest.

Inspiration made me lead my workforce with brilliance when the job was thankless and harsh. It keeps me wanting to help others despite the consequences. And without it, many people can become a shell of themselves.

The best thing about inspiration - about the things that can revive us, lift us and heal us - is that there is an unlimited supply. These things are always out there in the world, we just have to be willing to let them in and accept them. They do not discriminate or fail to live up to their promise; they merely touch us when we need it most.

The inspiration and motivation from faith, family and friends will guide us through even the most terrifying changes in our lives.

When our belief in ourselves or the world or our mission in life goes awry, these things get us back on track, provide support when nothing else does and are unfettered by the sometimes evil and murky waters of life.

## Health, Diet and Exercise

Diet and exercise sounds like a great commitment and idea to whip ourselves back in shape, but we actually have to get the ball rolling, stick to it and be patient to reach the desired plateau.

It is important to note: I'm no expert on the topic of health and fitness, but I have kept and can keep it simple for the casual busybody and workaholic alike to be able to make both priorities in their busy daily lives.

Fair or not, we live in a superficial world, and our ability to play that game factors into our survival and success. One can never have too many things going in their favor, and having a handle on your health and fitness helps for a multitude of reasons. A handle on these facets of life is one of many factors that can play into how you are perceived but also how capable you are of carrying out your daily mission of being the best version of you.

At some time or another, it is fair to say we have all likely struggled with our personal image. Considering how much emphasis is put on looks in our society, considering how we all pass through awkward stages in our growth and development and we reach points when our body reacts differently to changes in activity, stress and diet, the health game has importance across many components of life.

There are a variety of conditions and occurrences we have no control over, such as genetics or forced inactivity due to injury, yet an approach to controlling what we can control from a health perspective is beneficial on numerous levels. Like anything else, consistency, tweaks when necessary and tracking aid greatly in this essential part of living.

We've all come up with excuses or reasons why we disregard various parts of our health: we don't work out because we don't have time. We don't eat right because we're always on the run. Sure – coming up with a system that works for you, for your body and your life will be challenging. But like my dear mother always told me, we make time for what matters.

The gains in energy alone are enough of a reason to sell yourself on becoming more active in a way that benefits your body and lifestyle. The energy we can get from natural foods like fruits and berries and from activities like running or walking or weights are healthier and more impactful than your cup (or carafe) of coffee. (Though, believe me, I haven't stopped buying my Folgers.)

For, that is what is comes down to, right? Selling yourself on the change?

Many of us are able to buy a gym membership, eat well for a few days, go for a couple of jogs…but then we run into a night out with friends, a holiday with family or just a TV marathon on the couch and the whole thing goes to pot. But I have news for you: it's easier than you are making it, you're not a bad person for taking a day or two off here or there and doing the same old workout every single day *is* a bore.

There is a fix.

You do not need some special diet you pay money for. You do not need some gruesome workout routine you hate. In fact, unless you want to be a bodybuilder or model you will not be devoting every second and every thought to this endeavor. Like anything, the trick to change is having a game plan, charting a course and being consistent in the approach.

The advent and prominence of the Internet and Smartphones have made it worlds easier to track your progress in this day and age. I started in 2005 with an Excel spreadsheet and used an online website to look up how many calories were in the foods I was putting in my body.

When you start anything, you have initial momentum and drive. It will wear off; you just have to be prepared for that and tweak your process or revisit your motivation to ensure you stay on track. You will encounter bumps in the road and brick walls in your journey; but remember – it's not a diet. It's a regimen. It is a way of life.

The first part is selling yourself: your increased confidence, stamina, energy and perception of yourself will make an enormous difference that those around you will notice. Frankly, the differences it makes within you are the most important ones: you feel better. And what you exude to the world because of that fact will be what makes the biggest difference in your life; people will perceive you as happy with an energy they want to be around.

The diet piece does not have to be as difficult as we make it; many of us have a perception that we will be eating nothing but fruits or vegetables or salads. We think we will always be confined to small portions. We believe we will get bored very quickly with the foods we can choose from. Not so.

Pick a plethora of foods that are good for you that you enjoy eating. Again – the Internet comes in handy because you can research how many calories and how much fat is in the foods you are eating now (and see why they are taking such a toll on you) and you can find foods that you are able to eat (in case you have any allergies) that you enjoy and recipes with these foods so you can change it up and prevent boredom with this regimen.

If you have a Smartphone, download an application that will interact with you on your diet and exercise; there are countless these days that will help you in figuring out those very items. They will also track how many steps you take and allow you to input exercise activities and foods and beverages you intake. Fitness band trackers will keep your step count and tell you calories burned. It takes out the guesswork and turns it into simple math.

Portion control is not as important as simply not eating to be full. Eat to be satisfied. Your body will soon adjust to this new sensation; it will also feel a lot more comfortable than being so full after meals that you are unable to be your best.

A good analogy I have heard on this topic is like feeding wood to a campfire; you do not throw more logs on the fire at any given time than it can handle or that can be burned or processed. You feed the fire as it needs to be fed; you may very well transition from eating six smaller portions of food per day than having three huge meals. This keeps your body burning food, processing it into your energy and you will lose weight rather than bogging down your body.

There are also so many great gains to be made that we may not give a second thought to. Take the stairs instead of elevators and escalators. Find excuses to walk more and become active. Choose activities that you enjoy doing and make them more of a part of your daily routine. Literally, just move. Finding foods and activities that you actually enjoy remove the stigma of "having to" diet and exercise because you will find yourself looking forward to them. And they will pay dividends.

Furthermore, making your new food choices and exercise activities enjoyable and desirable will make it easier to sell yourself on making the time to make this important. There are 24 hours in a day; 168 in a week. Let's say we work 50 and sleep 56; this still leaves 62 hours for the other items on our agenda. We all have additional people and tasks to attend to, but find me someone who cannot allocate 5 of those 62 hours toward exercise activity.

Face it: we make excuses not to make the time. But if you get a taste of how great it feels after a solid workout – specifically the next day when you have that good pain – or a week of healthy eating and a visit to the scales, you know you want to replicate that feeling. The difficulty comes when you pass the doughnut shop or your cubicle neighbors are ordering pizza for the fiftieth day in a row or everybody wants to do beers and shots after work every night. Here's the deal: you do not have to jettison everything you enjoy from your life. You just have to be consistent in your new choices.

I still indulge from time to time in things I wouldn't on a strict diet, but I eat pretty much whatever I want whenever I want. That is where the consistency and the tracking come in; you will have bad days. Many diets brand this your "off day" (though I have seen some take the off day just a little too literally). My proposal: don't focus on an "off day" per se as much as you focus on some "off meals" with the commitment to consistency. Sure, I'll have a little bit too much stuffing and potatoes on Thanksgiving, but I'll run a little bit harder and eat significantly fewer calories the next day to bring balance back to my world. Like business, like sales – consistency is key.

Finding your mix of caloric intake and workouts boils down to your height and weight, ideal weight, typical activity levels and calories burned during workouts. Research or consultation with a physician is recommended to determine your perfect balance; I derived mine through online research and interaction with my calorie monitoring websites and applications.

Workouts will also have several different incarnations. You will reach many points – probably beginning at just a week or two or three in – where you have no desire to work out and you just want to eat an entire pizza. Take some time off – that's perfectly fine. Change it up a little – integrate different exercises in to what you do. It's actually effective to shock your body into different routines. Research what will have the most impact in the area you wish to focus.

One of the most important things to realize in this process (outside of the fact that yes – it is a process) is it takes time and it is a long-term decision and regimen. You will not see the immediate changes you want; you may not drop ten pounds right off the bat. Your body will make adjustments to compensate for the changes you are making that can preclude you from seeing the end result right away. Just like we never ask for the sale (the end result) immediately because we nurture the relationship and build toward the close, we make our new eating patterns, our exercise activities and holding ourselves accountable a permanent fixture in our lives. It's a science and consistency in effective process will yield results.

It does not matter how many reps you do in your workout or how far you run in the early going; what matters is hitting your limits and reaching exhaustion – whatever level that may be. As you continue in your journey, as you temper it with rest, your limits will increase and you will be able to do more and more. Rest is key to your body's reactions to workouts. Work to exhaustion as often as you can but when you need a day or two off, take them.

Just as you will hit brick walls with your newfound eating habits, you may with workouts as well. Keep things fresh; add new activities to your program, change it up, swap workout notes with friends or research new techniques online. Determination of what you enjoy doing and can perform physically that burns the most calories – running, sit-up's and crunches, jumping rope – and integrating it into your routine makes the most significant impact against your overall plan.

Finding and changing up food selections in the major food groups like your cereals and grains, utilization of steamed white rice, fruits, vegetables and roughage in the midst of your dietary regimen will provide the body the necessary fuel and energy while keeping it running smoothly.

Once you are able to find a system that works for you on a caloric intake level and exercise activity level, you have ingrained this process and your responses to the roadblocks into your daily life and you have consistently adopted and practiced this process, you are well on your way to mastery of the health and fitness game.

Its benefits will be reflected in every area of your life and career.

**Patience**

Axl Rose and Company were not lying when they gave us the poetry that all we need is just a little patience.

For those of us that are go go go, Type-A personalities that want and need the victory and the success and the money yesterday, learning the virtue of patience is not always an easy thing to do. Many of us are career-oriented or sales professionals and that description certainly fits.

Take it from me: there is literally no telling where your life or your career will take you. Sometimes, it is completely out of your control. There is a reason for everything - even if you do not like it or see it - but when you find a great distance between yourself and your goal, there is really only one thing you can do.

Start walking towards it.

Every journey has a beginning; you cannot reach or attain the grail you seek unless you begin the adventure. Sulking about why you are where you are, letting fear inhibit you from even embarking - these things only serve to stifle the greatness that resides in you.

Believe me, I understand more than most that exhibiting and practicing patience is not an easy thing. However, the foundation must be put down for a building to stand. The practice must be put in to prepare us for the things we do in life, no matter what our calling.

To become a sales professional, an effective leader, or even an author required me to summon patience I had no idea I had. The reason is because you want to conquer the sales charts and enjoy the six-figure year right away. You want to enrapture the masses immediately. You want to finish that 300-page book and sell it and change people's lives without the wait. But life does not work like that.

All our lives, we invest of ourselves and our talents in areas we think we fit or can make a change or a significant mark. Some of them pay off, others do not. The people in the world who are famous were often in the right places at the right times and they may have tried more times than those who didn't reach that level of acclaim; it is not to say others have not tried to do a lot of the same things. You just have not heard about them. Maybe not yet.

Patience means making the investment, planting the seed and waiting for it to grow.

Patience means understanding that the butterfly cannot emerge until enough time is spent in the cocoon.

Having a goal is fantastic; knowing what you want out of life is a big thing. But knowing how to get there, continuing on the course regardless of the setbacks and obstacles and naysayers and haters and objections - that is how we become great.

Often, to get the best results out of anything we do, all we need is just a little patience.

What's next? What should I do? What do I do now?

How many times in life have you asked yourself those very questions or some semblance thereof?

Even for someone like me, whose very job is to act like I have it all together and know all every day, those questions are commonplace in my thoughts. And I am here to tell you: that is OK.

Life is full of challenges; so full, in fact, that we never stop facing them. You cannot just be weathering a storm and waiting until "someday" to do something or take a leap or gamble. If you do, someday becomes never.

The real questions to ask are: what are your goals? What talents do you bring to the table? If money was no object, what would you want to do with your life? What are the steps you can take daily to head in that direction and still satisfy all of your obligations?

Everything takes investment of quality time, patience and nurturing to watch it grow. A garden does not sprout overnight and Rome was not built in a 24-hour period. Those, for instance, who set out to lose weight or be healthier adopt a process; they follow that process and it leads to results based on following that process. The weight stays off because of continued dedication to that process, in spite of evolution of process due to changes.

The reason it is OK to not know necessarily what is next is because we all face the uncertainty and decisions, and there is no set-in-stone-tablet set of rules to follow to take us to our dreams. Sure, people are splattered over big and small screens alike that have made dreams come true, but they are a small sampling of our population. For some, conquering the pop culture world is realization of a dream. For others, the noble life of a family man or woman is that dream.

For some of us, we still have no idea what that dream is.

Take a deep breath and imagine yourself happy. What would it take? Financial obligations aside, what do you want to be working toward?

## In Conclusion

People define success in so many different ways, but money is not always in that equation. Sure, we have to pay our bills and rent and support our families, but there is always time we can make to follow our dreams. And – who knows – if we apply enough, do enough, and keep sticking ourselves out there, they can come true sooner rather than later.

You will never reach success if you are not walking toward your definition of success – every day, in every way.

We may and will be knocked back 2, 3 and 10 steps every day. As long as the number of steps you take outweigh the ones you lose, you are headed in the right direction. At the end of the day, that is all we can hope for.

If you aspire to something, whatever it is, and your love of that dream is pure, following pursuit of it as best you can is the answer to your questions. It will not be easy, but nothing worth anything is.

Take each and every day and challenge at a time. A day or challenge achieved or endured is a day or challenge won. Tomorrow, God willing, you'll wake up and have another set of challenges to face. Handle them all the same – as they come, with a big picture mind of the future but planted firmly in mastering the present.

And all of that, my dear daughter, is what I call the surviving game. I pray your road will be smoother, your happiness happier and your destiny even greater. All my love,

Dad

# EPILOGUE

692 DAYS LATER

December 18, 2013

"So… I guess I'll start at the beginning.

"I am an only child. I grew up a prodigy to perfect parents. I guess that sounds great or glamorous or a lot of people would be envious of that predicament, but it always made things more difficult and whether they were pressuring me or I was pressuring myself it was no picnic.

"I won't complain, because my parents are great people and I certainly wouldn't want to be like everybody else… but being blessed with gifts makes you know you've got to figure out how to use them and it makes it all the more frustrating for everyone when you're not sure.

"I skipped a grade. And I always wondered what would have happened if I hadn't. I do a lot of wondering – if I'm doing the right things, if I've done the right things. I've always felt like I've been destined to do great things… something significant and game-changing… and yet I've never felt good enough or like I'm anywhere near where I'm supposed to be. I've done some cool things but then I get derailed and have a hell of a time getting back on track.

"I was always insecure. I was a late bloomer. I had darker, redder hair, braces, glasses… and my best friends were in the class I left behind. I felt out of place. There were these two kids that would not stop picking on me in high school. I hated them. I once was going to commit suicide… until my best friend just happened to call me and talk me off the ledge. Looking back, I wish I could have helped my younger self put stupid stuff like that into perspective.

"I never really tried in school. I didn't have to – not until college and by then I still had no idea what I wanted to do with my life and so I still didn't try very hard. I didn't declare a major until I was a junior and picked business management because I had the most credits toward that degree…graduated, moved to Minneapolis with my girlfriend and my best friend, and my friend's aunt helped me get a decent job with a huge company. Come to think of it, I was really happy then…

"When I do something, it has to be perfect; it has to be the best. I have a hard time admitting when I'm wrong and I can't let anyone see me do anything less than perfect. I'm not a complainer and I don't ask for help.

"I started in sales because it's the job I got – I thought it was a customer service job; I had no idea I'd be any good at it. At first, the scare tactics they used in training and all of the unethical behavior I saw shocked me. The job was excruciatingly awful and 90% of my training class quit. But I was good at it and did it right. In fact, I was so good I broke records, set records and still hold the records – even the people who did it dirty couldn't beat me. And it confounded them to the point they had to try to attack me to bring me down. I was promoted and promoted and promoted again; I was the youngest Associate Director in the company. I had paid my dues and things were paying off.

"Back then I was only focused on myself and making a fortune. I didn't put a lot of effort into my relationship and I guess I expected her to change but wasn't willing to change myself. I kicked her out of my apartment… and then I wanted her back. And when I couldn't have her, I didn't know how to handle it. I couldn't handle it. I couldn't process defeat; especially defeat that was completely out of my control. I didn't like it – and I swore I would never face it again.

"Years went by and I married myself to my career to avoid that very defeat. I could control what I put into business; I couldn't control love.

"Once I started making over $100,000 a year every year and partying with all of these kids that worshipped me and had women all around me I thought I had cracked the meaning of life. Looking back, I don't know how I was so wrong… but I guess that's what life is: growing up. Being able to put things into perspective. I was drinking every day and life was a party. I was so good at my job that I probably got away with far too much: I ran my teams how I wanted to, did not take criticism and told bosses what I thought of them. I had some doozies, and I called them on it.

"I've had issues with some of my bosses, but they never understood me. My work ethic was on another playing field and everybody speculated they were just threatened by me. On the same token, I know most of them were intimidated by what I could do. They would let me run wild for a while because it made them money and made them look good, but they would rein me back in from time to time. I can't say I blame some of them. But they also had no idea how to manage. I learned everything I know about leadership by doing and by watching them for cues on what not to do.

"I love being a manager. I love helping people, helping them be successful. Helping them put more money in their wallets and food on the table. I guess that's been my passion that has sustained me for so long at work.

"But what I don't love is the politics. I don't love being forced to do or say something I don't believe in. I don't love working for people who treat my employees like shit. And that's where I would always get into trouble; they would want me to write up or fire my people and I refused. I chose to coach them and develop them instead of having an itchy firing trigger finger. And not only did I defy them, but my results were the best in show – it pissed everyone off. I was the exception to every rule… but I threw it in their face, and that's where my immaturity would shine through.

"I think most every company starts off with a great idea, but too many of them get run into the ground by these assholes who have no idea what it means to be a leader. They have a good product or service, but they have bad managers who don't train their people, don't value their people and it just goes in circles. Then you get a few of these bastards who don't care about anyone but themselves and they snow the company and the customers until they get rich off cheating them. You get a few of these pricks and they stick together and form their boys' clubs; they promote each other and stick together… and you stand up to them and you're toast.

"So…I'm just motoring along, making money and living the party, and I wind up between two girls. One of them I think is my soul mate. The other gets pregnant… and I stuck with her. We fought like cats and dogs and were off and on for years – either in bed or in court. She cost me a considerable amount – emotionally and financially. I left her for the other one for fear I was missing out on my soul mate. Suffice it to say, I wasn't. She was only using me for my power player status and clout – my rising star.

"Everything was going so swell and…shallow, I guess, even though I didn't know it… until Elizabeth came along. She's my daughter… and she's the love of my life. The events surrounding her coming into my life sent me in a completely different direction but without her I would have never known real love. I've sacrificed everything for her, made decisions to benefit her that I never would have made otherwise and I have a fraction of the financial wealth I would have had but wouldn't change a thing. She's amazing. And I finally learned how to love something more than my career and myself. I finally understood unconditional love."

Vincent paused, making sure he would not allow himself to cry. Not yet.

"At this point, my career had really taken off. Everybody told me I'd run the company someday. I had built a dream team of managers. The only problem was our boss was a dictator from hell. He ran this commission scam, falsified records and would do anything to get his way and protect his secrets and boys' club. He threatened my team and retaliated against anybody who stood against him. My team plotted to overthrow him but they didn't have enough evidence. I did. I got involved, we were promised he'd be removed... and he wasn't. He fired me out of revenge, even though it decimated the department."

Vincent took a drink of water from a glass on the table to his right. He adjusted how he was sitting and continued.

"I thought I'd be reinstated pretty quickly once I presented the facts. I was wrong. I started the process to sue them. And it took a hell of a long time. *A hell of a long time.* And that time and the inability to have immediate justice and peace ate up every ounce of my ability to trust others, to believe in others, to believe in justice. I second-guessed myself and wondered if I should have just turned a blind eye to the illegal activities... and every so-called friend I had except for one or two completely betrayed or backstabbed or abandoned me. It was hell."

"After 13 excruciating months and applying to over 1,600 jobs, I finally got a district manager job paying substantially less than what I made before, with a cell phone retailer.

"I think in my work world, I allow myself to fall in love with potential and I fight to the death to make it work. However, I seldom do that in my personal life. Kind of funny if you think about it. I guess it's because I know all eyes are on me in business. I know people are depending on me. Or doubting me, and I can prove them wrong. That excites me. In relationships, I look for the reasons to escape before they can get rid of me... so I can leave on my own terms... and I avoid conflicts at all costs. Running from them...

"So the new job was a disaster. Nepotism, the blame game and complete and utter incompetence. I had a great team and marketing plan for the tiny budget they gave me, and I don't know how I kept it together as long as I did before that group shut down and was bought out. They didn't pick me up because I wasn't corporate enough; I wouldn't blindly fire people and I wouldn't throw my people under the bus. I wasn't corruptible... again.

"All of these companies talk about accountability, but when *you* hold *them* accountable – you lose. They brought in a guy and paid him half what they paid me. Since then, they've closed every single store I used to run and they fired my replacement. Obviously, it wasn't meant to be – for any of us.

"But I saw these people I was paid to protect... I worked with just these quiet, noble, humble people who made very little money and lived paycheck to paycheck; that's why I fought so hard. I knew they needed me and I was in a position to fight. When I got fired before, I fought for justice and what was right, but now I was fighting for these people's livelihoods.

"My supervisor in the whole thing – Jordan Wallace… at first, I was enamored by him. His demeanor, the way he carried himself and his cavalier approach to life. He embodied what I once was; what I thought I wanted to be again. Then, the shine came off the apple; I saw that he was just a show… he said and did things that I never would have done… I despised him for a while at the end. Then I realized he and I had a lot in common. He *was* me, a few years before. He lost it all – he showed me his cards and was defeated. *That* was real. And I doubt he really trusted many people with his actual self… but he did with me after everything went down, and I wish him no ill will. He made mistakes and had a downfall, but he discovered himself and rebounded. He actually went on to clean up his act, make good with his wife, become a Dad and start a reputable company. I wish him well.

"So, then I was unemployed again. Fortunately, I learned the system the first go-around. It only took me three months to land a better District Manager position with another cell phone company. I heard about them because my buddy Saul started working there, too. More money. What's funny is I beat the hell out of every interview I've ever done, but I was sure I didn't get this one. Their VP was a dick and he berated me in the interview, saying the hell I'd been through at my last job was nothing. He aggressively tried to poke holes in every single thing I said, so I was sure he hated me and I wouldn't get the gig. But somehow I did.

"I met so many great people there that were working here in Minneapolis. Wow. But I walked in and it was a disaster. They had been treated like shit and neglected by a revolving door of District Managers for years and I was like their savior. Familiar territory – walking into a bad situation and being charged with turning it around. I thrive on that stuff.

"Anyhow, I took over the 2$^{nd}$-to-last place market in the company… and we were #1 in the country my 2$^{nd}$ month there. I just did what I do – got to know these people, listened to their woes and fixed what I could. Held meetings and ran conference calls that just blew everyone away like nothing they had ever seen… and I wasn't even as good as I used to be.

"Meet with every single person who cares about their career or wants to advance – even if nobody thinks they have a shot in hell. Just investing in your people makes all the difference in the world. When you care about them, they care about working for you.

"I bucked the system. Hell, I rewrote the system. The VP got fired not long into my time there and my boss was practically nonexistent – which was good and bad. I liked the fact I could do things my way but I was expecting to be promoted any day with the lack of talent above me taken into consideration.

"There were so many of them that had been there for years – they were so jaded. And – like I've seen before – they didn't think I'd last; they had seen my videos and thought I was fluff like everyone else they had seen before. But I won the crowd; these jaded folks just needed someone to believe in them and champion them. When I got there, they were down one to two reps in every single store. I rolled up my sleeves and covered rep shifts, and held all-day interview blitzes of sometimes more than 30 candidates in a day by myself to get staffed up.

"One of my best moves was just investing a conversation in a lady who was a senior sales rep who'd gotten screwed over multiple times and put in her two weeks' notice. She just wanted a career path. I did the unthinkable – instead of lying and dangling carrots, I was honest with her, told her what I wanted and what my expectations were, gave her a timetable for follow up… and she came through with flying colors. I promoted her and she was one of the top managers in the company.

"And I have a story like that for every single one of them. I wasn't what I once was, but I was enough… they adopted my recruiting and hiring strategy for the whole company, I was making money hand over fist and everything was great. They even loved my lead generation program I adopted that I had used before at my previous company and committed to rolling it out to the entire company. And then the wheels fell off.

"Everything was great until they added too many layers and rules up top. It always happens. They have all of these folks at corporate trying to justify their jobs, so we have three different audits, a scheduling system that is in conflict with how many reps they will allow us to have and an HR team that wouldn't support us in the moves we needed to make. The marketing team promised lead generation in October *over a year ago* and dropped the ball so many times it never even happened. They bumped it to November. Then December. Then they asked me to summarize the program for them again – six months after it was supposedly rolling out they were just starting from scratch. I just let it go.

"And when you get a handle on things and your team's on top, they turn to socialism and break your team up to help peers who can't hack it while you have to develop and pillage and plunder the stores they failed to deliver with.

"It's always something, and I'm so tired of hanging on to people, places and things for their potential. You pin your hopes on potential and you are asking to be disappointed. I resisted; I did my usual program and ran things my way. We kept improving and making money – 170% year over year improvement while the company increased just 60% year over year total revenue – but I was spending every day fighting these battles and having to explain myself to people that had no freaking idea what we did or what needed to be done.

"And I'm not 25 anymore; I'm 35. My patience for this shit is gone. The 12, 14, 16 hour days every day started to break me down; they took away my will to live in the sales world anymore.

"I can't fathom why these people can't be content with their stars just making money. Leave us alone! Just appreciate us – stop beating the hell out of us! When you've struck oil, stop drilling! I've led my teams that way for 10 years – get in, get to know them, care, remove their obstacles, celebrate successes and repeat.

"Hiring people is like getting married – never settle. I had full teams I eradicated – dropped 5 deadbeats and hired 5 superstars. But these higher-up's can't leave well enough alone. They just have to keep meddling; they can't just sit back and enjoy the money. They pay these goons to come in your stores and just pick you apart – find something wrong and make it like you're not doing enough. I'm already working 7 days a week and these ass-clowns are barely on the clock for 40 hours and spend most of it just gossiping and socializing. I always loved how they celebrated on the Friday morning conference calls that it was Friday. Yeah, clearly you're not in the trenches working with us all weekend while we're making you money.

"Eventually, they hired a new VP of sales. He talked a good game. Most of them do. Ten years ago, I would have worshipped this guy. But now, I hear the words but look for the action to back it up. It wasn't there. Contradictions left and right, priorities changing every week – these people can't make up their minds what they want. And everybody preaches a different story based on their agenda. I could see right through this guy.

"The first day I met this jackass in person, he was visiting my stores. I always love when new bosses come to town and I'm #1 in the company. Imagine my surprise when this guy comes in and just rips apart everything in every store. Sure, you can always find something wrong with anything if you look hard enough, but this business isn't an exact science. You're bringing together a ragtag bunch of retail employees – most of whom are just doing this to pass the time until they get their real gig. You sell them on opportunity and hype up the job and hope for the best. But this guy comes in and just rips me to shreds – and I'm the best he's got. He tells me if I'm working 7 days a week, I'm just ineffective… and then he tells the whole company on a conference call a week later that we need to start working 7 days a week. He second-guesses some of my recent promotions based on walkthroughs of stores that were doubling their performance from last year. Who the hell is this idiot?

"I figured he just wanted to see if I could take it, so I endured and just kept doing my thing. It's not like I saw him often. His background was in clothing so clearly he didn't know what he was talking about. He told us he was going to do away with the arbitrary, bullshit quotas and rolled out this magical secret sauce only to change it every single month without fail so he could pay us as little as possible on goals that made no sense. He led through fear and intimidation, and made us get on sometimes three conference calls a day, 6 days a week. Of course – he wasn't on them. The guy didn't know the first thing about leadership – build the relationship. He never did that; he just pranced in and barked orders and wrote people up and blatantly lied to your face. Classy.

"So, one day I get a phone call from a guy I used to work with. Apparently a recruiter was calling around trying to fill my boss's position – behind his back! Don't get me wrong, my boss was a nice guy but I wouldn't even hire him as a sales rep. The only 'coaching' he ever gave me was, 'Maybe turn up the music in the stores a little bit.' I know I'm good, but come on; it would be nice to have someone in my career for once that can mentor me. I remember when he covered my annual appraisal and he said my opportunity areas were our district's outbound calling campaign and that I moved too many managers around. We were #1 in the company in outbound call campaign and the managers I moved doubled and tripled their new stores' revenue output.

"It was the right move to replace him. I've been caught in the middle before with bosses, so I straight up called him right away and told him what was going on. I also reached out to recruiters and planted the seed that if they were adding another Regional Director that I wanted to throw my hat in the ring. As the top District Manager in the company, I knew my time was coming.

"They all told me the position didn't exist, which was confusing considering more people contacted me about these recruiter calls. I am decently well connected in the Twin Cities from a sales perspective, so to have contacts reaching out telling me this role was real certainly had me believing it.

"One day, my boss gets demoted. We all report directly to the VP – which was awful enough – until he finds a replacement. I reached out again and not only did I not even get an interview, he tells me I'm not ready yet but I'm the most influential person in Minneapolis to pacify me. From what I understand, that's his own patented carrot-dangling line. That he's going to bring in someone to develop me to the next level. I attempted to explain my relevant experience, what I had done before and in my current role – but he was having none of it. He didn't care. He was not interested in the best candidate; he wanted a boys' club… I've been there before and I wanted no part of it.

"At this point, I'm like 'fuck you.' I could do *his* job with my eyes closed only working 3 days a week better than he's driving the ship into the iceberg now. To add insult to injury, I asked for a raise since I was the top District Manager in the company and he tells me, 'If we gave you a raise, we'd have to give everyone one.' Point taken. My team told me the company didn't deserve me… and they were right.

"It would have been one thing if this guy was a leader; if he had just met with me and talked to me and actually invested the tiniest bit of time in me. After everything I'd done for the business, the millions of dollars they had made off me, the fact I rewrote their recruiting and marketing and was doing the interviews for three markets at once mostly by myself… they owed me that. But the fact I didn't even get an interview spoke volumes.

"My passion and drive and love of my teams go through the stratosphere, but it always conflicts with their desire to run a cookie-cutter organization. They'd rather have control and conformity for the purpose of mediocrity – and that's not me. It will never be me.

"I couldn't get out of there soon enough. What was worse is I was starting to hate every facet of sales – we were peddling terribly inferior service and the company kept cutting costs and outsourcing overseas and laying people off but only to fund plan changes! It didn't go into improving their service or improving their God-awful computer systems that crashed on my employees numerous times every day in the stores.

"Capitalism in its purest form is beautiful, but this version of it is so watered-down and muddied it's pathetic. They were short-sightedly skimping the people who could have made them so much more money, in favor of squeezing out as much profit as they could at our expense through bloated quotas and reduced commissions. If only they had cared about the people, the profits would have been there in droves.

"It pissed me off because I was sleepwalking and was #1 in the company… and they just couldn't leave well enough alone. I could have stayed there forever and made a lot of money but they just had to keep jacking quotas up to pay us less, not giving us the support or resources we needed or continuing to over-manage us to death. They'd ask us to study the traffic patterns in the stores and set hours based on the statistics; then, they'd just change the hours themselves to the maximum even on stores where the plazas opened late or closed early and we found out about the changes when the new signs arrived – not from our bosses.

"They would even commit to marketing events and my guys would plan and strategize and get all excited… and days before the events we'd find out marketing hadn't even enrolled us.

"We're told we can't staff; then we can. I go in to staff us better and get cut off inexplicably or have to spend an hour on a call with someone just explaining why we need more people to grow the business, do events and actually take this to the next stage. That concept was totally lost on these people – growth. They looked at me like I had two heads when I talked about how we could do outreach with a few more people; they didn't want a sales organization. They wanted a cookie-cutter retailer.

"We had two small business reps; one of them couldn't close a screen door and I had to take his place with one client because they refused to even talk to him. The other caused drama at every turn and was an HR nightmare.

"I had brand new managers that I wanted to coach and develop but I didn't even have time because these twits up above were burning up my time with pointless conference calls and reports about nothing. Commissions were wrong like clockwork. It was unacceptable on every level. It was counterproductive.

"They claimed we were family; they said we were 'owners.' That's laughable; they just wanted lemmings to do their foolish, misguided bidding. Initially, I was going to ride it out, but they made it so unbearable and obvious that I was just another piece of shit to them – it was time to go.

"I wanted to find my real calling. But how do you do that at this point in your life? Hell, I didn't even know what I wanted to do. The same could have been said when I was in college; I just fell into sales and went with it. I'm looking into marketing manager jobs, management consulting, writing… but no matter what I looked into, I was rejected, told I'd have to start at the bottom, low-balled or ignored.

"What's worse is that right before my last job, I was actually recruited by Apricot Innovation – one of the most respected companies in the world where people would kill to work – and I turned them down to make more money at another bad cell phone company. I reached out to them again recently but – like everywhere else – I've heard nothing.

"It's like 'Bittersweet Symphony' by the Verve: 'You're a slave to money, then you die.'

"For a guy like me to wake up in the morning and not be able to bounce out of bed to attack the day... it told me something. And it had me asking myself: is there *any* of the old Vincent Scott left? I was making money but I was miserable. And the relative freedom I had being able to go to which stores I wanted when I wanted was getting buried with all of this minutiae and bullshit... all of these pointless reports so someone somewhere could justify their job. Seriously, pick a way of doing business that actually works and manage it; don't just change it every week on a whim.

"I got to that breaking point – I didn't care what it was. I had to leave. It's a shame, too, because when I first got there I loved it; I was making an impact, I was making a difference and forming good working relationships. I could even tell I was growing as a leader; one of my peers did everything he could – including fraud – to try to catch me on the sales report. The old me would have publicly humiliated and openly battled him. I just kept doing what I knew I should do and he got busted and fired and I came out on top again. I also didn't have to be the guy who spoke on every company conference call to talk about why we were #1 in nearly every category; I took a step back, let others shine and let myself be asked about our superior go-to-market strategies.

"But it all got bogged down in overblown bureaucracy and I had to get the hell out of there on my terms before they took me out for unwillingness to unfairly write people up or to manage in the wrong way.

"I wanted to find something that I'm passionate about, and helping others find success is my greatest career reward. There was a consultant firm I had talked to in the past that was one of the many places I reached out to in my new search.

"I'd known these guys for close to two years; we had started talking while I was looking for something else and I was at a doomed Cellular Horizons dealer. The first time, it was just not the right mix; they didn't seem on the same page on what they wanted to do with me, and the second-in-command wanted to bring me on as a 'business development' director, meaning straight commission and the minimum payout. There was not much going on with them. We parted as friends.

"This time, when I reached out to the head boss, he told me things were exploding – he needed someone to come in and run their sales trainings, their seminars, give speeches, and the role was a VP title. I was passively looking and didn't even plan on taking the job until things just got so horrendous where I was that I had no choice. When my boss got demoted and the VP didn't even consider me for promotion even though I was the top District Manager in the company and I hated my job and was working 70 hours a week, I didn't care if it sucked; I couldn't get out of there soon enough.

"It was a risk, but the risk took me away from something I knew I couldn't do for another second. There was such a sense of relief when I was able to put in my two weeks' notice to that smug, lying, arrogant bastard. The feeling must have been mutual; he hated me enough that he didn't even announce my departure to my team until after I was gone and he got me out of there fast. My old boss's name was still on our sales reports though he had been demoted weeks before but he pulled mine off immediately. Good riddance. I left on top and did it my way.

"And I was optimistic – a new adventure. It was a gamble; a new potential career path. But hell, these guys were the #1 small business consultant firm in Minneapolis. Or so they claimed on their website and materials that they had been voted that.

"And on Day 1, it unraveled from the word, 'go.' I walked in and these people who just weeks prior had sold me that this was a great opportunity were part of the most dysfunctional team I had ever seen.

"The leader was anything but a leader; he was disheveled, had no control and was as motivating as a doorknob. His sidekick was a useless stooge who brought no value or clients and all he did was tell stories about his past in sales and make useless spreadsheets. He gave a presentation on Q2 results and year-to-date results and… there was nothing going on. Everybody was jumping ship; three of them quit in the first week I was there.

"I found out the '#1 consulting firm' bit was a lie; they had been *nominated*, and the nomination came from their own people. They sold me I'd make more money there than I did in wireless… he told me last year everyone's average income was $100,000 and surely I'd make even more… and then I find out their top earner had actually made a little over $1,000 in 9 months. *Total*.

"They had prepped me it would take a month to get my first check after I got on with the projects they were putting me on, etcetera. Turned out there were no projects. I found a lead myself that the two top guys snaked from me and claimed as their own 'whale,' cutting me out completely even though what the new client needed was sales training. Then it became 2 months until I'd get paid, 4 months until I'd get paid. Simply put: I took a gamble and it didn't pay off.

"And there was no going back. I knew I made the right decision leaving the hellhole I came from. I knew the game – I just had to bite the bullet and play it.

"It's amazing how quickly the wheels can fall off. It's like after you interview someone for a job; they show up in the interview and play the part of a superstar and you see them weeks later and they perform like a dud. They look different. The look in their eyes is different. They talk different. These idiots sold me on a greener pasture and I fell for it; I took a chance and it was even worse than the hell I was already in – if that's possible.

"And it left me even more jaded and angry and lost. I didn't even mean to start in sales; I got a job at a big company and found out I was the best at it. I kept getting promoted, kept making more and more money… kept climbing. But then I got a look at what the top looks like. I wanted to run the company – until I found out what it took to be that kind of person. I've seen all of this filth; all of this lying and deceit and cheating and crime. These people make Gordon Gekko look like a saint.

"It's enough to make you want to give up on the human race. But there are good people out there… I know a lot of them. And I'm trying my ass off to be one. I just don't understand why this shit has to keep happening to me. I understand trials and tribulations, but this is ridiculous.

"And it's definitely taught me you have no idea what's going on in someone's life if they don't let you know. Even those who appear to have it all can be masking massive pain. People never see me bleed, but it doesn't mean I'm not gushing blood from these wounds of the last several years. I just want it to stop.

"Between work and fighting and court and my Dad and Abby and learning more and more about how this world works… it's enough to drive the most motivated man in the world crazy. I never used to worry about anything; now I find myself paralyzed by thought and fear.

"I got a few bad reviews on my book…and you add that to my career and relationship woes and it's like – what am I good at? What can I even do? I don't know what I want or even what I enjoy doing or want to do anymore.

"I'M EXHAUSTED. I'm a complete wreck. I don't even really remember what it feels like to trust someone completely and blindly and have faith in others.

"And all the while through this shit, I've got my wrongful termination case hanging over my head like a dark cloud. It took 1,229 days until I finally faced them again. 3 ½ years of waiting for some semblance of justice.

"I had been illegally terminated from a department I built because I helped my team stand up to a corrupt dictator… and afterwards I doubted everything I had ever known – justice, faith, humanity. I was initially so blinded by inconsolable rage and wanted nothing but revenge. But by this point, I was just emotionally drained. The pain had been with me so long I didn't know a world without it.

"The court process was horrific. It was nothing like TV or the movies; not like that's news, but it was so long, so expensive, so… filled with the unexpected. I won. Everyone knew I would. But I got a fraction of what I deserved after years of suffering. At least I got closure.

"I was sitting in that room with their 'final offer' after haggling back and forth with their attorneys for 10 hours. I had to listen to the warped, disgusting, inconceivable way they were going to defend themselves against me and the way they were trying to paint me.

"I could have suffered through it even longer, endured that and made ten times what I made had I gone to trial, or I could have potentially gotten nothing and been stuck with their attorney fees. It was actually somehow a gamble and – quite frankly – after 1,229 days of that place and that anger having its hold on me, and already dropping $20,000 in attorney fees, I said 'enough.' My lawyer said he'd go back in and he squeezed out a little more afterward and I knew it was the best I'd get without rolling the dice of taking it to court.

"I looked out the window and just knew it was time to let it go. It was less than I wanted and deserved, but I didn't want to live in it anymore. I couldn't wake up one more day with this shit weighing on me. *Not one more.*

"Their depositions of me were two 12-hour days, grilling me with every question under the sun about who I was friends with, who I had slept with, what people had said while plotting to overthrow my boss and when they said it – every sin or hint of dirt they could try to drum up on me from several years and many repressed memories ago. I originally wanted to depose my old boss; I thought it was necessary to see him again for my closure; I wanted to look him in the eyes while he answered for every crime he had ever committed. But then I realized: I'm going to drop thousands of dollars just to watch this sick, demented, horrible piece of filth squirm? What's the point? He's not worth it. He lives with his boyfriend in some ritzy house and cheats on him with every new pretty boy he can in the office and appoints his buddies to undeserved positions and he ran my department into the ground until they finally shipped him off to a figurehead role where he couldn't hurt anybody anymore. Everybody knows what a vile piece of shit he is and there is a special place in hell just for him. I'm over it. I'm over him, and he didn't beat me.

"Only in the movies do you get that 'final showdown' with the villain or the neat and tidy happy ending. Here you just reach hurdles, you find a way over them or around them and you continue until you find more of them. The best revenge is living well.

"I guess I'm maturing. I'm past it; I'm past revenge. I'm finally really starting to realize how the world works – which is terrifying. When times were great, I was relatively clueless because I was just drunk off the success… The world is a disaster. My political and religious beliefs continue to be challenged every day…but I see that money and politics govern all. And there will always be good fighting evil, just ever-so-slightly tipping the scales enough in good's favor.

"Even though I felt the initial relief, I thought after I let go of that pain, everything would get better and the confusion and depression would end. But it didn't end. It got worse.

"I started questioning everything in my life outside of my relationship with Elizabeth. I realized all of my relationships were shit because I didn't ever let anyone in, I pushed away everyone who tried to care and I came up with some excuse to keep them at arm's length at all times. I'd been burned and used by a lot of people and I held their sins against everyone else. Of course, after I won, everyone who left me during the dark times suddenly wanted to be my friend again. I just don't have any room in my life anymore for people who have never been there for me.

"I even questioned my career. Was working for horrible companies that had no idea what they were doing, had no idea how to treat people and were run by incompetent idiots my lot in life? I realized I had hated every single day of my career for years. I had fought so long and hard to get back to making the money I used to make. I finally got to the point where I made even more… and I couldn't put up with it for another day. Not another day.

"So I took a chance and left sales and walked away from the best financial situation of my life to branch out to management consulting only to find they misrepresented themselves in criminal fashion. No sense looking back; I cut bait and bid them adieu.

"For the last few months, all I've done is tirelessly network and apply to jobs and meet with people and get rejection after rejection after rejection. I know I'm doing the right things, but that's little consolation when nothing's popped yet… and I don't even know if I want it to. I don't even know who I am anymore; I don't know what I want to do in my life or career. I guess I never figured it out.

"I realize that I don't remember the last time I wasn't making sacrifices for others and not focusing on me. Part of that comes with the territory of being a Dad and being a manager who cares about his people, but I've been fighting my tail off for so damn long… and I don't have any fight left. None. Zero. Zilch. I'm done in.

"I've spent so much time in hospital rooms visiting… so much of my hard-earned money helping *other people*… so much time working… so many 14-hour days… and all I've gotten in return is grief and pain and loss and being taken advantage of… and doubt and loneliness.

"I don't love sales anymore; at least, not what this world has turned it into. A guy hits me up about a pyramid scheme who's never talked to me before in my life and claims he worshipped my Dad to get me to listen to him and sell his product. He tells me what an amazing person I am – how the hell would he know?

"The deceit, the lies, the manipulation; I'm sick of it. I don't want to become the person I'd have to be to be that guy who can sell anything to anyone.

"I thought I wanted to be a writer; I spent years of my life putting together a book, contacted a thousand publishers and I sign with the best offer I got…one who sold me a bill of goods… didn't put my book where they promised it would be, doesn't pay royalties on time or often at all, and blatantly lies to me about everything from marketing to total sales.

"And I realize now that I literally set fire to my entire career. I burned nearly every bridge without hesitation and took a dive from the top of the mountain, freefalling for years… and now I barely recognize those times. I barely recognize that version of myself. I don't even know who I am anymore; and I never had to stop to think about it before. It was such a whirlwind I was caught up in… so fast-paced. The money and the liquor and the ladies and the people and the standing ovations and the promotions and the power…… I had everything. I was the center of attention. I had the girl everybody wanted and every girl wanted me and every guy wanted to be me. I was going to run the company. I was the boss; I made it happen. I was in demand; my phone constantly ringing off the hook and my calendar full. Everyone wanted a piece of me.

"And then one day it was all gone. Nobody called. I was a curse word in the house I built. One year, 20 of my 'friends' showed up at Elizabeth's birthday party; the next year 3.

"I don't know if I was lost then, if I'm lost now or if I didn't realize I was lost until after I lost everything I thought was real. I certainly miss being at the top of that mountain, but now that I know it was all fake I would never want to re-create it. I'd do it differently. I'd be less trusting with the wrong people and more humble.

"Life in that world was a mile a minute, and life unemployed went a mile every million minutes.

"Life since then has been a struggle; I'm not going to lie. It's been hell. And the only thing that made me want to live was my kid. She is my universe.

"I know I have my blessings. She's #1. I have a great family. I have talents, though I don't know what the hell I'm supposed to do with them anymore. I thought I did, but… you know.

"In a way, becoming a Dad was a beginning and an end… I have never fully been in love with anything but being Daddy. I loved fragments of what I thought women in my life were but they turned out not to be. I've loved my friends, though the list has shed hundreds of names in just the last few years.

"My God, I've aged so much in the last few years and I didn't even realize it.

"At least I did finally make some peace with Abby – Elizabeth's Mom – even if it was too late. I hated her for so long… but when I had the chance to deliver the knockout punch in court I relented. I could have taken everything she had and broken her for what she had put me through … but I stopped. We were totally different people when we met… we didn't even know each other. I was so focused on what I had given up for her and never gave a second thought to the fact she was forced to give up her 20's… while I got to enjoy every minute of mine. She was pissed because I moved on so quickly, and everything went so fast back then that we never stopped to catch our breaths in our game of one-upping each other…until years later… and then the cancer."

Vincent stopped. His eyes watered and he took a drink.

"For so long, every day I woke up and I had somewhere to be; something to do. Then, for what seemed like eternity I had the fight and the lawsuit hanging over my head – I couldn't think of much else. It just made me completely numb.

"And now – I have neither.

"And it's rampant – my circle of friends are all in their own versions of disarray. My dear friend in the Navy, Jack, loves his job but it keeps him from his family and it's tearing them apart. My lifelong buddy Eddie is living his dream teaching back home at our old high school but his wife's career may take them elsewhere. My friend Ted got laid off from his dream job and can't find work; he's forced to start over and going back to the call center we worked at 10 years ago. My buddy Jeff has moved from sales job to sales job because they are all disasters. And then there's me: I never pictured it being this difficult.

"Everything I've ever believed in has come into question; business, politics, religion, people – I don't know how I feel about anything anymore. Four years ago I loved my life… or, at least, I thought I did. Now I know it was all artificial; I was being used, I was high on the power and the money and the lifestyle. My confidence was legendary; now I'm riddled with doubt and anxiety and my OCD is ten times worse than it used to be. I don't believe in myself anymore. I'm flat out depressed when I'm not playing workaholic but I'm sick of giving myself to these companies that aren't worth it.

"Life's compromise, it's rolling with the punches, but I'm laid out on the mat again and this time I don't know what to get up for."

Vincent paused again in reflection.

"I have Elizabeth… I'm in the best shape of my life… I know I have these gifts and talents for a reason. I know I've made some difference in this world but I feel like I have so much more to do – like I'm up against the world.

"I've seen the impact I had on the places I've worked; they collapsed and closed up shop after I left. The department I built? 75% of the staff laid off, a loss of hundreds of millions of dollars after four straight years of huge growth under me. The Cellular Horizons retailer who didn't choose me for their new dream team when they bought out my company? They ended up closing every single store I once oversaw after they ran them all into the ground. My old VP who wouldn't even consider promoting me or giving me a raise after I took a market from worst to first? Brought in a buddy for that Regional Director role and they are successfully tanking the place, destroying the morale and staff I built and losing their shirts. They've been hitting 70% to goal since I left. My 'replacement' is dead last in the *entire company* and he's just running around trying to fire everyone on my former team so he can misplace the blame.

"It's the same pattern: I am appreciated by the people who work for me and we have unparalleled and unmatched results. After I'm gone, the place goes to shit and rather than value me, the bosses I had fire everyone loyal to me.

"I know what I bring to the table; I just have no idea what to do with it and don't want to start all over somewhere to 'prove myself' again.

"I thought winning the lawsuit would make me whole again – but it didn't. It just sealed off that part of my life. I was looking at old pictures the other day trying to find more of Elizabeth and I came across my surprise 30$^{th}$ birthday party… pictures from the bar scene… old girlfriends… old friends. It just seemed like another life. They all seemed like so long ago. Everyone does. Like just people I once knew.

"And that was once my whole life. Both places I worked since had locations right across the street from my old offices… it was like the place wouldn't let me go. Or I wouldn't let it go. But – now it's completely out of my system. And I know I'm ready to move forward… I just don't know what to.

"My settlement should have been enough money to never work again, but it wasn't. And while I could take several years off, that's not my style. I know I'm supposed to be doing something of importance. I just don't know what it is. I've never been more confused or lost in my entire life.

"One thing I'd be remiss not to be thankful for is the fact that I could leave these terrible jobs. Everyone I worked with; we were all under extreme duress worked to the bone. We were cooked. We hated it. But they have to stay there… for their families… their kids in school… But I didn't. I have this freedom; but while the freedom is liberating it is scary. I've taken a step away from my prison of what sales has been in my life but I don't know who I am without it. In fact, I'm just on probation. I can leave for a while, but… I have to go back. There's nothing else I can do.

"Too much of my life is spent pretending the pain doesn't hurt, that what is completely broken inside me isn't and accepting the horrible circumstances I cannot change no matter how hard I have tried, while I constantly sacrifice myself to only my detriment. However, I have noticed I care a lot less lately about playing the game and putting on the act.

"I've given so much of myself – to everyone. And I've gotten very little in return; each time I make a deposit somewhere else I've got a little less in the tank that never gets replenished. I'm all for making sacrifices, but I need something for me now.

"I've always wanted to get to the point where everything's perfect – where I have it all. I really thought I could pull it off… but now I know I can't. Nothing's perfect. Relationships aren't perfect. We work to survive and pay bills and support the people we care about; we don't have to love every facet. But we have to love facets of what we do. Teachers are underpaid and taken for granted, but they do it for the love of teaching. I want that same feeling for something.

"People tell you what they think you want to hear and then they just keep going about their agenda. I was never like that… and I don't want to be. And I won't change myself for anything or anyone; I won't become like them.

"And it pisses me off that I was going to stay at one company my entire career and retire from there, and them firing me illegally turned me into a job-hopper. I've been at three dead ends since then in four years… and I don't even know what I want to do next.

"I killed myself to get back ahead of where I was… only to realize I didn't want to be there if it meant being somebody I'm not.

"I feel guilt for just the slightest escape from work. I feel guilt for having a sliver of happiness or joy so I cannot fully enjoy it… I'm always thinking or worrying about what I should be busting my ass at in that given moment. I feel like I can't rest until I reach my destiny.

"I've realized I've been burned so many times that I'm naturally paranoid about anyone showing an interest in me.

"I understand I'm better off than most anyone I know… that there are a lot less fortunate out there. But I've fought my ass off more than most anyone I know, too. I deserve success and I just can't seem to get to a place I'm happy with.

"My business life has been a sporadic disaster filled with amazing highs and horrifying lows… same with my personal life. But I'm thankful that no matter what, I've had lots of time to spend with my daughter. She's my heart. It didn't matter what I did or how out of this world I tried to get in my pursuit of success and greatness. My daughter kept me grounded on planet earth where I belong. I cringe to think what I would have become had she not come along.

"These bullies will always be there. They are practically the same person and they do the same things…selling their soul for the almighty dollar and promotion. I will never become that person."

Vincent stopped, thoughtfully blinked and took another sip of his water.

"I'm sorry –I've monopolized this entire conversation. I just don't have anybody I feel like I can burden with all that crap and everybody just expects me to magically figure everything out for myself or keep suffering through it…"

"That's OK – you're supposed to monopolize the conversation. And I certainly don't want you suffering. You were on a roll and I didn't want to stop you. Truth is, you are in touch with your emotions and thoughts in a way a lot of people aren't, even though you don't share them with anyone and you bottle up too much of it. We need to work together to find positive outlets for you; it sounds like your writing is one of them.

"You're your own worst critic – and nothing you do will ever be good enough to satisfy you. That's great in business; terrible in relationships. You know what you have, which is good. You know yourself better than you give yourself credit for; now you just have to figure out what to do with your life. You've got to figure out what makes you happy on a personal and creative level.

"But you've got to stop beating yourself up. You've got to stop hating yourself and thinking about the past and what you cannot change. You've got to stop caring about what anybody else thinks – they haven't walked in your shoes and it's like lending credence to the least qualified spectator. You've got to come to peace with your pain – no one can just give you that. Would you change anything you've done if given the chance?"

Vincent thought about that for a moment.

"No. It's all made me who I am today. And I like who I am becoming more than the guy I've been."

"There you go. Now you just have to spend your time focused on what you want to do with your life. You've got to think about what will fulfill you. You've got to commit to something like you've committed to being a good Dad."

"I was hoping you'd tell me what to do," Vincent cracked.

"No, but hopefully I can help you remove the obstacles so you can figure it out for yourself. You've dramatically shifted from one end of the spectrum to another; you went from trusting and carefree to untrusting and cynical all in the matter of the last few years. We need to find a happy medium; pardon the pun. We need to learn how to truly accept everything that's happened to you and move on from each part of it, bit by bit. We need to explore methods by which you can center yourself, focus on your priorities and stop letting the things that are out of your control keep you down. You have been through more than most because you put yourself out there more than most. It comes with the territory, but I'd imagine you're not going to stop being a crusader anytime soon."

Vincent laughed. "No – probably not."

"Trust me – we'll figure it all out. In the meantime, list out the things in your life that make you happy and the things you want to accomplish in your life. We're going to work on making those things front and center."

"Thanks, Doc," Vincent said, standing. He shook hands with his new psychiatrist, Dr. Fleming. The BLUE SKIES band still adorned Vincent's wrist and his diamond-studded Top Gun ring was on his ring finger. "Same time next week?"

"See you then."

Vincent walked out into the world, feeling better for having unloaded his years of pain on someone. Fortunately for him, his dance card was free and he went to Elizabeth's school to pick her up upon her release.

He arrived near the front of the line for parent pick-up and perused his missed calls and messages. Mid-swipe, his phone started to ring with a number he did not recognize. Typically, he would not answer these, but something told him to.

"Hello?"

"Vincent Scott," came the voice. "It's Nate Schulman – Apricot Innovations. Long time no chat."

"Yeah... absolutely... how are you, Nate?" Vincent managed, hiding his surprise.

"Nothing to complain about, sir. So, I got your call - you're really a free agent again?"

"The rumor is true," Vincent responded. "I'd say I'm passively looking but wanted to see if there was any way to discuss a career path with Apricot again."

"Interesting. I can't believe anyone would ever let you go – you're a find."

Vincent laughed, "Thanks. Still looking for the right place to call a permanent home."

"You turned us down once before – something that doesn't happen too often," Nate continued. "Are you talking with any other companies?"

"I'm not," Vincent answered. "Nate, I've thought about it for a year and a half. I made the wrong decision, but got more experience that would make me an even better fit for your team."

"I like what I hear. When can you start?"

"Daddy!" Elizabeth Scott shouted in her beautiful little voice. Vincent turned as she ran to embrace him and he scooped her up in his open arms.

# AUTHOR BIOGRAPHY

Carson V. Heady, 35, was born in Cape Girardeau, MO and first put in front of a typewriter at age 3.

He entered the sales arena at age 22 and has found success at every level, from award-winning sales representative, manager and director to multi-state division leader at multiple companies and management and marketing consultant. Once Carson realized his aptitude in the game of sales, he decided to write his first novel – *Birth of a Salesman* – which told the story of a young man who came into prominence in sales and sales leadership and doubled as a self-help sales and management advice manual to guide others to the level of success he achieved. His articles have appeared in several noteworthy publications such as SalesGravy, Smash! Sales, Salesopedia and the Baylor Sports Department S3 Report.

Carson lives in St. Louis, MO, with his daughter.

www.ingramcontent.com/pod-product-compliance
Lightning Source LLC
Chambersburg PA
CBHW051633170526
45167CB00001B/177